# THE CASTRATO
# AND HIS WIFE

# The CASTRATO and His WIFE

HELEN BERRY

OXFORD
UNIVERSITY PRESS

# OXFORD
## UNIVERSITY PRESS

Great Clarendon Street, Oxford OX2 6DP

Oxford University Press is a department of the University of Oxford.
It furthers the University's objective of excellence in research, scholarship,
and education by publishing worldwide in

Oxford New York

Auckland Cape Town Dar es Salaam Hong Kong Karachi
Kuala Lumpur Madrid Melbourne Mexico City Nairobi
New Delhi Shanghai Taipei Toronto

With offices in

Argentina Austria Brazil Chile Czech Republic France Greece
Guatemala Hungary Italy Japan Poland Portugal Singapore
South Korea Switzerland Thailand Turkey Ukraine Vietnam

Oxford is a registered trade mark of Oxford University Press
in the UK and in certain other countries

Published in the United States
by Oxford University Press Inc., New York

British Library Cataloguing in Publication Data
Data available

Library of Congress Cataloging in Publication Data
Data available

Typeset by SPI Publisher Services, Pondicherry, India
Printed in Great Britain
on acid-free paper by
Clays Ltd, St Ives plc

ISBN 978-0-19-956981-6

1 3 5 7 9 10 8 6 4 2

*For my lovely goddaughters,*
*Lucy, Ella, Beattie, Delphi, and Bessie*

Heard melodies are sweet, but those unheard
Are sweeter...

JOHN KEATS, 'Ode on a Grecian Urn' (1819)

# Contents

# List of Plates

1 The rooftops of Monte San Savino, the Tuscan hill town where Giusto Ferdinando Tenducci lived as a boy. The bell tower of the church of Sant'Agostino is in the foreground.

2 Michele Foschini, 'Interior of the Teatro di San Carlo, Naples', c. 1762. Oil on Canvas. Museo Certosa di San Martino, Naples, 23908.

3 Attributed to John Vanderbank, *'Portrait of Senesino, Cuzzoni and Berenstadt'*, c. 1723. Etching and engraving (214 x 262mm). Handel House Collections Trust, London. English audiences flocked to hear performances by castrati but their bodies were the subject of much cruel satire.

4 Charles Townley after Richard Cosway, *Portrait of Elizabeth, 1st Baroness Lyttelton*, undated. Etching. Tenducci was implicated in her separation from George, 1st Baron Lyttelton.

5 Francsco Bartolozzi after Giovanni Battista Cipriani, 'Ticket for Tenducci's benefit concert', 1786. Etching and engraving (128 x 116mm). Yale Center for British Art. B1978.43.743. Tickets were saved as souvenirs by fans as mementos of an expensive night out. For the Georgians, patronage of Italian music was a mark of taste.

6 Title page, Thomas Arne, *The Winter's Amusement*, c. 1762. Beinecke Library, Yale University. Ma31 Ar6 S81. Through his performances of popular songs in English Tenducci succeeded in building a fan base beyond the opera houses.

7 John Finlayson after J. Bruscett, *Giusto Ferdinando Tenducci*, 1770. Mezzotint (346 x 251mm). British Museum, Department of Prints and Drawings, 1889.0603.289. A slender Tenducci holds a copy of 'Water Parted From the Sea', the aria from Thomas Arne's *Artaxerxes* (1762) which made him famous.

8 Anon., *Fitz-Giggo or, the New English Uproar*, 1763. Etching (190 x 265mm). British Museum, Department of Prints and Drawings, 1868.0808.4276. Tenducci (centre), Peretti, and the soprano Charlotte Brent, are interrupted by rioters during a performance of *Artaxerxes*. The diminiutive male figure on stage is the composer Thomas Arne, appealing (unsuccessfully) for calm.

9 Thomas Gainsborough, *Portrait of Giusto Ferdinando Tenducci*, c.1773-75. Oil on canvas (766 x 640 mm). Barber Institute of Fine Art, University of Birmingham, 44.3. Tenducci as a man of sensibility exercising his most seductive talent—his voice.

10 John Nixon, *Signor Tenducci*, 1796. Engraving (192 x 126 mm). Holburne Museum of Art, Bath, FB41. In contrast to the society portraits which focus upon his character and taste, here Tenducci's identity centres upon the 'lack' in his breeches.

11 Anon., *The Ladies Lamentation for the Loss of Senesino*, 1737-8. Etching and engraving (328 x 202 mm). British Museum Department of Prints and Drawings, 1868,0808.3506. Castrati had the reputation of attracting crowds of female admirers from their first appearance in London.

12 Letter from Giusto Ferdinando Tenducci to Dr. Charles Burney, undated. Beinecke Library, Yale University OSB MSS 3. A rare surviving example of Tenducci's handwriting, the singer seeks advice from the eminent musicologist on vocal technique and composition.

13 Frontispiece to *A True and Genuine Narrative of Mr. and Mrs. Tenducci*, 1768. Dorothea Maunsell's teenage account of her elopement with the castrato Giusto Ferdinando Tenducci.

14 Extract from the London Consistory Court archive, LMA/DL/ C/558/21, of the original Italian deposition by Tomasso Massi, taken down in Florence on 23 October, 1775 (For full details and translation, see Appendix).

15 Valentine Green after Maria Cosway, *Maria, Baroness Cosway*, 1787. Mezzotint (460 x 330mm). British Museum, Department of Prints and Drawings, 1941.1011.65. A concert impresario fluent in five languages, the Baroness was a friend of Tenducci during the later stages of his career.

16 Thomas Beach, *Giusto Ferdinando Tenducci*, early 1780s. Oil on canvas (749 x 610mm). Garrick Club, London, G0796. Tenducci as an eminent tutor and composer in his later years. His rich suit of clothing and solidly respectable appearance belied his recurrent problems with debt.

# Picture Acknowledgements

# Prelude

*O*n this January night in 1735, the Spanish ambassador, Count Motijo, is hosting an assembly, a social gathering that will feature politicians, diplomats, and members of the nobility.[1] The star attraction is the castrato singer Carlo Broschi, also known as Farinelli, who possesses by common consent 'the first voice in the World'. Formerly the principal chorister at the Vatican, the opera star had arrived in London only recently, in the autumn of 1734. He had been received by the king and the royal household, and rewarded 'with vast Applause' at a private concert which he gave for His Majesty. Farinelli's royal approval sealed, he had made his first appearance in public on 31 October, performing in an operatic production at the Haymarket Theatre, where expensive season tickets were snapped up by the nobility. The London press reported the enormous fees which Farinelli commanded that year: £1,500 guineas for the season, representing a healthy annual income for an English lord.[2] Tonight, in return for appearing at the Spanish ambassador's private function, Farinelli will be paid a handsome sum, supplemented with gifts from admirers in the form of rare jewels, precious ornaments, and other expensive luxuries. Among his fans is the Prince of Wales, who within a few months will present the singer with 100 guineas in cash and a fine wrought-gold snuff box, richly inlaid with rubies, containing a pair of brilliant diamond knee-buckles.

Guests start to arrive at the Spanish ambassador's residence, Powis House, near Great Ormond Street, a three-storey neo-Palladian mansion and one of the grandest addresses in the West End. Wearing their best clothes and adorned with silk, diamonds, and lace, they step out of their *sedan chairs and pass through the grand front entrance. The guests ascend the staircase, the walls richly decorated in Italian rococo style, to the Great Apartment on the first floor. There are card rooms for gambling, and all kinds of refreshments are provided for the assembled company. In a private room, a magnificent supper is set out to which only twenty men and women of the 'first Quality' are admitted. As they move from room to room, the procession of guests is extravagantly guided by hundreds of candles.*

*At a certain point in the evening after supper, the company adjourns to the concert room. Liveried footmen open grand double doors, revealing glittering chandeliers and a room overwhelmed with the heat, perfume, and odours of bodies crowded together. Upon entering, all eyes are drawn immediately to the guest of honour, Signor Farinelli. He is the centre of attention, with the host at his side and the most important assembly-goers wanting to make his acquaintance. He is also easy to spot in the crowd since at over six foot tall he towers head and shoulders above the people around him. Finely dressed and au fait with the rules of courtly deportment, his physical presence alone is enough to cause a frisson of excitement, as exotic an addition to the company as a Persian prince. This is a celebrity event—a chance to see up-close the most recent star of the London stage, whose name features regularly in the newspapers. Some men, and a remarkable number of women, throng around him, eager to get close to this handsome singer, who is the talk of the town. Some of those present are perhaps hoping for drama: castrati have the reputation of being temperamental both on- and off-stage. With his imposing physical presence, and his personal charisma, Farinelli cannot pass unnoticed.*

*The guests have all gathered. The figure of the castrato is subjected to the intense gaze of all who are present. For in the person of Farinelli, controversies that raged across Europe at this time collide, in disputes over the nature of art, music, politics, and religion. Like the host, the Spanish ambassador, the singer is a Catholic with close associations to the Vatican, and is therefore a potential enemy to his audience, the Protestant English. Newspapers and popular pamphlets foster the widespread rumour that Catholic spies infiltrate gatherings such as these. When the castrato Senesino had quarrelled with George II's favourite composer Handel, he was accused in the public prints of being 'No Eunuch, but a Jesuit in Disguise'.[3] Farinelli also provokes strong reactions as a castrated man, a* castrato. *For many English men and women, the fact that his body has been mutilated, deprived of his manhood in the name of high art, evokes all that is artificial, barbaric, and Popish about Baroque fashion. But Farinelli's magnetic presence is confirmed by all who meet him: they praise him not only for his talent ('a revelation . . . for I realised that till then I had heard only a small part of what human song can achieve'), but for his 'agreeable and clever manners', being 'civille and well bred', and (as one dowager duchess noted), 'I think him handsome too'.[4] And so, the members of the audience take their seats, fans fluttering in the candlelight. There are a few last-minute coughs. The host rises to make his introduction. The castrato dabs his brow with his handkerchief. And then the room falls silent, and he begins to sing.*

♪

*Sometime in 1735, the same year as Farinelli's London concert, in a room hundreds of miles away near Siena, Italy, there is the altogether different and more brutal sound—of a woman in labour. The woman's husband, Signor Tenducci, is a servant, and their household is a humble one. She gives birth to a boy. Without the expense of formalities, the couple baptize their newborn son privately according to their Catholic faith. They give him two distinctive names: Giusto Ferdinando.[5] The infant's origins are obscure, and the odds are that he will be destined for poverty and obscurity too. However, this baby is destined for greater things. The fashion for Baroque opera that created Farinelli will also shape the destiny of this infant boy, Giusto Ferdinando Tenducci.*

♪

The extraordinary, forgotten story of Giusto Ferdinando Tenducci is at the heart of this book, but this is not a biography of Tenducci. Instead, in the pages that follow, a 'microhistory' unfolds of an exceptional and now-obscure figure. Within its wider context, Tenducci's story opens up bigger questions about the mental world of eighteenth-century Europeans.[6] Due to a singular musical talent, and the peculiar circumstances into which he was born, Tenducci the servant's son was destined to rise in the world in a way which few men or women achieved before modern times, when social mobility was still the exception. This is a story of one man's entanglement in a complex web of competing economic, cultural, and social forces in a rapidly changing world. His fortunes were to take him from servants' quarters in a remote village in Tuscany, to the palaces of popes and kings, and the opera houses of Rome, Milan, Florence, London, Dublin, and Paris. He befriended some of the leading composers of his day, including Mozart and J. C. Bach, sang for Marie Antoinette, and was honoured for his contribution to music with a title by the Grand Duke of Tuscany.

The lack of evidence about many aspects of Tenducci's life requires us to move beyond the usual historian's reliance upon written texts. The story contained in these pages is based upon several hundred contemporary documents ranging from original archival material and court records to printed sources, including musical scores, and other kinds of material evidence, such as contemporary portraits and engravings. Research for this book started in England, but soon became more 'entangled' in the mental worlds of many different societies, cultures, and time periods. The trail widened to Italy, France, Ireland, Scotland, and America. But Tenducci left no cache of letters, no diaries that speak of his personal experiences and public career. His voice—which was both his fortune and misfortune—has been difficult, but not impossible, to recover across the centuries.

♪

From a vantage point overlooking modern Siena, it is possible to glimpse a panoramic view over the city, over the rooftops of the houses occupied by its poorest citizens. The medieval heart of Siena, its narrow, winding streets, hemmed in by high walls, are crowded with families living cheek-by-jowl. The Tenducci family, like their neighbours, would have been familiar with these streets, struggling against hunger, dirt, and illness, with little respite from their daily struggle to make ends meet. But there are close and visible signs of an altogether different world, of high art, riches, and power. Looking to the horizon, one landmark dominates the skyline of Siena: the towering *duomo*. Just next to the cathedral, a separate building, the baptistery, appears like a Christening cake, a Romanesque and Gothic extravagance. Its white-and-pink marble façade has been here for nearly five hundred years. This is the place where newborns have been brought by generations of local families.

Escaping from penetrating sunshine into the cool hush of the cathedral baptistery, the visitor's eye becomes accustomed to the gloom of the interior: the frescoed walls soon emerge, bright with angels and the figure of the risen Christ. In the centre of the main room, the size of many lesser cathedrals, is a great hexagonal Renaissance font, adorned with bronze panels by Ghiberti and Donatello. A timeless ritual takes place here: a priest sprinkles a baby with holy water from the font, a richly dressed family looks on and smiles with satisfaction as the lofty building reverberates with the cries of their much-anticipated male heir. From birth, this baby's world is open to art, music, and the comforts of luxury.

There were two worlds in eighteenth-century Siena: one, aristocratic and wealthy, family rituals celebrated with elaborate and expensive formality and tangible legacies in the form of buildings, paintings, books, and archival documents; the other poor and obscure, leaving few written and material traces. For a Sienese boy of humble origins like Giusto Ferdinando Tenducci, the ambition of moving between these worlds would have been an almost impossible fantasy, one which was to require a very particular and brutal kind of sacrifice.

*Chapter One*

# The Pig Man Arrives in Monte San Savino

The town of Monte San Savino is situated in a long, wide valley, the Valdiciana, one of four that make up the *Terra di Arezzo*, the Arezzo region of Italy. Today, as far as the eye can see, the valley is a mosaic of fields, vineyards, and olive groves, with a horizon patrolled by lines of tall green cypress trees. Set against the sloping fields are hill towns capped in bright Tuscan red, a lasting remnant of the early medieval process of *incastellamento*, whereby hilltop villages were gradually fortified with high walls to ward off would-be attackers.[1] At the focal point of each scattered settlement is a church tower, and at regular intervals the sound of bells echoes across the valley.

Some features of this place have remained the same for centuries. Only nine thousand people live there today: in the eighteenth century it was smaller in size, with most of its citizens living behind the medieval walls. St Catherine's fair took place annually in late November, when local peasants stocked up on the goods needed for their homes that they could not produce themselves, together with valuable items such as tools, clothes, and cattle.[2] The grandeur of some of Monte San Savino's municipal buildings, fronted by solid stone *loggia* capped with imposing Corinthian columns, and the scale of the palaces inhabited by its leading citizens, complete with formal

6

gardens and shaded inner courtyards, are lasting indications of the town's one-time wealth and administrative importance.

Monte San Savino was a centre of feudal government in the area during centuries of struggle over its control by competing local potentates. It was originally under the control of the Sienese, who became overlords in the fourteenth century. During the sixteenth century, the town made its own contribution to the Italian Renaissance—one of its most famous sons was the poet and architect Andrea Sansovino. (Sansovino distinguished himself through many achievements and one failure: he tried unsuccessfully to carve something out of the immense and impossibly hard marble block from which Michelangelo eventually succeeded in making his statue of David.)

In 1644, the town was seized finally by the Medici family: the Grand Duke of Tuscany, Ferdinand II, granted lordship to his brother Mattias de'Medici. Feudal jurisdiction was transferred in the female line to Vittoria della Rovere, upon whose death in 1694 it was absorbed into the Florentine state under the jurisdiction of a special Commissioner (*Commissario*) nominated by the Grand Duke.[3] From this time to the mid-eighteenth century, the medieval office of *podestà* or local justice was united with that of the *Commissario*, who dispensed his rule from the Palazzo Pretorio.

By the year 1748, Giusto Ferdinando Tenducci's father was employed as a servant to the *Commissario* of Monte San Savino.[4] In this part of Italy a quasi-feudal social structure continued into the eighteenth century, with a very small social élite employing retinues of bureaucrats and administrators who oversaw the business of government. Since the sixteenth century, there had been no distinction between the centres of government and the private households of the leading families: hence the most powerful banking families of Europe such as the Rothschilds effectively ran their businesses from their palatial homes.[5] Likewise, the leading representatives of seigneurial offices such as the Commissaries of the Duke of Tuscany kept large and complex households requiring retinues of staff. It is therefore difficult to say whether the Commissary of Monte San Savino employed Tenducci's father as a long-standing and trusted retainer, or whether it was a much more impersonal arrangement, where master and servant hardly had any contact. In 1747 and 1748 there were two successive Florentine *Commissari*, Filippo di Lorenzo di Domenico Pissi and Giacomo Lorenzo di Giovanni Filippo di Lorenzo Gamucci.[6] Tenducci's father must therefore have been employed by either Pissi or Gamucci. He was just one of a countless number of employees whose invisible labour made the daily business of the Commissary's household function smoothly, providing routine maintenance to the building, cleaning repetitively, and serving food and drink to the family and visiting dignitaries.

It is possible to infer from other sources of evidence what kind of family and household Tenducci grew up in, given his father's lowly occupation. In southern Europe (unlike in England at this time), it was common for female servants to continue in service after marriage.[7] In England and other parts of northern Europe during the mid-eighteenth century, couples delayed marrying until they were in their mid-twenties or even later, so limiting family size. In Mediterranean countries the custom was quite different: people married young by northern European standards, perhaps in their mid- to late teens, and consequently tended to have large families. Eight, ten, or more pregnancies could result from a single marriage (though shockingly few children survived to adulthood), before the death of either the husband or wife ended the union.[8] It was not unusual in early modern Italy for couples to remarry, and for several generations to live under one roof, with grandparents, uncles, aunts, and cousins muscling in to sustain the household with their labours.[9] The parish records of the Arezzo region indicate that a family with the surname Tenducci was living east of Siena during the 1740s. Valentino Tenducci, originally from Pisa, and his wife Maria, from Portoferraio in Livorno, had four children baptized in the church of St Agata during the 1740s: Aldegonda (1742), Anna (1743), Francesco (1746), and Maria Rosa Angelica (1748).[10] These could have been the aunt, uncle, or cousins of Giusto Ferdinando, and it is not impossible that these were his parents and siblings. The same distinctive family name and geographical proximity to Siena suggests at least close kin.

In Catholic countries with extended family households, a man who fathered many sons was thought to be especially virile and blessed: his reputation for sexual prowess, 'heat', and vigour enhanced his reputation in his local community, and did him no harm in his standing among men. Historically, attitudes towards large families have differed in the Catholic south from Protestant northern Europe, where nuclear families consisting of just parents and children have traditionally been more common. (By contrast, in pre-industrial England the poor were censured for marrying young in case they ended up petitioning their local parish for a subsidy to pay for children they could not afford.[11]) It is highly likely therefore that Tenducci's father and mother married relatively young, perhaps in their late teens or early twenties, and had already had several children before Giusto Ferdinando was born. Given his fate, it is possible to infer that he would most likely have had at least two elder brothers, an heir and a 'spare'.

In terms of Giusto's standard of living as a boy, undoubtedly it would have been a struggle for his family to make ends meet. The servants of the rich could have high status, particularly if they were literate and performed administrative tasks, but Tenducci's father was unlikely to have been among their number. Those who met Tenducci's father later recalled that he referred to himself as a 'poor man'.[12] In the Tenducci household, basic necessities such as food and clothing would have been scarce. The rituals and observances of the Catholic Church, with its days of feast and fast, its Saint's Day celebrations and Lenten abstinence, would have regulated the minutiae of the Tenducci family's daily lives, determining when they could lawfully eat meat (on the rare occasions that a neighbour slaughtered an animal), and even when husband and wife could have sex.

♪

Tenducci, like all boys as they grow up, would have received strong messages within his own culture about how to be a man. His ideas about masculinity were shaped on a daily basis by witnessing the roles undertaken by his father and brothers, by other men in the community of Monte San Savino, and by the instruction of the local priest who undertook his education. Agricultural communities such as those found in eighteenth-century Tuscany often reserved the most prestige and power for men who exhibited the greatest physical strength. In the popular songs and legendary stories that were part of the folk culture of ordinary working people across Europe, male heroes were celebrated for demonstrating enormous feats of strength and stamina. François Rabelais drew upon an oral peasant tradition which celebrated this quality when he wrote *Pantagruel* (1532) and *Gargantua* (1534), about a father and son of gigantic height who could perform unrivalled feats of strength, such as lifting dumb-bells made of lead weighing 870 tons, and wrestling wild beasts to the ground.[13] The priority of families and the wider community was to grow enough food to subsist, and to have sufficient manpower to defend villages when faced with an external threat. The importance of having a healthy and strong male at the head of a household was thrown into sharp relief by the lament of one European peasant, directed at the opponent who injured his hand in a fight: 'What have you done to me and my small children?'[14]

These ideas would have been impressed upon Tenducci from an early age by his parents, and by the teachings he received from the Catholic Church. Childhood, especially for poorer children, was not a time for leisure and play, but for learning to toil alongside their parents.[15] For boys, the expectation was that they would do no better nor worse than their fathers, and that they would take up the same occupation as the other men in their household, or at least a related one. Tenducci would have learned that men gained honour and respect from other men by marrying and fathering children. Among rural

10

families who still had a connection to the land, good 'husbandry' (in itself an etymological reminder of the historical importance of a married man being a skilful farmer) remained important. In urban areas, new opportunities were opening up with the growth of towns across Europe following the Renaissance. If they had a little education and managed to save a little money, some men took to shopkeeping. Those who had the good fortune to be well educated took up careers as bureaucrats, army officers, and physicians.

At the upper end of the social scale, well beyond the social milieu of the Tenducci family, customs and types of masculinity changed more rapidly, and were produced and reproduced in literature, art, and music. Embedded in European culture were ideas about the ideal political man, someone who could exercise qualities of fairness and reason, and elicit respect. Baldassare Castiglione's *Book of the Courtier* (1528), for example, recommended that men wishing to acquire a courtly demeanour should be 'very bold, stern, and always among the first' when confronting an enemy, but at other times 'gentle, modest, reserved'.[16] The eighteenth-century polite, bourgeois man was the inheritor of the ideals of civility popularized during the Renaissance. He exercised restraint towards servants and those in his debt, and was not unduly deferential to social superiors, but disposed himself well and thereby established his credit, much like the citizens of ancient Rome.[17] Among the most influential champions of politeness was Anthony Ashley Cooper, the third earl of Shaftesbury, who proposed that masculine discernment and good taste should 'be ever the great employment and concern of him who covets as well to be wise and good as agreeable and polite'.[18] Later in the eighteenth century, among the growing ranks of the middle classes, a man's dedication to hard work, and Christian sensitivity to the suffering of others, was seen as a virtue at a time of revived interest in evangelical religion. 'Hardness of heart, and insensibility of temper conceal themselves under the appellation of manly fortitude', wrote Vicesimus Knox, reflecting the new vogue for men to display their sensibility in public, even by crying on appropriate occasions.[19]

Culturally dominant ideas about masculinity in Europe at this time were therefore remarkably malleable, and required élite men to adapt their behaviour over time. Among the vast majority of the population, including ordinary folk like the Tenducci family, people adapted more slowly to changing ideas about the proper social roles of men. But the lives of boys from humble origins were no less shaped by gendered expectations about how they should behave than their rich counterparts. The influence of these masculine ideals varied across cultures, as men who travelled across Europe found out, but could frequently overlap. It was a fairly universal expectation across Europe at this time, for example, that a man was free to experiment sexually before marriage, provided he did not compromise the reputation of the woman he intended to be his future wife by fathering an illegitimate child upon her.[20] Another of society's norms was that he would at some point marry and father children, thereby establishing his own household. The blueprint for men's lives was in many respects cross-cultural in Western Europe, but when it came to the lived experience of individual men, the social expectations of idealized manhood often proved difficult to achieve.[21]

There was also one particular category of men who offered a notable exception to the principles by which male honour was established in a community through marriage and fatherhood. Catholic priests were expected to remain celibate, and could have high status within their local communities. In many parts of continental Europe, the Church of Rome offered poor boys the chance for an education and for social advancement if they proved to be talented scholars, though in return they usually surrendered any hope of having a family of their own. And so it proved for Tenducci. Some time before the age of 11, he entered Holy Orders, which was a recognized pattern for younger sons in poor households.[22] The Church provided a living and an alternative source of maintenance. At that age, he would have been an acolyte or lector, minor orders to which many boys destined for a lifetime of service in the priesthood belonged.

We can therefore picture the young Tenducci as a 10-year-old altar boy at one of the churches in Monte San Savino, possibly the grand church of Sant'Agostino, where local dignitaries were entombed (Plate 1).[23] His duties would have included assisting the priest during Mass. He also sang in the choir and received a basic education in music, at which he evidently excelled, and which drew attention to his pure, unbroken voice. Since Tenducci did not write down how he felt about his boyhood talent, we must rely upon the account of another boy singer, Balatri, who composed a verse-autobiography that expressed his own point of view as a young chorister: 'My voice is high, clear, and without fault... | I sing at Mass. | Everyone begins to praise me, and pride begins to give me its hand.'[24]

As Tenducci reached 11 or 12 years old, when puberty was about to take effect, someone in authority—his priest, perhaps—raised a question that would have a decisive and irreversible impact upon his life. Should young Giusto be castrated to preserve his talent—the purity of his unbroken voice?

♪

Human male castration, the surgical removal of testicles, was banned upon penalty of excommunication (a prospect which terrified God-fearing people), and the marriage of eunuchs in the Catholic Church was explicitly forbidden by Pope Sixtus V in 1587.[25] The practice of castration, and eunuch marriage, were also prohibited in judicial codes across Europe as abominations which went against natural law. Under-taking deliberate mutilation of the male body was regarded as perverse and dangerous, as much for the body politic as for the individual victim. The formation of a lawful Christian marriage was deemed to be impossible without the intact male organs of generation, since the possibility of conception was regarded as a necessary part of sexual congress in order for consummation to be valid in canon law.[26] The expectation was that married couples should set about producing children according to the divine injunction to 'be fruitful and multiply': if by accident or design a couple took steps to avoid conception, or if the husband was incapable of consummating the union, it was no marriage.[27] Upon these fundamental building blocks consisting of lawful marriages that produced children, ordered societies were founded in western Christendom.

It was for these reasons that eunuchs—castrated men who had been deprived of part or all of their genitals—were regarded as the antithesis of the values represented by Christian patriarchy.[28] Eighteenth-century Europeans knew about eunuchs by reputation: many had read or heard stories about them passed down from the courts of the Roman and Byzantine emperors. Eunuchs were known to have numbered among the entourage of servants employed by Chinese rulers, and to have been present throughout the Islamic world in the households of powerful men, where they were employed most often as guardians of harems. Eunuchs were also known to early modern churchmen since they featured in the Bible: one African eunuch, a high-ranking and literate servant to a royal Ethiopian court, was converted to Christianity by the apostle Philip.[29]

The ambivalence of Western readers towards Oriental and Middle-Eastern eunuchs is apparent in a variety of fictional and semi-fictional accounts written at the time. The eunuch was often portrayed in Western cultures as embodying all that was supposedly cruel and barbaric about non-Christian societies. Many writers capitalized upon the exotic fantasies which eunuchs inspired. The wife of a diplomat, and fearless traveller in her own right, Lady Mary Wortley Montagu published her account of visits to Middle-Eastern harems, in which eunuchs featured memorably, for the benefit of an eager reading public. On a visit with the French ambassador's wife to the home of the Grand Vizier, she recalled that she was handed from her coach by a black eunuch. In her letters from Adrianople in the year 1717 she recorded her meeting with the Kuzlir Aga, or chief black eunuch, robed in yellow 'lin'd with sables'.[30] The French author Montesquieu epitomized the warped Orientalist fantasies of Europeans about Eastern cultures in his portrayals of white and black eunuchs in his *Lettres Persanes* (*Persian Letters*, 1721), who were featured as sadistic torturers of their female captives. It was from fictional accounts such as these that Enlightenment readers became familiarized with eunuchs, whose mention was associated with violent discipline and titillating descriptions of punishment in the all-female harem.

But castration for aesthetic rather than political reasons—to preserve the unbroken male voice—was quite a different matter, a European practice which could not be blamed on the barbarism of the Grand Seignors of the Ottoman Empire. It involved the surgical removal of both testicles, and sometimes the spermatic ducts, to prevent the onset of puberty, usually when a boy was aged between 7 and 12.[31] The practice can be dated back to the church choirs of early medieval Constantinople, and to twelfth-century Spain, where the technique of using falsetto was developed by male singers to cover the highest range of notes in church music written for many voices. Some of these falsettists were likely to have been castrati, such as 'Manuel', a Spanish eunuch who turned up in Smolensk in 1137. The fact of these singers' castration was often concealed since the practice was almost always censured by the Church, before it was actually made illegal. Nevertheless, throughout medieval times, a small number of castrated men continued to sing in churches scattered across Europe.[32]

But it was during the Renaissance that the castration of boys to serve church choirs effectively became an industry in Italy, first supplying the Vatican in the sixteenth and early seventeenth centuries. Women were expressly banned from the Vatican church choirs, but this imposed limitations for composers of polyphonic choral music when it came to supplying the highest vocal parts: soprano and alto. Many composers and choirmasters found the high voices of the Spanish choristers who sang falsetto to be unsatisfactorily forced and artificial. In 1589, Pope

15

Sixtus V authorized the recruitment of four Spanish castrati in the choir of St Peter's Basilica. A turning point was the employment of the first Italian castrato in the pope's private chapel.[33] Matteo Fornari, a tenor in the papal chapel in the first half of the eighteenth century, claimed that the first-ever Italian castrato to be hired by a pope for the Sistine Chapel choir, Girolamo Rosini (1581–1644), had been castrated as a boy not to preserve his voice but 'because of an illness' ('*per infirmità*').[34] There is some evidence that hernia operations were often pretexts for castration at this time. The famous sixteenth-century anatomist Gabriele Falloppio hypothesized that castration could cure intestinal hernias, noting as he did that some friars who sang very loudly could suffer from hernias, since these ruptures were commonly caused by 'tiring and violent strains and loud screams'.[35] One Spanish surgeon alleged that he had witnessed a dishonest hernia surgeon perform such an operation at the behest of a local priest, and there is evidence of the emergence of hernia-doctors in Italy specializing in castration.[36] By the early seventeenth century, Italian castrati outnumbered Spanish singers in the Vatican, and those who turned out to have exceptional voices attracted rich patrons among the cardinals and crowned heads of Europe.

During the Renaissance, to be able to hear a castrato sing was an élite privilege, a private pleasure reserved for powerful men whose bodily senses were attended to with all forms of luxury. What pepper and spices did for the tongue, and furs did for the touch, the castrato did for the ear, and sometimes the eye as well. At first the best castrati were treated as jealously guarded commodities by aristocratic and royal patrons, and were kept almost as pets in some of the wealthiest houses of Europe. During the sixteenth and early seventeenth centuries, cardinals often maintained a castrato in their private musical establishments. As early as 1571, Cardinal Madruzzo employed a castrato in his service: the employer of Girolamo Rosini, the earliest Italian castrato to sing in the Sistine Chapel, was Cardinal d'Aragona.[37] After d'Aragona's death, Rosini transferred to the patronage of Cardinal Pietro

Aldobrandini. It is probable that cardinals 'shopped' for a favourite castrato in the pope's private chapel and singled one out for special attention, having been drawn by ear, or eye. Pietro Montoja, for example, was in the Sistine Chapel choir before leaving to live in the household of his patron Cardinal Francesco Maria Del Monte. It was Cardinal Del Monte who commissioned Caravaggio's *The Lute Player*, an androgynous beauty whose appearance may have been inspired by Montoja.[38] There was a long-standing association of castrati with homosexuality, and some had been the lovers of powerful men. Grand Prince Ferdinando de Medici, himself an accomplished musician, met the castrato Domenico Cecchi ('Cecchino') at the Venetian carnival in 1687. So enamoured was Ferdinando of Cecchi that he neglected his wife and failed to produce an heir. Since his younger brother Gian Gastone showed a similar lack of interest in the female sex, this marked the end of the House of Medici.[39]

Though many within the Church found the pleasures of hearing castrato voices (not to mention their personal qualities as lovers) to be addictive, precisely how these men came to be procured as boys for castration remained a mystery. The Church created the original demand for castrati, but their supply was something from which the Catholic Church distanced itself. As a result, there is almost no information about the history of this illicit practice.

The operations to castrate boys were shrouded in secrecy due to the illegal nature of the procedure. It rarely took place if a boy was set to enter Holy Orders, since the Code of Canon Law decreed that for a man to enter the priesthood he had to be physically intact, with no genital or other deformities, and capable of consummation and procreation were he to marry.[40] This regulation, still in force in modern times, required would-be priests to undergo medical examination, and discouraged men from taking extreme measures to avoid carnal temptation. Self-castration to draw the 'thorn in the flesh' (St Paul's description of sexual temptation) was not unknown among the Church Fathers. For example, there was much casuistical discussion in scholarly literature, not to mention the popular press, regarding the story of Origen. Such was Origen's zeal for God that he castrated himself to avoid sexual sin, but, subsequent commentators wondered, did he commit a greater sin against God by self-mutilation? Most agreed that he did. Ever since St Augustine had confessed his lifelong struggle between the pleasures of the flesh and the dictates of scripture, there had been much high-minded debate among theologians as to whether the dictates of the body, sexual desire and Christian devotion were mutually incompatible. In the medieval love story of Eloise and Abelard, which was widely known across early modern Europe, Abelard was forcibly castrated by his lover's male relatives for his illicit sexual relationship with Eloise, and rebuked her subsequent protestations of worldly as well as spiritual love, as befitted a priest in Holy Orders.[41] Castration was therefore regarded within the Christian traditions of western European society as a righteous punishment or renunciation, a legitimate and even logical anatomical extension of the biblical injunction 'If your hand or your foot causes you to sin, cut it off and throw it away.'[42] When performed so that a boy could remain sexually chaste and offer his body, and unbroken voice, in lifelong service and devotional worship to the Church, it could even be framed as a holy sacrifice, and was sometimes depicted as such by contemporary commentators.[43] Perhaps unsurprisingly, the petition made to the Duke of Modena in 1670 by one Rinaldo Gherardini, requesting his own castration so that he could preserve his vocal talent, was highly unusual.[44]

By the early eighteenth century, the demand for castrati, according to one (no doubt exaggerated) estimation, was such that some 4,000 Italian boys a year underwent the horrific procedure.[45] During the Renaissance, the French regarded it as an Italian custom, even though many of the earliest castrati came from northern France. The Spanish also blamed the Italians, even though the first castrati to be employed in the Sistine Chapel in the sixteenth century were from Spain. Charles Burney the musicologist enquired on his European travels how and where castration took place: 'I was told at Milan that it was at Venice; at Venice that it was at Bologna; but at Bologna the fact was denied, and I was referred to Florence; from Florence to Rome, and from Rome I was sent to Naples.'[46] Several musical conservatories where castrati trained were in Naples; one rumour was that parents could take their sons for an audition in the town, then visit a local shop displaying the sign '*Qui si castrono ragazzi*' ('Boys castrated here').[47] This was an unlikely urban myth, given the severe penalties that could follow from being caught.[48] Burney found out from the British consul in Naples that the Neapolitans also denied any association with the practice of castration; instead, he was told, 'young Castrati come from Leccia in Puglia'. Others thought the operations took place in Bologna, since it was a city full of musical agents and impresarios.[49] Still others whispered that castration happened in the remote Umbrian town of Norcia. The unique account by the castrato named Balatri drew a veil over the truth of how he came to be castrated with the fable that there were cockerels named *Norcini* who laid eggs that hatched into castrati.[50] It was a commonplace that the men of Norcia knew about one thing in particular: the rearing and butchering of pigs. (The tradition continues to this day in the production of a famous local salami, and in the colloquial Italian reference to any butcher as *un nurcia*.) One of the skills of pig-keeping was and is castration, performed on male swine in order to keep the pork sweet. If these rumours were true, it was an early and morbid example of the entrepreneurial application of transferable skills by the men of Norcia.

♪

In the year 1748, Pietro Massi, an itinerant barber-surgeon, arrived in Monte San Savino, the Tuscan hill town where Giusto Ferdinando

Tenducci was living with his family. Pietro's journey could have brought him from Siena, sixty kilometres to the south-west, or from Perugia, in the south-east. It is less likely that he came from the south, from smaller settlements such as Montepulciano that produce famous wine, but slim pickings for a travelling surgeon in search of business. He may have approached on foot or horseback from the bustling provincial capital of the upper Arno region in the north-east, Arezzo, or more probably from the city of Florence to the north, near where the Massi family had a house in Figline Valdarno.[51] It would have been easy for Massi to have hitched a ride on a cart or wagon carrying goods across these well-worn trade routes, but the journey into Monte San Savino from any direction would have been arduous, punctuated by meandering roads and steep hill climbs. From late spring to early autumn, the climate in this part of Tuscany is hot and humid, and wearies the traveller, particularly on the final ascent up the hillside and the winding road into the town.

Pietro doubtless earned a living by advertising his services in teeth-pulling and other painful procedures requiring a strong arm, a sharp knife, and a quick hand. These operations were the staple of wandering barber-surgeons throughout Europe at this time, men whose training was less likely to be in the ancient universities of Padua or Rome than on the battlefields of successive continental wars, where soldiers needing amputations were in plentiful supply.[52] But Pietro had a particular skill that was in demand in centres of ecclesiastical power with their church choirs: for this reason, he may have made it his particular concern to visit the more important towns with a *duomo*, such as Siena, and the lesser satellite hill towns in the region, such as Lucignano, with its cathedral church of Santa Maria, fewer than ten kilometres south of Monte San Savino. His particular skills are hinted at with the detail of his identity: he was described as 'Pietro Antoni[o] Massi of Nurcia'.[53] It is certain that in the surgeon's tool bag carried by Pietro Massi on his travels would have been the necessary equipment for the job of castration on animal—or human—victims: special shears kept sharp for the purpose.

The surgeon Pietro Massi did not travel alone: his work required the services of his son Tomasso, who was then aged about 17, and who was learning the surgeon's art from his father.[54] It was the young Tomasso's particular task to assist in the after-care of patients, visiting them and dressing their wounds to check upon the healing process.[55] Tomasso later remembered that he had helped his father with operations to castrate patients on several occasions: 'after he made his Operations in order that I might become proficient therein he used to send me to attend upon and Cure those persons he had Castrated and to heal up their wounds'. Perhaps nervously aware of the illegality of the operation, Tomasso emphasized that he acted to heal the patients post-operatively 'according to the rules of the profession'.[56] Also travelling with Pietro Massi the surgeon was his servant, Gaetano Mugni. Gaetano was illiterate but useful for his strength: his job was to hold the patient's body as still as possible while his master performed the operations.[57]

Unlike the open vista of neighbouring Lucignano, for the approaching visitor Monte San Savino has the character of a fortified town, one that keeps its secrets hidden. Set back from the traveller's eye at the base of the hill upon which it is built, the town is enclosed by high, sloping medieval walls surrounding an ancient castle keep. If it was summer, Pietro and his two companions would have come on a dirt track, noticing as they approached the town walls the ripe purple *chianti* grapes ready for harvest in the vineyards that in one direction stretched far into the distance, and in the other ran right up to the town walls. Massi and his fellow-travellers would have been aware that they had arrived in a place of some significance as soon as they passed through the *Porta Fiorentina*, an imposing stone gateway. Overhead, the sky would have been filled with the piercing cries of hundreds of swallows that nest each year in the overhanging eaves of farm buildings and local dwellings.

21

Pietro Massi and his companions found their way among the narrow medieval streets of Monte San Savino, orientating themselves by the church tower until they reached the market square with its stone obelisk, a monumental reminder of the Medicis who had ruled here over a hundred years earlier. The travelling trio made their way to the house where the Tenducci family lived.

Nearly a quarter of a century later, Tomasso recalled in middle age that it was here, in the Tenducci family home, that:

> My ... Father Pietro Antonio Massi did ... in my presence Castrate Mr Giusto Ferdinando Tenducci by making an Amputation of both his Testicles and the Spermatick Ducts to which Operation Gaetano di Antonio Figlini a Servant and Assistant to my said Fa[ther] was present and held the said Tenducci fast and secure at the time of the said Operation that the said might be done Effectual[ly].[58]

The details of the procedure were corroborated by the other surviving witness to the operation, the servant Gaetano Mugni, who remembered that 'I did actually hold fast [Tenducci] the son of the ... servant of the Commissary' while he underwent the procedure. When pressed to say more about the details of the surgery, Mugni went on:

> I clearly saw that ... [the surgeon] made two Incisions between the Thighs, and the Body next the Groin, and when these two Incisions were made I saw the said Mr Massi take out the Testicles one at the time, and which I clearly and without a possibility of being deceived saw them in the Hands of the said Mr Massi who afterwards put them in a plate which was ready for the Said Operation.[59]

The operation 'being happily Executed', the surgeon's son Tomasso explained what happened next: 'I ... by way of my ... Father did upon the successive Days after the Operation as often as was necessary go to the House where ... Tenducci resided', in order 'to Apply his Plaisters and do whatever Else was wanting to the Incision of the Wound given to ... Tenducci at the time of Castrating him'.[60]

Thanks to Tomasso's ministrations, unlike many boys who had suffered the same operation, Tenducci survived his trauma. Once his physical wounds had healed, young Giusto left his Tuscan home and journeyed south, to the city of Naples. There, he entered a conservatory and began his musical training. It would take more than brutal surgery to transform Tenducci from an ordinary boy into a *castrato*.

---

## Chapter Two

# Schooling Angels in Naples

In the year 1748, as a boy of about 13, Giusto Ferdinando Tenducci was admitted to the Conservatorio della Pietà dei Turchini, one of four great musical conservatories in Naples.[1] These four conservatories, Santa Maria di Loreto, San Onofrio di Capuana, Poveri di Gesù Christo, and Tenducci's own, Santa Maria della Pietà dei Turchini, had their origins as orphanages founded by the Catholic Church in the sixteenth and seventeenth centuries. Some vestiges of this tradition survived through to the eighteenth century; boys at the conservatories were known as '*figliuoli*' ('little sons'), an allusion to the idea that these institutions assumed the role of a family in the case of orphans, or had given the conservatories sanction to act *in loco parentis*.[2]

From the mid-1600s, the character of these foundations changed. The best students started to be retained for large fees as tutors. Scholars were no longer only orphans and poor boys, but fee-paying boarders, who were recruited from as far afield as Spain and Germany. Gradually, the schools were transformed into prestigious and professionalized fee-paying musical conservatories.[3] Out of these hothouses for talented boys, Naples produced famous composers such as Alessandro Scarlatti, who was Director of the San Bartolomeo opera company in Naples from 1683, Leo, Vinci, and Pergolesi, whose sacred music is still well-known to modern audiences. Another graduate of the Neapolitan conservatories, Porpora, was the most famous music teacher of his generation, and a leading figure in the world of European Baroque music.[4]

Tenducci's admission to Santa Maria della Pietà dei Turchini was therefore both a remarkable opportunity for a poor boy, and a rite of passage. It was marked by an elaborate ritual which was afforded all the solemnity of a priestly investiture. This began with confession, followed by Mass. As Tenducci knelt at the altar beside the rector, he placed his cassock and surplice over his arm. The moment when he first put on these garments would symbolize his new life and vocation. There were prayers, his vestments were blessed, and the other boys chanted '*Veni creator spiritus*' ('Come, holy spirit'). At the climactic moment of dressing, he was helped into his robes by two assistants in the Mass, and a prayer was said to the Virgin ('*Ave Maria*'). This was followed by a psalm which celebrated the joys of fellowship between brothers, underscoring the fact that he had entered a community that would now be his family. The service was concluded with a blessing by the rector, and the very next day his training as one of the *figliuoli* of the conservatory began.[5]

Even before his admission to the conservatory, Tenducci was already familiar with the discipline of being in Holy Orders. This was doubtless a good preparation for the quasi-monastic dedication which his life as a conservatory pupil now required. Every day without fail he rose early in the morning, at 6.30 a.m. in winter and 4.45 a.m. in summer, dedicating the new day to God by singing *Laudate pueri Dominum* ('Boys, give praise to the Lord!') while performing his ablutions. He then put on a distinctive uniform: a black habit, shoes, stockings, a red belt, and distinctive 'Turkish beret' (an exotic touch that was in keeping with the name of his conservatory, *dei Turchini*, 'of the Turks'). He attended morning Mass, the first of many communal prayers which continued throughout the day. Besides prayer, the rest of his days were spent undergoing gruelling training. Though the original purpose of the conservatories was to school boys in preparation for church choirs and a lifetime of divine service, there was another purpose behind Tenducci's musical education: to turn him into an opera star.

♪

Where and how opera came to be invented as a new musical genre is something which has excited much curiosity and speculation. Early modern theatrical productions, as Shakespeare's plays remind us, featured songs, but opera took this to a new level, in effect creating a new theatrical genre. It is usually agreed that opera was invented in Italy during the early seventeenth century, by composers and librettists who were inspired by an earlier tradition of musical dramas in ancient Greece. Opera was distinct from other forms of theatre in its use of *recitative* (sung dialogue) to advance a plot, interspersed with arias which provided soloists with the opportunity to display their vocal talents. Early operatic experiments consisted of *intermezzi*—interludes of singing and dancing between performances of drama—which were staged in the gardens of the Pitti Palace in Florence. Performances of early operas were noted for their spectacular effects and lavish costumes, which were in keeping with the emergent Baroque style in the visual and performing arts at this time. The essence of Baroque was spectacle, artifice, and luxury, the experimental application of different technologies, motifs, and materials to create a dazzling sensory experience. Strongly associated with Catholic devotion, the origins and fullest expression of Baroque style were in Italy, exemplified in the ecstatic sculptures and sinuous architecture of Bernini. During its heyday, Baroque art, architecture, and music were adopted and appropriated widely, due largely to the global reach of European imperialism. As a consequence, it has been called the first truly global style, as its influence spiralled across Western Europe, the Indian subcontinent, and Latin America.[6]

The composer Monteverdi (d. 1643) is usually credited with developing the form of Baroque opera in Mantua under the patronage of Duke Vincenzo Gonzaga. One of his earliest works, *L'Orpheo* (1607), featured a castrato in the leading role as Orpheus. This new art form was enthusiastically embraced across the courts of Europe by royalty and the aristocracy, whose dynasties were closely related by marriage, and whose tastes transcended differences in language, religion, and nationality. From the beginning, opera was associated with aristocratic luxury and expense. Venice's commercial culture and well-established patronage networks favoured private investment in public entertainment: four new opera theatres opened in the city between 1637 and 1641, each with a capacity to hold an audience of 2,000–3,000 people. These early Venetian operatic productions featured elaborate moving stage scenery, sound effects such as thunder and lightning, and even the appearance of the occasional camel on stage. The Teatro Novissimo opened in 1641 with a production of *La Finta Pazza* ('The Feigned Madwoman'), which wowed audiences with four appearances of gods descending to the stage in machines during the performance.[7] Quick scenery changes were made possible by painting vividly coloured stage sets on sliding wings, and changing backdrops via pulleys overhead. Theatres competed with one another to provide more and more stunning effects, so that a typical opera performance could feature marine gods rising from trapdoors in the stage, illuminated clouds, lit from within, descending from on high, and loud thunder claps emanating from above the heads of the performers.[8]

Naples already had a reputation as one of the leading venues for opera and theatrical performance, which had flourished there from the mid-1600s under the patronage of the Spanish viceroy. There were four theatres in Naples: the San Bartolomeo, Fiorentini, Nuovo, and della Pace, of which the Teatro San Bartolomeo was the most influential. San Bartolomeo had the closest links with the royal court and special privileges over the performance of stage works and their profits. During the early decades of the eighteenth century, the theatre had benefited not only from the successes of local composers such as Scarlatti and Mancini, but from imported talent of international fame, including guest performances by leading castrati such as Carlo Broschi (Farinelli) and Francesco Bernardi (Senesino).

In 1735, the city of Naples government changed hands, passing from Austrian to Spanish control. Charles Bourbon, son of Philip V of Spain, became King of Naples and proceeded to set up court there. As Charles III (1734–59) his plan was to extend the reputation of the city as a leading centre of European culture. One of the main means of achieving this was through his patronage of music, especially opera.[9] Shortly after his coronation, Charles quickly commissioned a new opera house, the Teatro di San Carlo, which opened its doors in 1737 (Plate 2).

This lavishly furnished building, situated within sight of Tenducci's school,[10] was one of the grandest of its kind. Its original interior featured six tiers of boxes, arranged in a horseshoe shape around the proscenium. The richly carved and gilded interior was illuminated with hundreds of candles, which were not extinguished during the performances: the point was to people-watch and be seen. The most prestigious seats were reserved in the gilt-and-brocade festooned royal box, at the focal point of both the performers on stage and the audience, to the centre of the second tier. Other boxes were paid for by the nobility, and could not be relinquished without the King's express permission. It was the court in microcosm, with ordinary folk crammed in to watch the spectacle from the margins of the uppermost tier, the hallways, and backstairs.[11]

The Teatro di San Carlo championed the most influential musical and theatrical genre to have appeared across most of eighteenth-century Europe, *dramma per musica* or (more commonly) *opera seria*, that is, opera with a serious plot that was often tragic and always dramatic. This was in contrast to *opera commedia* and *buffo* performances, consisting of raucous scenes whose primary purpose was to entertain by making the audience laugh, interspersed with ever-popular cavorting ballerinas. By contrast, the themes of *opera seria* were highbrow, and contained thinly veiled political allusions. The 'musical poets' who composed *libretti* drew upon themes from classical mythology to illustrate the historic struggles of great leaders, and the primacy of rulers who exercised absolute power. Martha Feldman summarizes the classic form of *opera seria* as 'tales of heroes, young and old, who make their way through a labyrinth of passions, from jealous desire to filial love, rage, joy, pity, sorrow, remorse, and piety', who suffer 'bitter loss, divided loyalty, sacrifice, and redemption'.[12] It is no coincidence that the most influential librettist of the eighteenth century, Metastasio, was poached from Naples by the Habsburg court in Vienna to write theatrical pieces that extolled the virtues of duty and autocracy. In *La Clemenza di Tito* (1734) Metastasio hoped to steel the resolve of the leaders of the Holy Roman Empire to turn the ongoing Polish War of Succession to their advantage by presenting the spectacle of Titus renouncing all personal happiness for the sake of ancient Rome.[13] The performances at the Teatro di San Carlo, under the patronage of the new King of Naples, were to prove no less political, both on- and off-stage.

The universal subjects of love, power, and fate that were the themes of *opera seria* evoked powerful emotional responses in the audience, for whom going to an opera was a highly participative experience. The fashion in *opera seria* was for high, piercing voices trained with great flexibility to provide the maximum expressive and intense effect, a tradition which in the early nineteenth century was given the retrospective term *bel canto* (literally 'beautiful singing').[14] The Italian school of *bel canto* emerged during the seventeenth century in Florence, and spread to Venice, Rome, Naples, and eventually Milan. The earlier church tradition of polyphonic choirs had presented melodies in sacred music that were sung by many voices. However, in *bel canto*, melodic lines were given to one, single voice. Though it was possible to find star singers in the sixteenth century among the many-voiced cathedral choirs, *bel canto* singing encouraged the emergence of the *diva* or *virtuoso*, with its greater emphasis upon individual talent and

29

technical mastery.[15] Soloists became increasingly well versed in the arts of 'florid song', about which instruction manuals began to be published and circulated, which shaped taste in music across Europe, and influenced the practical aspects of vocal and compositional training. By the mid-seventeenth century, a handbook on how to produce operas, *Il Corago*, had been printed in Venice. By the start of the eighteenth century, a lively debate flourished in print as to whether Italian or French opera was superior, based upon an entirely subjective judgement as to which of these two nations had the finer language and musical expression.[16]

Solos and duets in Italian *opera seria* were interspersed with rapid sung dialogue, with one character lapsing into 'lyrical effusion' just as another made a hasty exit.[17] The grandest, most impressive arias in which castrati and female sopranos displayed their most impressive feats of singing—in terms of both technique and expression—were saved for climactic moments in the plot, at the end of important scenes or entire acts.[18] Castrati were associated with a passionate style of singing, involving virtuosic trills, luxuriant sighs, and turns of phrase laden with pathos. Farinelli famously sent his audience into a swoon when he demonstrated his virtuosity by singing a single note for over a minute.[19]

The classic *da capo* format of an aria (an opening section, a second section, then a reprise) provided the opportunity for the castrato to demonstrate his skill in the Baroque methods of ornamentation and extemporization. The most brilliant castrati were also known for their ability to introduce trills, producing a rapid effect that charmed the ear, supposedly like birdsong. In this respect, castrati were 'co-creators' of the music, not just performers.[20] With a three-octave range or more at their disposal, the best castrati were able to sing a powerful and sonorous low register of notes as well as an undistorted high register, all the time maintaining clear and natural pronunciation. Castrato voices were not undifferentiated: there were alto and soprano castrati, and individual voices could change during the course of a career.

30

Carestini, who was brought to London by Handel in 1733, was said to have a 'powerful and clear' soprano voice that matured into 'the fullest, finest and deepest counter-tenor that has perhaps ever been heard'.[21] The fully trained castrato voice epitomized everything about Baroque style—artificial, sensuous, luxurious, and exotic.

♪

In order to reach the standard required of leading castrato singers, natural talent had to be augmented by repetitive and exhaustive training. Pupils at Tenducci's conservatory included not just young castrati like himself, but others of the same age who had not suffered the operation. All boys were supposed to receive a broad education in the humanities. In practice, the focus was inevitably upon music: learning a musical instrument, training the voice, and the fundamentals of composition, with extra tuition in harmony, keyboard, and a second instrument. During the eighteenth century, one Irish visitor, Michael Kelly, recalled that he visited one of the Neapolitan conservatories as a prospective student. He witnessed first-hand the chaotic din of a great number of boys simultaneously studying composition, singing, and playing instruments: 'There were several rooms, but in the great school-room, into which I was introduced, there were some singing, others playing upon the violin, hautboy, clarionet, horn, trumpet, etc. etc.' Kelly vividly recalled the effect of hearing so many pupils playing different music at the same time, and in different keys. 'The noise', recalled Kelly, 'was horrible; and in the midst of this terrific Babel, the boy who studied composition was expected to perform his task, and harmonize a melody given him by his master.'[22] Somehow among this racket (which was perhaps the misguided impression of a visiting foreigner), the young Tenducci mastered the harpsichord. This was an essential instrument for composing and performing Baroque music; many years later, when he became famous, Tenducci was able to buy a very fine instrument of his own by the German harpsichord-maker Americus Backers, much as a violin-player might buy his dream Stradivarius.[23]

Each day had a particular routine and discipline. In the morning, Tenducci spent an hour rehearsing difficult passages of music. Particular attention was paid to breathing and the fundamental techniques of Baroque singing: *passaggi* (repeated trills), *messa di voce* (vocal agility), and *appoggiaturas* (so-called 'grace-notes' just above and below the primary note on the score). The techniques he learned were designed to refine his voice into a flexible and nimble instrument. He then spent an hour practising his letters, and a further hour singing exercises in front of a mirror. The idea was to encourage him to attend to his facial expressions during performances, and improve his breathing technique through awareness of his posture, as well as refining the gestures and deportment that he would use in performances of sacred music and on stage. In 1723, a reform of acting methods used by vocalists had been initiated by the castrato Tosi, who complained about the poor standard of acting among operatic performers. A common language of gesture emerged in European theatres and opera houses: indicative gestures (such as pointing), imitative gestures (indicating the size or speed of an object or person), expressive gestures (indicating passion, fear, or anger), and gestures of address, emphasis, or commencement and termination (raising a hand to begin an aria, for example, or lowering it to indicate completion).[24]

Though to the modern eye these gestures would probably appear artificial and mannered, they were an important means by which eighteenth-century performers communicated the emotion and sense of their music to their audiences through the use of their bodies. The English playwright and actor-manager Colley Cibber praised the castrato Nicolini for his acting during opera performances: 'by his action, as much as he does the Words of it, by his Voice; every Limb and Finger, contributes to the Part he acts, insomuch that a deaf man might go along with him in the Sence of it'. Nicolini, not the most lithe of castrati, was nevertheless praised for his 'beautiful Posture'.[25] Opera singers were therefore prized not just for their voices, but for their full, embodied presence on stage. During his education at the conservatory, Tenducci therefore learned to master his body as much as his voice as an instrument for communicating the entire range of human emotions on stage.

Afternoons for Tenducci and his fellow-pupils were immersed in musical theory, including a time for practising counterpoint—a distinctive feature of Baroque music, which was essentially the art of improvisation. Another hour of counterpoint with the *cartella*—the musical equivalent of a slate for writing practice—was followed by another hour of study, which often included lessons in enunciation of words whilst singing so that expression and meaning could be drawn out to greatest effect.[26] Tenducci, like the other boys, was not allowed to rest before scrutinizing his conscience at vespers in the evening. He was also required to attend confession at least once a week, and to observe the strict rules laid down by his conservatory, which included a ban on spending the night, or even eating a meal, beyond the confines of the school walls.

Tenducci's music masters at the conservatory were Signors Fago and Brunetti, but he recalled that it was 'The celebrated Caffariello, under whom I studied Music from my infancy' who was his most formative influence during his education, most probably as his private tutor.[27] Many castrati sought a father-figure in their teachers, mentors, and patrons, and, perhaps as a result of their operations, regarded the construction of their own families of choice as a vital means of gaining support, both emotional and financial, which their birth families could or would not provide. Farinelli's exceptionally close relationship with his brother Riccardo, whose wife Farinelli chose in order to secure an heir for his own fortune, is one example of this. Farinelli also had an unusually close relationship with the librettist Metastasio, and for many years was under the direct patronage of the King of Spain, living in his household and singing at the monarch's bedside to alleviate his depression.

The famously temperamental Gaetano Majorano, called Caffarelli (1710–83), had attended the Conservatorio dei Poveri in Naples before his professional debut in Rome in 1726. He was employed by Handel for many years in London, and was later to play a pivotal role in advancing Tenducci's career in England. In his heyday Caffarelli had been a great singer, even replacing Farinelli on the London stage in 1737, and commanding a fee of £1,000 for a season performing for Handel in his opera *Faramondo*. He was however a man of 'capricious temper and uncontrollable arrogance'. Across Europe, Caffarelli was notorious for turning up late, or not at all, for rehearsals. His escapades included fighting a duel over whether Italian or French opera was superior, and humiliating his *prima donna* whilst on stage in Italy by using obscene gestures towards her (a shocking breach of etiquette which led to his imprisonment).[28] In 1739, during one religious service in a church in Naples at which a nun was due to take the veil, Caffarelli sacrilegiously assaulted a fellow-singer, Reginelli. A particularly low episode followed in which he received a rival singer Conti 'upon his close-stool, where he sat during the whole visit'.[29]

Like his master Porpora before him, Caffarelli sometimes took poor but promising boys under his instruction without charge as a form of charity, which yielded dividends if the boy went on to become famous. Porpora was a hard taskmaster, but among his pupils was the legendary Farinelli, so his training techniques were those of the undisputed *maestro*. According to one anecdote, Porpora confined Caffarelli for five or six years to exercises written on a single sheet of paper, after which time he sent his pupil on his way with the advice 'Go, my son, I have nothing more to teach you. You are the greatest singer in Europe.'[30] Though they could father no biological children of their own, a quasi-dynastic link was established between the greatest singers of the era as though from father to son, through which knowledge of the techniques and secrets of the castrato's art was passed on to the next generation. Through Caffarelli, Tenducci established a musical pedigree that linked him directly to Porpora, giving him impeccable credentials. While Caffarelli's talent was undoubtedly an inspiration for Tenducci's musical career, his master's character was less of a role model than a caution. Caffarelli's well-documented narcissism was unlikely to have provided a bedrock of emotional support for his young protégé. Effectively lacking a mentor, Tenducci may have been unable to trust or respect authority figures, a hint of which was revealed in his subsequent dealings with the daughters—and wives—of powerful men.

♪

Three of the four musical conservatories, including Tenducci's, were under the patronage of the King of Naples, and enjoyed special privileges as a result. They were commissioned to provide boys for the choirs and special ceremonial events in the city. In the autumn, the pupils were 'obliged to attend morning and evening, for nine days, at the Franciscan Church' wearing their uniforms. In return for participating at this festival without pay, they were exempt, by the King's permission, 'from all taxes on provision and wine, which are paid by every other class of inhabitants [of the city]'.[31] Within the annual calendar of obligations, young castrati could be especially profitable for their conservatories. They were especially popular dressed in white as '*figliuoli angelini*' ('little angel-sons' or 'angel children') for choral vigils or processions, perhaps because the angelic purity of their unbroken voices was associated with the idea of perpetual (enforced) virginity.[32] One student who entered Tenducci's conservatory in 1739, Nicola Reginella, was under the patronage of the Duke of Monteleone, who paid twenty-four ducats a year to have his protégé trained. Others were already commanding good fees for their performances before graduation, which surviving accounts suggest went straight into the coffers of the conservatory to which they belonged.[33] Tenducci himself sang at the marriage celebrations of the Duke of Savoy at Caligari in 1750 while he must still have been a pupil at the conservatory in

Naples, a mark of the trust which was placed in him as an outstanding student to perform well on this grand occasion.[34]

Among their peers at school, castrated pupils were treated to better living conditions than the other boys: they were given warmer clothing, better food, and attentive treatment should they catch cold or fall ill.[35] Because of their operation and altered physicality, they were thought to be more delicate than their fellow-students. Their voices were so prized that every pain was taken to ensure that they lived in relative comfort. Their treatment by the other boys must have been a curious mix of envy and ridicule. On the one hand, their uncastrated fellow-pupils could have been envious of them since they were cosseted like young racehorses, and enjoyed many comforts denied the others. But as the other boys entered puberty and started to display the bodily signs of maturing into men, castrati could not fully have been part of the all-male camaraderie of testosterone-fuelled adventure. As the other boys' voices broke, and they started to shave, the young castrati were excluded from the important rituals which attended the normal transition into manhood. Their cohabitation in close proximity with other adolescent males must have heightened their sense of difference during such rites of passage. Of course, this did not stop the student castrati from forming a strong camaraderie amongst themselves. In 1759, just a few years after Tenducci had graduated from the Pietà dei Turchini, the governors of his conservatory petitioned the King of Naples to stop their young castrati consorting with the ballerinas of the Teatro San Carlo, since the women were encouraging them to drink, gamble, and engage in other bad habits.[36] This small piece of evidence hints at a counter-culture of adolescent castrati on the town. 'Other bad habits' among Tenducci's peer group may have included some kind of sexual initiation that mirrored the loss of virginity that was a rite of passage anticipated by any teenage boy in Naples, where the sexual services of prostitutes were not difficult to obtain. Though their profitable image was of pious *figliuoli angelini*, the reality of adolescent castrati's lives may have been rather different.

♪

It was out of this hothouse environment that Tenducci emerged as a fully trained castrato, ready to test his talent upon the European stage. Like promising young athletes schooled in an academy from an early age, the education that Tenducci and his fellow-pupils received was highly specialized. It did not equip boys well for any other vocation if they failed to make their careers as opera stars. Some whose vocal talents proved disappointing went on to make a living singing in church choirs: others whose voices did not live up to expectations simply ended up destitute. The comparison of the castrato voice with pyrotechnics is an apposite one: fireworks, like arias sung by those few castrati who made it, cost a great deal of time, toil, and money to create a luxury art form which was, in essence, transient and wasteful.

Tenducci was one of the fortunate ones, since his vocal talent was among the minority that responded exceptionally well to training. Doubtless one of the most promising boys in his year, he was as yet untested in the highly critical and competitive world of commercial opera. In order to graduate from his Neapolitan conservatory, Tenducci had to compose a stage drama, drawing upon a sacred theme, but presented as an opera. This provided a transition into the world of professional singers in which he and only a few dozen of his peers were destined to reach international fame. It was the culmination of many years of training.[37] He most likely graduated in the summer of 1753, since his first professional appearance on stage was in the autumn of that year, at the Teatro Grimani di San Samuele in Venice. Here, he took a minor part in an acclaimed performance of *Ginevra*, a drama in three acts by Antonio Salvi, set to music by Bertoni. He also appeared in the Venice carnival the following year at the same theatre, performing in *Tamerlane*, with music by one of the leading Baroque composers, Cocchi, and *Adriano in Siria*, to a *libretto* written by Metastasio. By 1755, Tenducci had come to the attention of the famous librettist himself. Metastasio commented in a private letter to

Prince Trivulzi, dated 17 February 1755, that he had met a young castrato named Tenducci, who apparently at that time was commonly called 'the Sienese', a moniker he later dropped, perhaps to avoid confusion with the elder castrato Francesco Bernardi, also called Senesino.[38] Over the next three years, Tenducci continued to develop his repertoire of performances of *opera seria*, appearing at theatres in Milan, Padua, and as far afield as Dresden, as well as returning to the Teatro di San Carlo in Naples, to growing critical acclaim.[39]

♪

In 1758, Tenducci's career entered a new phase. He consolidated his reputation early in the year by singing at the Teatro Nuovo in Padua with the soprano Caterina Gabrielli, in *Demofonte*, a three-act opera by Metastasio with music by Galuppi, which by all accounts was a 'brilliant success'. Sometime during that year, his services were secured by the King's Theatre in London for the following operatic season, from October 1758 to June 1759. He was talent-scouted by one of the managers of the King's Theatre, probably Francesco Vanneschi or Giardini.[40]

It was customary for managers to send their agents to Italy to find the best young talent among the latest crop of castrati. During the mid-1750s, Felice Giardini (himself a famous violinist) was leader of the orchestra at the King's Theatre, and had toured the Continent in person, searching out the best performers. He later appointed an agent, Leone, to undertake the search on his behalf, a process which was critical to the success of the London opera season. Eighteenth-century productions of *opera seria* usually consisted of six or seven main characters. The *primo* and *secondo uomo* (lead and second man) were played by castrati, whose love-objects, the *prima donna* and *seconda donna*, were female sopranos. The cast was completed by one or two ruler-figures, who were usually played by older men with tenor or bass voices. Leone was therefore despatched to Italy to find at least half a dozen singers, armed with a fat purse and a list of 'ten commandments' which Giardini advised were the best maxims for an opera agent new to the game. Giardini's fairly bland exhortations included 'Never...be hasty', 'be civil to all', 'talk little, and hearken a great deal', and 'When Things go well, you will have Honour and Profit'. Giardini's commandment to Leone that he should exert 'Oeconomy with Decorum' was indicative of the fine balance which had to be achieved between offering a sum large enough to lure the best Italian singers to London and enhance the reputation of the King's Theatre, without bankrupting them.[41]

Leone was despatched in July, just a month after the previous opera season had closed, and travelled via Paris to the main centres of Italian opera in Turin, Bologna, Rome, and Naples, where he consulted the most famous singing masters about their latest pupils.[42] Though it varied according to the quality of the performer, a *primo uomo* (leading man) could negotiate a fee of between £950 and £1,500 for a London season. As a relative newcomer, the young Tenducci's fee would have been below the lower end of this scale in 1758, since he was hired as second man to another castrato, Pasquale Potenza. But it is likely that he earned more than £700 in fees for his first London season at the King's Theatre, since this was the usual level of fee commanded by the *prima donna*.[43] This fee alone was ten times the annual income that was needed at that time to sustain an entire middle-class family in England for a year. Tenducci would also have had the expectation of additional income from at least one benefit concert in London—a one-off event in his honour from which he would receive all profits from ticket sales.[44]

The unpredictable Caffarelli certainly played a role in promoting his young protégé at this critical stage in his early career. Tenducci later wrote his own account for the English public of how he first came to their country. He recalled that 'Caffariello...obtained for me, by the means of Master Cocchi, an invitation to England, as the Second Singer in the King's Theatre'.[45] Cocchi had evidently heard Tenducci sing in

Italy and wished to recruit him to perform his own compositions, since Tenducci subsequently performed Cocchi's *Ciro Riconosciuto* during his first London season. Tenducci was among several Italians—six principal singers and four dancers—recruited for the 1758–9 season. In addition to Potenza and Signora Mattei, the leading man and woman, there was a second woman to play opposite Tenducci, Signora Calori, a third castrato, Quilici, and a third woman, Signora Rosa. Tenducci signed a contract, most likely before he embarked for England, for which he received a down-payment on his fee for the season, and the promise of monthly payments by instalment of the remainder of his fee, unless the opera house burnt down. In return, Tenducci bound himself to perform day and night as required: 'I do promise and Oblige myself to sing as second actor in the . . . [King's] Theatre in all the Heroic Operas in Musick that shall be Acted in the said Theatre from the day of my Arrival there until the End of June of the Ensuing year.'[46] Having undertaken 'to go by the post to the City of London without detaining my self in any of the Cities in my Voyage except some days to rest', with the promise of fame and fortune ahead of him, the 23-year-old set out on the long journey by land and sea to England.

## Chapter Three

# The Castrato in London

It was no surprise that London was a magnet for the young Tenducci as he forged the early stages of his operatic career. During the eighteenth century, Italy had a reputation for producing the best singers and composers, while England had the reputation for paying for them. The German music connoisseur Johann Mattheson noted in the early 1700s that 'He who in the present time wants to make a profit out of music betakes himself to England. The Italians exalt music: the French enliven it; the Germans strive after it, the English pay for it well.'[1] There was some foundation to these national stereotypes. Opera has always been an expensive business, requiring capital to fund the building and upkeep of opera houses, and the lavish scenery and costumes that were eagerly anticipated in each new production. Though some 'recycling' was possible, with classical stage sets being reused time and again for leading composers such as Handel, previously unseen backdrops and ever-more spectacular costumes and props were expected with each new opera.[2] In addition, there were the large salary bills incurred by the employment of singers, musicians, and dancers, a cast which could number over one hundred performers. In one season alone, Beard's Company at Covent Garden employed 61 actors, 25 dancers, and 14 singers, including Tenducci and two of his contemporaries: the much-acclaimed female soprano, Mattei, and fellow-castrato, Quilici.[3] Opera in the eighteenth, as in the twenty-first century, was more likely to bring bankruptcy than riches to operatic speculators and impresarios.

But in Georgian London an entrepreneurial spirit was the order of the day. In 1758, the same year that Tenducci had his first English season, tax officials counted that there were precisely 21,603 shops, warehouses, and other retail outlets in the capital, selling foodstuffs and merchandise from all corners of the globe. Visitors and residents alike marvelled that London was rapidly becoming one vast emporium.[4] Among these emerging consumer markets in England was a new appetite for leisure and entertainment.[5] Instead of being born to pleasure and luxury among the ranks of the landed gentry, a wider cross-section of the population started to buy tickets to their entertainment of choice: the theatre or opera, assemblies and pleasure gardens, the Tower of London and British Museum. Depending upon one's taste (that watchword of the discerning Georgian consumer), it was possible to visit Don Saltero's coffee house in Chelsea or the British Museum to view the collections of artefacts and curiosities, peruse the galleries of the Royal Academy of Arts, or pay the admission fee to enter Bedlam Hospital in order to observe the destitute and insane.[6]

Since the days of the theatre-loving monarch Charles II, two hundred different venues had opened in London for entertainment, ranging from theatres, fair booths, and music rooms, to taverns and pleasure gardens.[7] A growing tier of 'middling' sorts of shopkeepers, tradesmen, and professionals—such as bureaucrats, lawyers, physicians, and officers—emerged to service a rapidly expanding metropolitan population. A disposable income was needed to spend on comfortable lifestyles and entertainment, and though this was still beyond the reach of the majority of England's population, within certain parts of the metropolis there emerged a new economy of pleasure. Some have called this the era of England's 'consumer revolution', with massive profits to be made in new markets for imported chinaware and decorative goods, commodities such as tea, coffee, and sugar, luxury textiles, and furniture. The scale of these new consumer markets for pleasurable diversion was demonstrated in 1749, a decade before Tenducci's inaugural London season, at the first performance of Handel's *Music for the Royal Fireworks*. Commissioned by George II to commemorate the Peace of Aix-la-Chapelle, the rehearsal alone attracted 12,000 ticket-buying spectators to Green Park, at an inflated price of two shillings and sixpence each.[8]

The story of how Italian opera came to influence English culture is an exceptional example of the influence of royal patronage upon the arts, and of the European-wide cultural influences to which Britain has always been susceptible. Across Europe, Italian opera was strongly associated with royal patronage. Queen Henrietta Maria, the Catholic wife of Charles I, had been an early fan of operas featuring castrato singers. Another devotee was Queen Christina of Sweden, a late convert to Catholicism as an exile in Rome, who vied with other aristocratic women to appoint the best castrati for private concerts. In Germany, the Dukes of Württemberg, the Electors of Bavaria, and Frederick the Great were among those aristocrats who had expensive opera habits. Before the mid-eighteenth century, Dresden emerged as one of the leading centres of Italian opera in Europe under the patronage of the Electors of Saxony. The preservation of opera as an élite leisure activity in this German city was ensured by an actual ban on payment for tickets.[9]

After the death of the last Stuart monarch, Queen Anne, in 1714, the English parliament had imported German princelings from Hanover to ensure a Protestant succession. Both George I and George II brought with them new cultural influences from the Continent in the visual and performing arts. Unlike their French and Italian counterparts, however, the Hanoverians were notoriously reluctant to support the arts and sciences financially.[10] It was due to the particular influence of the composer Handel that London's Royal Academy of Music was founded in 1719 under the patronage of George I, who gave £1,000 towards the cost of setting up the Academy specifically to promote opera under the directorship of the Lord Chamberlain.[11] With Handel as its musical director, the Royal Academy produced successful operas which were the height of fashion, although the expense of staging them meant that they seldom made a profit. Following the success of *Rinaldo* (1711), Handel continued to compose operas throughout the 1720s, such as *Julio Cesare in Egitto* (1724). Like Metastasio at the court of the Holy Roman Emperors, Handel used classical and historical themes to celebrate the grandeur and military successes of his royal patrons. His *Riccardo Primo* (Richard I) was intended to celebrate the accession of George II in 1727. His successes continued during the 1730s with *Partenope* (1730) and *Faramondo* (1738). Though he failed to produce new operas in the last two decades of his life, Handel's influence stretched into the mid-eighteenth century and beyond: Georgian men and women considered that his compositions were sublime, defining 'true taste' in music.[12]

♪

By the time Tenducci arrived in London in the late 1750s, castrati were no longer a novelty. Tenducci would not have surprised the English men and women whom he met and performed for simply by being a castrato, though men such as himself maintained their status as objects of curiosity and interest, if not novelty. Castrati had first been introduced to English audiences as early as the 1680s, though at first they performed at private concerts for royalty and at church services. They were instantly popular, if controversial.[13] In an era when the Royal Society encouraged speculation and enquiry into strange phenomena in the natural world and greater scientific understanding of human anatomy, the anomalous bodies of castrati aroused much speculation. Samuel Pepys, who was one of the first to hear two Italian castrati sing in London during a private concert at the home of Lord Bruncker, noted a comment by Sir Thomas Harvey on first seeing these 'Eunuchs': 'that

[he] . . . believes they did grow large by being gelt, as our Oxen do'.[14] Similarly, the first depictions of castrati on-stage in England focused attention upon the unusual physical characteristics of castrati, particularly their long limbs and disproportionately small heads (Plate 3).

Curiosity, fear, and prurient interest underpinned many of the fictional and anecdotal stories about Italian castrati in London. While some English commentators evidently greeted these Italian singers with scorn and ridicule, others raved about their spectacular voices, and their personal attributes. Samuel Pepys implied he was not like other people when he noted in his diary that he did not 'dote of the Eunuchs', although he later succumbed and engaged a castrato for a private concert.[15] Another famous late seventeenth-century diarist, John Evelyn, went especially to a Catholic chapel in London to hear the castrato Siface sing, noting rather diffidently that there was 'much crowding, little devotion' in church that day.[16] The Whig informant Roger Morrice noticed in his 'entring book' for February 1687 that an unnamed 'Italian eunuch' (most probably Siface) had sung at Whitehall several times before the King, and that 'he is reported to sing better than any man that this century has produced'.[17]

Over the course of the next two decades, the demand for castrati expanded in London from private concerts and royal performances to large-scale commercial concerts and expensive operatic productions. It was not just their curious bodies and exquisite voices that attracted attention, but the fact that they were almost without exception Italian.[18] It was Handel who made Italian opera acceptable to English audiences: *Rinaldo* had brought fame to the castrato Nicolini. Though the public flocked to hear Handel's music, reassured by his loyalty to their Protestant monarch, there was an enduring suspicion that Italian opera was a means for Romish priests to infiltrate the nation. The anonymous author of *A Protestant Alarm* (1733) urged the 'Nobility, Gentry and others whom it may concern' to take care that Handel and one of his leading stars, Senesino, were true Protestants 'well affected to the present Government'.[19] Since English audiences could not by and large understand the words of Italian operas, it was suspected that opera singers were hiding 'Jesuitical Quibbles, or other Papistical Legerdemain' among the words of the sung *libretti*. One solution, suggested the *Protestant Alarm*, could be for parliament to insist that people should not be allowed to sing 'in an unknown Tongue'. Since many of the leading castrati had risen to fame by singing in the Pope's private chapel, it was even suggested that opera was an alternative way of celebrating the Catholic Mass.[20] Though these comments were deeply satirical in character, the fact that the popular literature of this period chose to focus upon Italian opera as a flashpoint for religious, political, and social commentary is indicative of the wider awareness of imported fashion beyond the social élite, and the curiosity of the English towards this Baroque art form. Italian opera was imported not just into England but into other Protestant countries such as Sweden, where it likewise found enthusiastic audiences. The English seemed to be able to hold the contradictions in tension of despising all things 'Popish' but enjoying the exoticism of European imported style, which in large measure was due to the enduring popularity of the Grand Tour. From the mid-seventeenth to the end of the eighteenth century, the Grand Tour to Italy was a rite of passage for young English gentlemen of fortune, a formative experience that could last several months or many years, one that shaped their aesthetics, and completed their education by giving them (in theory at least) an appreciation of the art and architectural styles of classical antiquity.[21]

The influence of Italian style in late seventeenth- and eighteenth-century England can be traced across many different art forms. Henry Purcell composed Baroque musical odes which were performed at the court of William and Mary, which celebrated the saints (such as St Cecilia, the patron saint of music) beloved of the nation's Catholic enemies. Sir Christopher Wren's construction of the new St Paul's Cathedral as England's most stunningly Baroque building (designed to surpass St Peter's Basilica in Rome) raised concerns among some Anglican clergy. The purchase of paintings to add to the interior was later rejected (perhaps rather belatedly, given the surroundings) as overly 'Popish'.[22] While many English commentators despised Baroque style for embodying all that was idolatrous and absolutist, there was also the sense that, historically, when it came to art and music, Catholicism was the 'parent of taste'.[23] Part of the pleasure evoked by Italian castrati, the stars of the London opera houses, was therefore not only their vocal ability and the macabre novelty factor of their status as castrated men, but also their dangerous connotations of Popish decadence, and crypto-Catholicism.

♪

In the early 1700s, there were two theatrical companies performing plays, and another group producing Italian operas in London. The King's Theatre in the Haymarket (site of the present Her Majesty's Theatre) was the home of Italian opera in England. The building was frequently altered following its opening in 1705, and suffered fluctuating fortunes. During the good times of the 1720s and 1730s, Handel visited Italy in person to gather the best talent. Frederick, Prince of Wales was a direct patron, sponsoring entertainments for the nobility held at the King's Theatre. By mid-century, however, changing fashions and a succession of legal disputes and managerial handovers had jeopardized the fortunes of the theatre.[24] Garrick's Theatre Royal, Drury Lane (designed by Sir Christopher Wren in 1674) was more associated with dramatic productions than opera. Drury Lane was also the main venue for the new pantomimes that were much beloved of the English from their earliest appearance in the 1730s. While theatrical performances required in principle at least the sanction of the Lord Chamberlain, operas were customarily permitted as one-off, expensive forms of entertainment patronized directly by royalty and the nobility. John Rich's new Theatre Royal in Covent Garden (which eventually was remodelled into the modern Royal Opera House) provided a new venue for operatic productions after 1732.

The castrato Farinelli was already a singer of international fame when he made his London debut in 1734 under the auspices of a company known as the Opera of the Nobility, and was known for commanding spectacular fees. William Hogarth's second scene in his *Rake's Progress* series depicts a young man lost in financial ruin and moral dissipation, including his indulgence in Italian opera, through which he bankrupted himself by giving gifts to famous singers. Hanging over the back of a chair is 'A list of the rich Presents Signor Farinelli the Italian Singer Condescended to Accept of ye English Nobility & Gentry'.[25] Farinelli succeeded temporarily in outshining even the 'immortal' Handel, who produced other operatic masterpieces in the Italian style and, although he never wrote for Farinelli, composed for Senesino and Carestini, and agreed to have an aria from the *Messiah* transposed for his favourite castrato, Guadagni.[26] By the 1750s, however, Handel had not composed an opera for over two decades, and the influence of the Royal Academy of Music had declined. Italian opera was starting to become unfashionable, the popularity of 'florid song' waned in favour of a more direct and simple form of musical and vocal expression. Opera needed new young composers, and new talent, to revive the jaded tastes of the novelty-seeking English public.

♪

When Tenducci arrived in London for the season at the start of October 1758, he found a teeming city growing in wealth, numbers, and cultural confidence. As a major European trading port and capital of an island nation, London has always played host to diverse groups of immigrants.[27] In the Georgian period there was a close-knit community of Italians who provided Tenducci with much useful information on how to survive in a foreign city. He lodged at the home of a fellow-Italian, Lorenzo Lombardi, whose house was conveniently situated in the Haymarket, close to the King's Theatre.[28] Like other fashionable

Italians—singers, artists, and musicians—Tenducci probably worshipped on Sundays at the Catholic chapel in Soho Square. By the mid-1700s, this was more or less tolerated by English Protestants, except at moments of domestic and international political crisis, when Catholics and their places of worship became targets for street violence and vandalism by the mob. London thronged with Italian dancing-masters, musicians, and artists, who may have become even more prized mid-century due to the difficulties in travelling to Italy that resulted from the Seven Years War (1756–63).[29]

Tenducci would have known which coffee houses were frequented by his fellow-Italians, and where to buy delicacies of pasta, cheeses, and wines from his native country, imported by Italian merchants such as Filippo Mazzei, who took particular pride in supplying opera singers.[30] Tenducci's growing reputation through his performances at the King's Theatre brought invitations to give private concerts and an entry into distinguished circles frequented by élite Italians: diplomats, noblemen, artists, and politicians in exile. The detailed social diary of the redoubtable James Boswell, chronicler of Dr Johnson's life, sheds light upon the circle of eminent Italians and their patrons with whom Tenducci became acquainted over the years in the drawing rooms of the English nobility. Boswell witnessed Tenducci perform at an assembly in the presence of the Spanish Minister, Counts Carlucci and Piazza, two noblemen from Cremona, the Genoese Minister, and the musician and artist Gaetano Bartolozzi, son of the famous Francesco, a fashionable engraver. Several decades later, Boswell also recorded that he saw Tenducci at the home of General Paoli, an exile who was hailed by the English as a great patriot and freedom-fighter against the occupying forces of the Genoese in his native Corsica.[31]

As for the city itself, Tenducci's London centred around Covent Garden and the Haymarket, the theatres, concert rooms, and private addresses where he performed. His name first appears in the classified advertisements section of the London newspapers towards the end of 1758. The *Public Advertiser* announced on 16 December that 'Sig[nor] Tenducci and Sig[nor] Quilici' would appear in 'an Opera call'd Demetrio' at the King's Theatre in the Haymarket, by 'His Majesty's Command' (a formality respecting the King's licence issued via the Lord Chamberlain). The performance was also given the additional puff of social cachet in the advertisement with the suggestion that it was being staged 'By particular Desire of several Persons of Quality'. New dances were promised as part of the entertainment. In terms of special seating arrangements for what was anticipated to be a popular event, 'Pit and Boxes to be put together, and no Persons to be admitted without Tickets'. The doors opened at five o'clock in the afternoon, with the performance starting at half past six, allowing plenty of time for social mingling beforehand.[32]

The advertisement for Tenducci's performance of *Demetrio* in 1758 indicates how aristocratic opera-goers were separated from the general ranks of the well-to-do in the pit. Any further broadening of the social make-up of the audience in the best seats was unlikely, since tickets were expensive at half a guinea each, the equivalent of a week's wages for an agricultural labourer. Even the cheaper gallery seats were five shillings apiece. This arrangement was less usual than admission by season ticket, and may have been designed by the managers of the King's Theatre to showcase their new talent from Italy. In a measure to try to keep a slightly more orderly house than usual, they advertised that, on this occasion, 'No persons whatever to be admitted behind the Scenes' (which suggests that this was a fairly common occurrence). When the King's Theatre was at full capacity, Tenducci could have sung to an audience of 2,000 people at one time.[33] The close arrangement of pit, tiers of boxes, and front-of-stage action meant that singers and dancers on stage were highly visible and audible. At the Theatre Royal, Drury Lane, all of the action took place in the 6-metre-wide space at the front of the stage: the back of the stage behind the proscenium was reserved mostly for the scenery, and traditionally the stage scenery was treated as a backdrop rather than an integral part of the performance. In a style developed in the courts of Europe, the scenery was moved in pairs in

grooves on the stage, with the backdrop operated by hidden machines and a system of heavy ropes and pulleys. Trapdoors, balconies,
and other devices made unexpected entrances and exits possible.[34]
The intimate character of eighteenth-century operatic productions
was underscored by the relatively small size of the theatres. Even
those seated at the back wall of the boxes could be as close as 9 to 11
metres from the stage (such as at Lincoln's Inn Fields and Drury
Lane theatres), although as the century progressed, 18 to 21 metres
became typical.[35] Unlike most modern performances, there was
relatively little, if any, distancing between the stars of the show and
the general public, although the orchestra pit served to delineate the
proscenium (the part of the stage in front of the proscenium arch
dressed in the stage curtains) from the audience occupying rows of
benches in the fan-shaped pit. Up until the 1760s, it was not unusual
for the stage itself to be populated during the performance not just
by singers and dancers, but by members of the audience actually
seated alongside them in rows of chairs. There was little elbow
room and no health and safety concerns about blocking aisles with
additional rows of benches, which meant a large number of people
could be crammed into a relatively small space.

There is no surviving account of the public reaction to Tenducci's
voice when he first sang *Demetrio* in London. However, he shortly
afterwards appeared in *Il Ciro Riconosciuto* on 16 January 1759, a new
opera by Gioacchino Cocchi, the Neapolitan composer who had bro-
kered Tenducci's invitation to England, and who also happened to be
the musical director of the King's Theatre.[36] In this opera, Tenducci
performed the role of a male hero, Cambises, and was favourably
received in the London press.[37] *Ciro* was regarded by Charles Burney
as the best of Cocchi's productions of *opera seria* in England. He
judged one particular aria, a love song interpreted in sprightly fashion
by the soprano Mattei, to be 'full of spirit and passion', and recalled
that 'It was in this opera that Tenducci was first noticed on our stage'.
Though still only a young man (aged about 24 in 1759 when Cocchi's

work premiered), and second to the leading man, Potenza, Burney noted that Tenducci already 'had a much better voice' than the *primo uomo*.[38]

Shortly afterwards, in May 1759, Tenducci undertook to perform at a benefit concert for Signor Falco, an Italian violinist and fellow-performer, at the Great Room in Dean Street, Soho. Tickets, costing half a guinea each, went on sale at Mr Johnson's music shop in Cheapside (traditionally one of the parts of London that was a shopper's paradise) and the Prince of Orange coffee house at the Haymarket, a favourite watering hole for the opera-going public situated conveniently near the King's Theatre.[39]

By the end of his first season in June 1759, Tenducci had a growing fan-base among English audiences. Eighteenth-century opera-goers across Europe had a tradition of being highly vocal and engaged, and were moved to heckle, clap, and cheer between arias, and sometimes during them as well. In Italy, one of the audience's favourite cries of appreciation if a castrato sang a particularly pleasing aria was '*Viva il cotellino!*' ('Long live the little knife!'). There was no smooth transition between arias if the audience wanted to express their appreciation: applause was a signal for an immediate encore. At which point, one opera-goer observed in the 1750s, 'the orchestra ... returns to the prelude, and the *castrato* walks about in a circle, and sings the favourite *arietta* the second time. This is sometimes repeated even to the fifth or sixth time; and in these repetitions it is, that the singer exerts every resource of nature and art, to surpass himself at each repetition.'[40] Considering that at the height of Baroque fashion there could be as many as seventy-eight arias and thirty scene changes in a single performance, audiences were evidently determined to get their money's worth, and expected to make a long night of it.[41]

Tenducci worked hard in his first season to build a rapport with his English audiences. By the summer of 1759 he had already given no fewer than fifty-five performances of five operatic works at the King's Theatre: *Attalo* (billed as 'a new opera' but in fact a *pasticcio*, a performance cobbled together from favourite arias interspersed with incidental music, songs, and ballet), directed by Cocchi, in which Tenducci sang the part of Idaspe), *Demetrio* (with new songs performed by Tenducci and Quilici), *Il Trionfo de Gloria, Farnace*, and *Il Ciro Riconosciuto*.

An important part of Tenducci's success would be determined by his ability to attract prestigious patrons. At the end of his first London season, in the summer of 1759, the press spent several weeks issuing advertisements about the installation of the Earl of Westmoreland as the new Chancellor of Oxford University. For this prestigious social occasion, held at St Mary's, the University church, the Vice-Chancellor arranged for the entire 'Opera Band, Vocal and Instrumental' from the King's Theatre to be moved 'at prodigious expense' out of London so that they could perform the London production of *Ciro* with the original cast of singers and musicians in Oxford at the inaugural service. The *London Chronicle* reported that the 'academical exercises' were almost incidental to the occasion. Festivities had begun on Thursday, 12 July with an evening performance of Handel's oratorios honoured 'with a greater appearance of ladies of the first fashion, nobility, illustrious foreigners, and gentlemen of distinction than ever were assembled on any like occasion'. The *Chronicle*'s reporter listed 101 persons of note in attendance, including dukes and duchesses, the Lord Mayor of London, courtiers, and members of parliament, including 'a very splendid appearance of other gentry, too numerous to be here inserted'. Saturday was taken up with the performance of *Ciro* by Tenducci and the other members of the King's Theatre company, whilst Sunday was given over to sermonizing and sacred music at St Mary's, attended by 'the Vice-Chancellor, the Heads of Houses, Doctors, and Masters of Art, in their usual seats, and the ladies placed in the bachelors' galleries'. Signors Potenza, Tenducci and Quilici, the three leading castrati from the King's Theatre, sung the 'Latin Anthems' to accompany the investiture. By way of an encore, they stayed in Oxford on the Monday to give an additional performance imported from the London stage, of the opera *Farnace*. Though for some the expense of procuring Italian singers was extravagant, it was undoubtedly popular: the church, it was noted, was 'remarkably crouded', both morning and afternoon. The Earl of Westmoreland was reported to have left Oxford the following week having 'expressed the highest satisfaction at the polite reception he had met with from the University'.[42]

♪

Immediately after his success in his first season at the King's Theatre and the favourable reports of the investiture of the new Chancellor in Oxford, Tenducci's future looked promising. But already the precarious nature of a career as an opera singer, even for those of the first quality, would have been only too apparent to this new star of the London stage. He was not engaged again for the 1759–60 season, which was due not to his lack of talent nor lack of success in his first season, but to his involvement in a society scandal. Elizabeth, wife of George, first Baron Lyttelton (Plate 4), was one of Tenducci's earliest admirers among the English aristocracy, to the extent that at some point during his debut season in London she began writing him love letters.

We do not know the content of this correspondence, nor Tenducci's response, but they became public knowledge in the spring of 1759. Since this was not Lady Lyttelton's first indiscretion, it provoked her husband to sue for a formal separation. George Lyttelton wrote privately to his brother William in July 1759, informing him that he had obtained a Deed of Separation via his lawyer, and detailing his wife's 'ill conduct'. He confirmed that the latest episode was that 'she has again made herself the talk of the Town by writing Love letters to Signor Tanduchi [sic] a Eunuch, one of which has been shewn to several people'.[43] Though Lord Lyttelton was a senior Whig statesman with an influential network of powerful friends, he had not been able to 'obtain a sight of the Letter, nor get any body who had seen it to attest the contents of it'. However, he determined upon a private separation rather than his other, more publicly damaging option, one which was available at this time only to aggrieved aristocratic husbands such as himself: to petition for a divorce through parliament.[44] Remarkably (considering the voracious appetite of the Georgian press for rumours of sexual scandal in high places), this strategy paid off since it kept the details of the separation out of the newspapers. Another possibility, had there been suspicion of a sexual relationship, would have been for Lyttelton to prosecute a 'crim. con.' civil lawsuit against Tenducci in recompense for damage to his 'property' in the form of his wife. In English law at this time, wives were regarded among the chattels belonging to their husbands, and therefore sexual intercourse with someone else's wife was described by one judge at the time as 'the highest invasion of property'.[45] Since the level of proof for 'damage' in 'criminal conversation' cases was full heterosexual intercourse, this would have raised the unprecedented dilemma for the courts to decide whether a castrato was capable of performing such an act. In the event, Lyttelton wrote to his brother implying he had decided against divorce or crim. con. action since he believed that the letters from his wife to Tenducci did not make reference to sexual relations between them ('the Expressions which have been reported to me', he wrote, 'are not of an absolutely criminal nature'). It may be that Lyttelton felt his reputation as a man of honour was sufficiently safe, considering the fact that Tenducci was known to be a castrato and therefore presumed incapable of sexual relations. Nevertheless, the revelation of Lady Lyttelton's love letters was sufficiently damaging to her husband's public reputation that he 'determined to separate from her, [so] that my Honour may suffer no more by her Shame'.[46]

In June that year, the separation was mentioned by Henry Seymour Conway in a letter to his cousin, Horace Walpole. This confirmed that news had spread in London society that it was 'Signor Tenduchi' who was the object of Lady Lyttelton's affections. Conway had in fact acted as a mediator between the Lytteltons once the circumstances became known to both parties, since the marriage had already been under considerable strain even before Lady Lyttelton's correspondence with Tenducci was exposed.[47] For her part, Elizabeth Lyttelton may have only intended the love letters to be expressions of platonic affection, and Tenducci may not have been willing or able to reciprocate with passion of a sexual or platonic kind, but his association with an aristocratic woman's name was sufficient to pose a threat to the reputation of her husband. Doubtless it was the very fact of his status as a public performer of opera, an Italian (hence Lyttelton's careful reference to him as 'Signor'), and a castrato that made the love letters so scandalous, even though they did not imply that Lady Lyttelton's adoration of Tenducci on stage had extended to an actual relationship. Lady Lyttelton's version of events was unfortunately not recorded for posterity. By early summer, her estranged husband had tactfully exited the capital for a tour of the North. He wrote to his friend Elizabeth Montagu from Morpeth in August 1759, expressing his relief and satisfaction that he was now legally separated from his wife ('before I left London I signed and seald my Deliverance from the worst Uneasiness of my Life').[48]

The Lyttelton separation case illustrated how an alliance with a castrato could prove useful to some women within the confines of a society ruled by men, offering an escape route from patriarchal authority in the form of a disagreeable husband or father. Respectable ladies of high status who loved castrati could be ridiculed for their devotion to 'eunuchs', but they could also give vent to their emotions without incurring society's full moral censure. This would not have been the case were they to be implicated in a love affair with a 'normal' man. Whether or not it was done deliberately (for sometimes reason did not hold sway in matters of the heart), women like Lady Lyttelton had stumbled upon a loophole in the sexual double standard that they could use to their own ends. After her separation, Elizabeth Lyttelton lived for many decades in comfort upon £600 a year in alimony from her estranged husband. One of the few long-term disagreeable effects of the events leading to her marital separation was that she never trusted those she knew with her correspondence ('it is much more secure to trust to the Post, than to a friend').[49] In extreme old age, when infirmity finally caught up with her, she complained of ill health, poor spirits, and nerves, and wrote in a shaky hand: 'I am Such a poor Animal . . . I do not enjoy things (not even the Opera) as I used to do.'[50]

♪

Tenducci himself may have been completely innocent as the recipient of the love letters from Lady Lyttelton, a noblewoman who was nearly twice his age. It was however a forewarning of his ability to attract the devotion of women, and the ire of powerful men. Considering the circumstances, he had to depart for the Continent as a matter of urgent expediency.[51] And so, sometime during the summer of 1759, Tenducci fled London and headed back to his native Italy.

The details of what he did next are obscure, but it is evident from subsequent catastrophic events that, once back in his native country, he quickly began to run into debt. The hiatus in his career caused by the scandal in which he had become embroiled in England may have contributed to his impecuniousness. Like many other singers in the eighteenth century, even those who rose to the top of their profession, Tenducci's life and fortunes were characterized by boom-and-bust cycles that took him from luxury to penury and back again on a recurring basis. He was not unlike any modern celebrity who rises from obscurity but finds himself ill-equipped to manage his own finances and ward off ill-intentioned hangers-on. Unlike his mentor, the great castrato Caffarelli, who squirrelled away a fortune and retired to Calabria in Italy on his own country estate,[52] it seems that Tenducci had little financial acumen. He may have had a manager, although there is no evidence at any stage of his career of a Svengali figure in his life other than Caffarelli, either promoting his cause or actively extorting money from him. The problem was also cash flow: singers' pay was famously erratic, and theatre managers notoriously failed to pay on time. Mixing with the social élite required fine clothes, hired carriages, gracious lodgings, and access to expensive musical instruments for practice. Even this early in his career, the servant's son from Monte San Savino found that he had neither the family connections nor the education that would have enabled him to cope with the trappings of fortune and celebrity.

By early 1760, perhaps in order to escape his creditors in Italy, he had returned to London. In order to raise funds, a benefit concert was held for Tenducci in March that year at the King's Theatre, a mark of the esteem with which he was regarded by the company. One of the previous season's successes, *Farnace*, was performed by his former colleagues. Tenducci sold tickets from his lodgings.[53] Tickets were also sold at the King's Theatre box office, and were saved as souvenirs by Tenducci's growing number of fans among the opera-going public (Plate 5). The newspaper advertisements for Tenducci's benefit concert promised in advance that the singer would perform three new songs, in appreciation of his supporters. It was an early example of the way in which celebrities built their rapport with the public by placing advertisements in the press, a mechanism which was relatively new, but which Tenducci proved adept at exploiting over the course of the next three decades during the fluctuating fortunes of his career and personal life.

Though the sums raised from the profits of a benefit concert could be considerable, on this occasion they were not enough to pay off debts which he had contracted in Italy. Sometime shortly after his benefit concert, his creditors caught up with him: he was arrested and thrown into a debtors' prison. This event must have taken place before September 1760, since during that month the London press noted that 'Ferdinando Tenducci, an Italian Eunuch' had escaped from jail in Southwark. A description of his person and reward for

58

his recapture evidently worked, since he was quickly caught and re-incarcerated until the end of the year.[54]

Among the campaigners for reform of England's draconian laws affecting debtors earlier in the eighteenth century was Daniel Defoe, who was himself imprisoned by his creditors in his early unsuccessful career as a wine merchant and hosier. Defoe had highlighted in his *Essay Upon Projects* the absurdity of imprisoning a man for debt, thereby rendering it impossible for him to pay off his creditors by working.[55] Since Defoe's day, there had been some limited reforms, but it was still exceptional for a prisoner to obtain temporary release unless his 'friends' on the outside undertook to lobby on his behalf among those who could pull strings to secure his relief, and usually delved deep into their pockets to bribe the right people. Debtors' prisons were notoriously insanitary, and Tenducci quickly became ill. During the months in which he languished in jail, he would have been entirely reliant upon his friends, and upon bribes given to his warders in order to supply himself with even basic daily rations of food. In January 1761, he demonstrated his acumen in using the newspapers to appeal to his public. He issued an extraordinary advertisement, with the headline 'Ferdinando Tenducci, Musician' (indicating he anticipated that his name already had some public recognition), in which he made a pitiful representation of his 'Want of Necessaries and Attendance' in prison, and thanking the 'Charity of the Humane', those people who had supported him during a period of 'utmost Indigence and Misery'. Flattering his host nation, he begged their 'Leave to fly to the distin-guished Benevolence of the Nobility and Gentry of this Kingdom' towards himself, 'an unfortunate Stranger in Distress'. He issued his illustrious patrons with an invitation to a benefit concert which was being held for him at the Great Music Room in Dean Street, Soho later that month.[56] Among the distinguished 'Professors of Music' on this occasion were to be Mr Abel, the *maestro* performer of the viola da gamba who later went on to organize a famous annual concert series with J. C. Bach, youngest son of Johann Sebastian Bach.

Extraordinarily, Tenducci gained permission to be let out of prison temporarily so that he could appear in person at another benefit concert that was being held in his honour. Just one month later, in February 1761, he was released a second time to perform at a private function in the house of a 'Lady of Quality' in the premiere of Thomas Arne's new oratorio, *Judith*. Tenducci gave a preview to 'a numerous Assembly of the first Distinction' in advance of its first public performance at Drury Lane Theatre, and was very well received. The newspapers reported that an understudy had been at the ready on this occasion, one Signora Eberardi, in case on the night Tenducci could not obtain permission to be released from prison from the plaintiff who was suing him. Though new to London, it was clear that Tenducci had already built up a powerful patronage network by the early 1760s, and a degree of celebrity that allowed him to bend the rule of law that normally applied to others.

♪

In spite of the brief hiatus of the Lyttelton scandal and his imprisonment for debt, newspaper reports from the late 1750s and 1760s make it clear how quickly the doors to the most privileged venues in England were already open to Tenducci. His was not a long, slow battle from obscurity, but a meteoric rise, made possible by his early successes at the King's Theatre and immediate access to powerful patrons who saw him perform there. Charles Burney rated Tenducci's voice highly, and charted the singer's progress in the early years of his career. By 1761, having been freed from prison and performing again in England, Burney noticed that the young castrato's voice was 'much improved'.[57]

The numerous and prestigious venues in which Tenducci appeared during the course of his career, which was to flourish from 1761 until the 1780s are remarkable. Many of these venues were within a one-mile radius of the Piazza in Covent Garden, which was one of the main destinations for pleasure-seeking Georgians. Newspaper reports from the period contain over three hundred advertisements for operas, concerts, and other public entertainments featuring Tenducci by name, although the actual number of his performances was far greater, allowing for under-recording of repeat public performances and the unadvertised private engagements which he undertook in the course of his career as a singer and as a composer in his own right. The abundance of newspapers in this period make it possible to identify over two dozen venues in the capital at which Tenducci performed. One mark of his success is that, within just a few years of his arrival in London, Tenducci had performed at the four leading theatres: the King's Theatre, Haymarket, the Theatre Royal Covent Garden, Drury Lane Theatre, and the Theatre Royal, Haymarket.[58]

During the 1760s and 1770s, Tenducci came to be associated with one London venue in particular: Ranelagh. Located in Chelsea, Ranelagh was the more prestigious of London's two leading pleasure gardens (the other, less prestigious one was south of the River Thames at Vauxhall). In 1742, Ranelagh had opened its famous Rotunda and Gardens with a celebratory public breakfast. It immediately attracted the cream of London society. Horace Walpole reported that he went 'every night constantly', and that 'you can't set foot without treading on a Prince or Duke of Cumberland'.[59] The Rotunda was an extraordinary structure made entirely of wood resembling a covered amphitheatre some 46 metres in diameter. Inside its cathedral-like interior, finely dressed men and women paraded, took tea, and ate bread and butter and fancy cakes in one of fifty specially constructed booths. The whole edifice was illuminated with chandeliers, so that 'painting, carving, and gilding, enlightened with a thousand golden lamps that emulate the noonday sun' dazzled the assembled company. Once refreshments were over, concerts were held at half past six or seven o'clock in the evening. After dark, these entertainments were followed by fireworks in the Gardens, with the trees festooned with tiny lanterns.[60]

It was in the magnificent Rotunda at Ranelagh that Tenducci sang popular songs in English, some by Thomas Arne, and others of his own composition (Plate 6). These were expressive, sentimental ballads, competently set to music in a style suited to the taste of the day, telling stories of love lost and found. One popular song by Tenducci, 'Fair's my Lucy as the Day | Brighter than the Glooming May', found its counterpart in another of his compositions, 'O Cruel Maid thy scorn forbear | Nor thus my tender bosom tear . . .'. The public rushed to John Johnson's shop opposite Bow Church in Cheapside to buy copies of the sheet music at three shillings a time. Once purchased and taken home, the songs could then be sung again at social gatherings in the privacy of polite drawing rooms, accompanied by the harpsichord and bassoon and other instruments suitable for amateur domestic performance.[61] The *London Magazine* and *Public Advertiser* began serializing the words of Tenducci's songs 'to oblige our Readers and frequenters of Ranelagh'.[62] Meanwhile, the socially aspiring customer paying in cash for his silk waistcoats at Mr Lorrain's, a tailor's shop in the Strand, could finesse his fashionable gentility by picking up a copy of 'The favourite songs now sung at Ranelagh by Mr. Tenducci'.[63] The *British Muse*, a magazine containing a miscellany of 'knowledge and pleasure', included an extract of the musical score and words to a new song premiered by Tenducci at Ranelagh in 1763, presumably to enable readers to perform it at home.[64] Tenducci even makes an appearance in Tobias Smollett's novel *Humphry Clinker*, when the heroine Lydia Melford writes to a friend that she has fallen in love with the singer after hearing him 'warbling so divinely' at Ranelagh.[65]

Another commentator at the time used Tenducci's concerts to contrast the fortunes of paupers and pleasure-seekers in this part of the metropolis. Disabled soldiers and sailors from the nearby Chelsea hospital, casualties of the recent Seven Years War, could be seen on the streets of this part of West London, and were a visible reminder of the cost of Britain's expanding global empire. Meanwhile, down the road at Ranelagh, Tenducci was in concert, 'cloathed in angelic sounds' which caused 'the intelligent beings who formed the audience' to melt into raptures, with cries of 'Divine! This is heaven! Encore!

Encore!' The author of this commentary reflected that men had sacrificed limbs, robbing 'existence of its comforts and death of its terrors',
while the 'gay crowd' at Ranelagh were lost in pleasure. Tenducci was
an emblematic example of 'the refinements in taste imported from
foreign nations' in which the British were urged not to indulge *too*
much, lest they were deflected from their serious pursuit of useful
activities such as 'learning, sense, and commerce'.[66]

Other public complaints were made about Tenducci singing excerpts
from Handel's *Messiah* at Ranelagh due to the 'Impropriety and
Indecency of performing this solemn Piece of Musick' at a pleasure
garden. Tenducci responded by changing the bill: arias from Handel's
*Acis and Galatea* and *Coronation Anthem* were performed instead of
the *Messiah*.[67] These examples of Tenducci's use of the press to engage
with his English audiences suggest his sensitivity to public opinion and
willingness to tailor his performances to please his host nation. More
generally, the controversies over his performances cited here bear
witness to the rise of 'social distancing' that was taking place between
different parts of English society in the second half of the eighteenth
century along two lines in particular: class and religion.[68]

Since he was now profiting from his growing popular appeal, and in
reciprocation for benefit events held on his behalf, Tenducci was able to
undertake a large number of charitable engagements. These took the
form of benefit concerts for other singers and musicians, at the smart-
est public concert rooms, such as the Hanover Square Concert Rooms,
Hickford's Great Room in Brewer Street, the Great Room in Dean
Street, Soho, and Pasquali's Rooms in the newly built Tottenham Court
Road. He also performed sacred music in churches for commemor-
ations, such as a special service held at the Lock Hospital Chapel.[69]
Within just a few years of his first London season, he had succeeded in
gaining a reputation as one of the most famous performers in the
capital, and was engaged to sing whenever a prestigious event was held.
The inauguration of the new Freemasons' Hall was a case in point,
although the strong association between opera and Freemasonry that

was later immortalized in operas by Mozart had its limitations for Tenducci. He, like all castrati, was debarred from becoming a Freemason, even if he had wished to do so, for reason of his emasculation. This gave rise to unfortunate *bons mots* about the need for masons to be capable of carrying 'stones'.[70]

♪

The big break in Tenducci's career came in 1762, when he appeared as the hero Arbaces in Thomas Arne's opera *Artaxerxes*. In some respects, the production adopted the classic form of Italian *opera seria*, a reworking of the *libretto* to *Artaserse* by Metastasio which told the story of ancient intrigues at the court of Artaxerxes, king of Persia. Arne's production of *Artaxerxes* was highly experimental, since it was the first all-sung opera in English. The plot, like so many eighteenth-century operas, was extremely convoluted and explored questions of honour, duty, and sacrifice, played out by royalty and with resonances for contemporary politics among the dynastic struggles that were then taking place between and within the great houses of European monarchs. Tenducci, as Arbaces, played the part of a young man fighting to clear his name when faced with a murder accusation, and to win the hand of his sweetheart Mandane.

*Artaxerxes* proved an instant success, with which Tenducci became for ever associated. His touching rendition of the aria 'Water parted from the sea' was a lament which found universal appeal in its expression of sentimental longing for home. So beautiful was the aria that one anecdotal story was that Charlotte Brent, Arne's mistress, who was playing the part of Mandane, became jealous during rehearsals and flew into a rage 'because he had given the best air in the piece to Tenducci'. Arne allegedly went away immediately and composed her an equally beautiful aria to pacify her.[71] Successful arias such as these found a market way beyond those who actually went to the opera: catchy melodies that proved popular in the opera houses were quickly issued in bulk and sold in shops as popular renditions of songs from the pleasure gardens, not to mention home performances and tavern singing-clubs.[72] In John Johnson's shop in Cheapside, for example, a popular songbook of arias from *Artaxerxes* was advertised alongside works by Haydn and Purcell, transposed for amateur performance.[73] The degree of popular celebrity which Tenducci came to enjoy as a result of the widespread popularization of his aria in *Artaxerxes* is reflected by one contemporary recollection that, in Dublin, every barrow-boy was said to be humming 'Water parted from the *Say*'.[74] Right into the nineteenth century, Arne's aria popularized by Tenducci became a favourite drawing-room piece for performance at home, such that Jane Austen confessed she had grown tired of *Artaxerxes*, she had heard it so many times.[75] Tenducci began performing his 'hit' from *Artaxerxes*, together with songs of his own composition, to large crowds at Ranelagh. His music thereby reached wider audiences than would have been possible in the opera house alone, so that like other popular musicians and artists of the day he eventually became a celebrity pin-up, his portrait engraved and sold as a single sheet for his fans to display in their homes (Plate 7).

Tenducci's growing fame among the English public in the early 1760s was furthered by the publicity he received concerning a riot which took place during a performance of *Artaxerxes* early in 1763. This was provoked by the decision of theatre managers to refuse customary admission to people at the end of the third act of a play for half price. In the 'great uproar' that followed, the *Gentleman's Magazine* reported that the mob had torn up the pit benches, shattered the chandeliers and glass lustres on the walls, and shredded the linings of the boxes, in all causing four people to be arrested and an estimated £2,000 worth of damage.[76] Without such dramatic incidents, mused the anonymous author of the verse which accompanied *'Fitz-Giggio'*, *A New English Uproar*: 'Pray what would Eunuchs e'er have gain'd | By Bravo and Encore?' In the *New English Uproar* (Plate 8), Tenducci and his fellow-castrato Peretti are featured on stage, their imposing presence indicated by the spectacle of two tall male figures wearing exotic costumes—including turbans. Arne himself, recognizable by his extremely slender frame (a physical characteristic which was a gift to the satirists), is shown on stage alongside the performers, trying in vain to quieten the rioters, some of whom are in the process of leaping over the orchestra pit.[77]

♪

By the mid-1760s, Tenducci had forged a colourful and successful career in England as a rising star of the London stage, consolidated with a popular following gleaned from the pleasure gardens of Ranelagh. Already he was no stranger to controversy involving sexual scandal and the mob, and had a cautionary spell in the debtors' prison behind him. He had proved his ability to use the press to promote his concerts through advertising, and was aware of his status as a public figure with a growing fan-base of music lovers willing to sponsor him via subscriptions and benefit concerts. His association with Ranelagh, and with Arne's new experiments in 'English opera' won fans among new middle-class audiences, with melodic arias such as his signature 'Water parted from the sea' becoming popular songs beloved by aristocrats and commoners alike. The old suspicions that Italian opera was a mask for crypto-Catholicism were confounded when people could understand and be moved by the simple, pastoral sentiments of Tenducci's most famous arias and his own compositions. His talent as a vocalist and composer, his charisma and personal attractiveness were other valuable assets that contributed to his rise to fame. But if Lady Lyttelton was one of the earliest, most illustrious, and least discreet, among his female admirers, she would not be his last.

*Chapter Four*

# Fancying Tenducci

Tenducci's citation in the marriage separation case between Lord and Lady Lyttelton was just a foretaste of his future entanglements with the fair sex. Throughout the rest of his life, there were repeated rumours of his relationships with women, at least one of which turned out in spectacular fashion to be true. In spite of his physical predicament as a castrato, and in opposition to the precedent set for men such as himself by centuries of law and custom, it seems that Tenducci refused to accept that he could not have a relationship with a woman like other 'normal' men. In the decades that followed, his adventures in love were to provide a valuable insight into his character and temperament, and the wider expectations of the society in which he lived regarding the boundaries of what was deemed acceptable in heterosexual relations. More than this, by his actions, he was to present a challenge to the institution of marriage itself.

For now, though, the evidence is only that Tenducci was the object of Lady Lyttelton's affections; his own part in the affair remains a mystery. But the fact that he attracted such a high-profile female admirer does invite speculation regarding Tenducci's sex appeal, as to whether—and why—some women who met him and heard him sing found him personally attractive. Such questions are of themselves perhaps natural, but immediately reveal a certain prejudicial attitude towards castrati that has a long history. It was—and is—often assumed that castrati were inherently freakish and must therefore have commonly aroused disgust rather than desire. More fundamentally, the inherent assumption in early modern and modern times alike, and across many cultures, is that full manhood—that most culturally desirable of attributes—requires intact and unequivocally male genitalia.[1] So the fact that not just Tenducci but a number of eighteenth-century castrati were adored by women fans was met with defensive or aggressive responses from the press and contemporary social commentators. Whether they met with nervous ridicule, or outright hostility, such reactions suggest that castrati touched uniquely upon some raw nerves in the history of heterosexuality. In England, these criticisms were overlaid with the exoticism of their culture and religion, as Italians with strong links to the innermost sanctum of the Catholic Church. Many famous castrati had actually started their careers as choristers in the Pope's private chapel. Moreover, Baroque fashion in music, art, and architecture was unequivocally associated with the Church of Rome, its full-blown ornamentation expressing a heady combination of luxury and Catholic devotion which some found to their taste, but which others reviled. George Thomson, a contemporary and friend of Robert Burns, recalled from personal memory that 'Tenducci's singing was full of passion, feeling, and taste', 'his articulation of the words was no less perfect than his expression of the music'.[2]

Of course, as Thomson's admiring comments show, castrati appealed not just to women, but to men as well. Without a broad mixed-sex fan-base, they could never have attracted the kind of mass audiences that made them so commercially successful. Among Tenducci's male fans was the Edinburgh publisher William Tait, who also recalled being moved by the singer's 'passionate feeling and exquisitely touching expression of the melody'.[3] It is highly likely, given the size and diversity of Tenducci's audiences across Europe, that he had male admirers whose feelings towards him were more than platonic. 'Such

Musick—O Heaven it breathes the very soul of voluptuous effeminacy',
sighed the bisexual William Beckford, one of the richest men in
England, upon hearing Pacchierotti sing. Beckford was so in thrall to
the castrato that he arranged his Grand Tour around Pacchierotti's
performances in different Italian towns. He hired not one but three of
the most famous castrati of the day—Tenducci, as well as his beloved
Pacchierotti and Rauzzini—to sing at his twenty-first birthday party, an
event that cost the princely sum of £40,000 and which Beckford later
fictionalized as the epitome of decadence in his Gothic novel *Vathek*.[4]

Though love or desire in any form was not illegal *per se*, men's desire
for castrati was rarely recorded for posterity beyond the realm of aristocrats and cardinals, particularly if this extended to a sexual relationship.[5]
But in spite of the historic association between some castrati and
homosexuality, there is much evidence in terms of his sexual orientation,
self-identification, and behaviour throughout his adult life that Tenducci
was exclusively heterosexual.[6] Francis Michael Passerini, a 'master
and professor of music' of Stephen's Green, Dublin, who knew Tenducci
in the mid-1760s, recalled that he had often been at music parties and
other social occasions with the singer. They were on intimate terms,
and Passerini recalled that he 'repeatedly heard [Tenducci] . . . declare
that he could very safely sleep with a woman, as he could not get her
with child . . . being (as he also declared) an eunuch or castrated person'.[7]
Sexual boasting in all-male company, particularly in the alehouse
or club, was a common pattern, an attempt to win 'approval and
admiration from other men', as historian Elizabeth Foyster has
observed. Court records have revealed that men, particularly younger
and unmarried ones, harped on their supposed sexual conquests
and 'Venus sport', and regaled their peers with tales of excessive 'wench-
ing'.[8] The diarist Roger Lowe described how he discussed 'how to
get wives' in an alehouse with his male friends, and how he and
his friend, a fellow-bachelor, 'talked of wenches'.[9] Tenducci's comments
to Passerini therefore tailored a well-recognized pattern for asserting
manhood to fit his own circumstances. As a known eunuch, he was at an

obvious disadvantage when it came to establishing an honourable reputation among men.[10] His physical incapacity as a castrated man was the most obvious source of what were often cruel satires against him and his fellow-castrati. But this reference suggests that Tenducci actively sought to make the best of his lot in establishing his identity as a man, not only in his relationships with women, but among other men.

It is through evidence such as this that we encounter a new route into understanding what it meant to be a man in Tenducci's time. 'Tell me, is it possible for me yet to make myself a man?' wondered the friend and biographer of Dr Johnson, James Boswell.[11] Honour, credit, and manly reputation had to be earned, and in this regard Tenducci was no different from other men of his day. The singer was helped in this endeavour by the emergence of a culture of sensibility in the second half of the eighteenth century which valued the faculty of taste, whether in music, literature, or other arts. This was an alternative to the culture of 'drinking, fighting and sex', of competitive wrestling, shin-kicking, badger-baiting, and bare-fisted boxing that had hitherto characterized a particular kind of youthful and libertine manhood.[12] The Georgian period gave rise to a kind of polite masculinity to which castrati not only subscribed but acted as admired cultural leaders. Novel ideas concerning those attributes that were most desirable in men were gradually becoming accepted within British culture. Taste, argued the Scottish moral philosopher David Hume, was the basis of rational discernment, which had long been regarded as one of the most desirable qualities in a man. Hume observed that some men 'feel not the proper sentiment of beauty', which he put down to their 'want of that *delicacy* of imagination, which is requisite to convey a sensibility of . . . finer emotions'.[13] Hume argued that it was the imagination, rather than the body, that was the source of finer feeling. This presented an opportunity for those men like Tenducci whose bodies were incapacitated in some way to express their equality with others of their own sex. Addressing his patrons on the publication of *Amintas*, an operatic work in English that he compiled from the best music of the day, Tenducci wrote in the preface that he dared 'to flatter himself... [of] the superior excellence of the music which he has chosen for the opera he now ... present[s] to the town'.[14] A similar level of self-pride in his own powers as a man of taste and sensibility may be traced elsewhere. 'I can tell you,' Tenducci wrote to the protective father of one of his female music pupils, 'my notions of women's behaviour are full as delicate as yours can possibly be.'[15]

♪

The most superficial aspect of Tenducci's attractiveness was the question of his physical appearance. It is not easy to piece together what this rising Italian opera star looked like during his formative years as a young man embarking upon his career in London. Although no painting of him survives from this early period of his life, we can make inferences from later portraits and descriptions by people who knew him. Castrati were inclined to be fat, and some, like the castrato Nicolo Grimaldi, would certainly be classified today as obese.[16] In his early to mid-twenties, Tenducci was a slender youth, with dark hair, dark eyes, and a sensitive, pleasant face. Like many other castrati, he was notably tall, since he did not go through the normal processes of physical maturation. Growth not only starts, but stops, according to the normal hormonal changes that take place at puberty. As a consequence, many adult castrati had disproportionately long limbs, making their heads look small in relation to the rest of their bodies, a characteristic which was exaggerated still further by cartoonists who mocked their appearance (Plate 3).[17] Another of the characteristic physical features of castrati was a tendency to be barrel-chested, a result of the years of intensive vocal training in breathing techniques that were designed to increase lung capacity. Tenducci seems not to have suffered from any such problems: he was sufficiently handsome to play romantic male leads convincingly on-stage, and to attract comment from women. One social commentator attended a private musical concert at Lady Brown's London residence in 1771, and remarked, 'Lord Cranborn...is as tall and thin as Tenducci.'[18]

One portrait in particular, painted by the leading society portraitist in England, Thomas Gainsborough, associated Tenducci with the culture of sensibility which was coming to dominate the tastes of British society in the realm of art, literature, and music, in the new vogue for expressing feeling above formal politeness, sincerity rather than dissembling manners. Gainsborough painted a number of amateur and professional musicians while he was living in Bath, where his close association with the musical life of the leading spa town in Britain brought him into contact with Johann Christian (J. C.) Bach, youngest son of Johann Sebastian Bach and court musician to Queen Charlotte between 1763 and 1782, of whom Tenducci was a lifelong friend.

Gainsborough's distinctive style, the delicate brushstrokes building a composite image, was popular since he tended to portray his subjects in a sympathetic and flattering light, producing studies in liveliness and personality which broke the strict conventions of formal portraiture. This unfinished study (the hands are mere sketches) is of Tenducci exercising his most seductive and engaging talent—he is singing (Plate 9).[19] The sensitivity of the singer is conveyed by his slightly raised eyebrows, his emotional absorption in what he is doing. Unlike portraits where the gaze of the sitter is direct, Tenducci seems to invite his audience's attention while simultaneously being oblivious to their presence, lost as he is in music. It was extremely unusual to portray a sitter with his mouth open at this time, gaping, open-lipped smiles (particularly among female subjects) being regarded as uncouth, and associated with low morals. In an era of poor dental hygiene, the attractiveness of the sitter would not usually have been improved by showing their teeth.[20] Here Tenducci's open-mouthed posture is acceptable since it is shown for a reason: he is engaged in the polite activity at which he excelled as a *virtuoso* opera singer. His dress is typical of Gainsborough's restrained palette of sepia and cream, with just a hint of sensuality around the mouth, accented in the red fabric of the chair behind him, and the understated luxury of a fashionable brocade waistcoat, picked out with a highlight of embroidery. The softness of Tenducci's features, his smooth skin and rounded cheeks, hint at him being a castrato, but there are also masculine qualities in his dress and posture: he is broad-shouldered, and no more coiffeured in his periwig than any other fashionable Georgian male.

We cannot know the full range of responses of eighteenth-century viewers of Gainsborough's portrait, but it shows Tenducci in a sympathetic light: here is a sitter in his full humanity, a dedicated musician, an attractive personality, a pleasing countenance, not exactly handsome, but certainly appealing. Most likely commissioned by an admirer, it marked his admission to the world of high society and fashion during the early 1770s, when he was in his mid-thirties and at the height of his fame. Gainsborough's depiction of Tenducci's vocal and personal qualities was consistent with the verdict of those people who heard him sing.

♪

The personal qualities which Gainsborough was evidently eager to convey in his portrait of Tenducci sit uneasily with the contemporary comments of those who sought to ridicule castrati, of which there were many. Castrati were insultingly and routinely described as 'a neuter', 'a thing', unsexed and essentially unappealing, a living testimony to the horrors inflicted upon man by his fellow man in the name of luxury and art. For all her admiration of his singing, Lydia Melford, Smollett's fictional heroine in *Humphry Clinker*, described Tenducci as 'a thing from Italy—It looks for all the world like a man, though they say it is not'. But there is much evidence that these neutered men had a powerful sexual appeal to many people, both men and women. There seems to have been no sense in which European audiences found the casting of castrati as male romantic leads to have been problematic, even though they were often mocked for their physical status as 'capons', 'geldings', or other kinds of neutered animals.[21] Castrati, with their boyishly smooth faces, statuesque height, and exquisite voices were thought by many at the time to be highly desirable and convincing love-objects. The ambivalence which their voices aroused: desire, without the promise of consummation, was expressed by Lydia Melford, for whom Tenducci's voice 'to be sure, is neither man's nor woman's: but it is more melodious than either . . . while I listened, I really thought myself in paradise'.[22]

Throughout the eighteenth century, there was an enduring popular belief in the Aristotelian model of the four humours (hot, dry, cold, moist) from which combination all bodies were believed to be concocted. The interpretation of Aristotle's humoral model had been challenged by the physician Galen, who questioned the implications for human reproduction. Aristotle construed men to be the producers of 'seed' and women the passive receptacles for nurturing the embryo, whereas Galen promoted the theory that men and women both produced semen, which when combined with the heat generated during sex produced a conception.[23] In both models, the exact role of human reproductive anatomy was obscure. By their own experiments in dissection Renaissance anatomists were beginning to challenge the received wisdom of physicians from antiquity, but the majority of non-medical folk at this time continued to imagine and interpret the body, its temperament, and illnesses in this way. Falloppio warned that castration was a danger to boys since it deprived them of the natural 'heat' commonly thought to be the disposition of most men. Eunuchs were therefore considered to be cold, moist, and therefore passive, more akin to women, although if they experienced bodily manifestations of sexual desire (such as erectile function), or character traits which society construed to be marks of manhood, such as courage, this would have been interpreted within the humoral model as vestigial, masculine 'heat', for which the possession of testicles by a man was by no means certainly necessary.[24]

Though their castration was thought to have rendered castrati 'colder' and more effeminate than other men (an idea which in modern times became stereotypically associated with homosexuality), according to early modern ideas effeminacy in a man was actually a sign of being deeply attracted to women. The caricature of the fop was of a man of fashion in thrall to Italian luxuries who became effeminate because he loved women too much, not because he eschewed them altogether.[25] In many respects castrati matched the aesthetics of an idealized form of male beauty beloved by eighteenth-century Europeans, and were convincingly staged, to contemporary audiences, as romantic, lustily heterosexual heroes. Women were thought to be more responsive and attracted to men who displayed signs of effeminacy, although their actual views on the subject usually went undocumented (unless they were actresses, prostitutes, or playwrights with no sexual reputation to lose). Experiences of female desire must have been as variable as they were numerous. One rare appreciation of the fashionable ideals of male beauty written by a woman is among the *Letters from Italy* (1776) by Lady Anna Riggs Miller. Lady Anna recorded her damning verdict upon the famously muscular statue of the Farnese Hercules: 'if all mankind were so proportioned, I should think them very disagreeable and odious'. By contrast, she was drawn to the lithe and youthful statue of the Apollo Belvedere, which epitomized the contemporary ideal of male beauty, exuding 'angelic sweetness'.[26] In this era, being tall was associated with male authority, a remnant of the time when martial valour was a test of aristocratic male virtue and virility.[27] Charles II, who was among the minority of six-footers, found his height to be a natural advantage in commanding respect and authority among his diminutive subjects, and it certainly did his reputation no harm as a monarch capable of commanding troops in a crisis. The castrato's body was therefore something of a paradox. In some respects, men like Tenducci cut fine figures of manhood which conformed to idealized notions of male beauty and bearing at the time, but other aspects of their physiology inevitably meant that they became cruel targets for comments inspired by the spectre of castration. Rather understandably perhaps, this was especially the case among male authors and commentators at the time. The Georgians of course lacked the language of modern psychoanalysis to describe 'castration anxiety', but fear of lost manhood certainly found different types of cultural expression over a century before Freud. It certainly loomed large in the imagination of the eighteenth-century English novelist Lawrence Sterne. Sterne's *Life and Adventures of Tristram Shandy* (1759–67) features the eponymous hero being accidentally circumcised as a boy in a bizarre accident that takes place while he is urinating out of a sash window. In the same novel, Tristram's uncle Toby is altogether emasculated by a fateful wound to the groin at the siege of Namur.[28]

A similarly grotesque preoccupation with castration was crudely portrayed in one particularly cruel popular print of Tenducci, which sought to emphasize what he lacked, rather than his positive talents and qualities. In contrast to Tenducci's elegant society portrait painted by Gainsborough, this roughly drawn caricature gave prominence to the folds of Tenducci's empty breeches, suggesting none too subtly that the singer was in possession of quasi-female genitalia (Plate 10). This print invited the viewer to laugh at his physical emasculation, rather than admire his talent, even as he was performing his art. Just as some were transported beyond the physical when they heard a castrato sing, for others it was impossible to separate the castrato's talent from his bodily deficiency. This depiction of Tenducci featuring the suggestion of feminized genitalia emphasized his failure to belong to the world of men. Though castrati were not women, some commentators made them analogous to the female sex, and subordinated them by turning them into figures of fun.[29]

Critics did not have to look far for further evidence that castrati were highly effeminate almost-women, since their roles on stage were often interchangeable with female sopranos who took 'breeches parts'. In certain circumstances, gender roles could be reversed, with female sopranos playing male leads, or castrati playing female parts, but in England this tended to be if there were no other options available.[30] As manager of the King's Theatre, Giardini's instructions to Leone, his agent in Italy during the 1760s, were to hire either 'a Woman of a good figure' who could 'occasionally perform in Mens Cloaths' or 'a young Castrato with a good voice' who could sing both male and female parts.[31] Another illustration of this was the shared arias in the repertoires of Tenducci and a leading female soprano, Charlotte Brent, mistress and muse to the composer Thomas Arne. In 1762, the words set to a 'Scotch air' in the overture to *Thomas and Sally*, a successful pastoral opera composed by Arne, were sung in Italian by Tenducci at Ranelagh and in the same season at Vauxhall Gardens in English by 'Miss Brent'.[32] Each, however, sang different lyrics to the same tune. Tenducci's was a general paean of praise to love, sung in Italian, in terms that would have been appropriate for any male singer (though few in the audience would have been able to translate his high-minded sentiments). Charlotte Brent meanwhile sang the same air in the part of an innocent country girl, Sally, fending off an over-lusty suitor. Given that Charlotte Brent's lyrics were in keeping with the plot of *Thomas and Sally*, it suggests that the *libretto* was reworked specifically to make it more suitable for Tenducci to sing as a male vocalist. Only once did Tenducci sing a 'female' role: that of Mary, Queen of Scots, although in the course of his entire thirty-year career this was exceptional.[33]

Another leading female soprano, Mrs Mattocks, sang the 'breeches' part in Tenducci's most famous role, Arbaces in *Artaxerxes*, inviting critical comparison between her interpretation and Tenducci's.[34] This could work both ways: Tenducci sang a male part in Bath, that of Alphonso in Samuel Arnold's *Castle of Andalusia*, which the press referred to as 'Mrs Kennedy's Part'.[35] At the centre of fashionable eighteenth-century culture, there was therefore a close professional connection between castrati like Tenducci and the leading female vocalists of the day, such as the formidable Gertrude Mara.[36] Though some castrati were known for performing women's roles on stage, Tenducci's overwhelming preference during his career was for playing romantically doomed classical heroes, such as Orpheus, and legendary men, including (memorably), in one of his last triumphs, Montezuma, king of the Aztecs.[37]

In terms of how they were regarded in wider society, there were some similarities between the lot of castrati and that of female actors and vocal performers. Neither group had much expectation of being received permanently into polite society, although whereas castrati could earn respect as ornaments to a social occasion, actresses were seldom received, especially at private functions, when there were respectable women present in the room. Though women were banned from the stage in many parts of Europe (in the Papal States, this continued to apply until the end of the eighteenth century), in England the presence of female actors and soprano singers on stage following the Restoration continued to excite much debate and comment from foreign visitors and Britons alike. Until recently, historians have studied female singers less than actresses, but the behaviour of *prima donnas* held a strong fascination for the Georgian news-reading public. The rivalry between the mezzo-soprano Faustina and the soprano Cuzzoni, for example, led to the two women actually fighting on stage in 1727, an episode which divided London society according to which protagonist was the victor. The Countess of Pembroke led Cuzzoni's supporters, while her rivals rallied around the Countess of Burlington, a factionalism which was said to overshadow the rivalry between Whig and Tory, or support for George II or the Jacobites.[38] Over time, these female performers, their escapades on and off stage, were made highly visible through reporting in the press. Their public profiles effectively created a new public arena for wider debates on the proper role of women in society and their representation in the visual and performing arts.[39] With their frequently tangled and unconventional love-lives, actresses and *divas* were often regarded as little better than prostitutes, common to all-comers for the price of a ticket. In this respect, however, castrati like Tenducci were regarded more like men, in spite of their physical mutilation, since the sexual double standard remained resolutely in place. It was debatable whether castrati were *fully* men, but unlike women they were not expected to be guardians of chastity by virtue of their sex alone. Though they carried the whiff of scandal by virtue of their public careers, generally they were regarded as sexually harmless, and therefore risible rather then reckless. But actresses and female sopranos who performed on stage inevitably bore the taint of immorality, and permanently reminded virtuous women of the peril of losing their reputations.

♪

Women were a visible—and vocal—presence among theatre and concert audiences that flourished in London and provincial towns during the Georgian period. Opera performances were a significant opportunity for élite women to meet one another and exchange news, as is evident in a letter from Susanna Phillips, née Burney, to her sister Fanny. Susanna reported how Fanny's new novel, *Cecilia*, had been received: 'though your praises were not <u>sung</u> at the opera on Sat[urda]y night, I heard nothing [else] <u>talked</u> of'. She heard this first from a visit to 'the Eldest Miss Bull, who has a delightful Box on the ground floor just over the Orchestra', then Lady Mary Duncan, who said 'she was sure you'd never have acquired so much knowledge of the world', and then finally 'After this I made a Visit to the other Miss Brett who was in Lady Clarges' Box'.[40] Though they were somewhat atypical, coming from an exceptionally musical and literary family, the Burney women were keen documenters of the wider social and sexual mores of London society, and showed how connoisseurship of opera could be a mark of good taste for others of their own rank and sex, albeit with bluestocking inclinations. Susanna Phillips found Covent Garden 'so improved' after refurbishment in the 1780s that she opined: 'I thought myself in Italy— there is so much symmetry & Elegance in the Whole building, that it seems to me, though <u>in little</u>, compared with the Italian Theatres, to be equal in beauty to any one I ever saw on the Continent.'[41] Just like men who had been on the Grand Tour, society women demonstrated their knowledge of Italian art, architecture, and opera to indicate their refinement, even though very few of them ever had the opportunity to undertake Grand Tours of their own.[42]

There is therefore a reasonable amount of contemporary evidence to suggest that the popularity of castrati was in large measure due to their appeal among women, to which there was a romantic, if not explicitly erotic, dimension. Earlier in the century, an Englishwoman had notoriously shouted from the audience during an operatic production by the greatest castrato of them all, 'One God, one Farinelli!', at a stroke breaking the taboo against a woman raising her voice in public, blaspheming, and making a spectacle of her desire, in a manner which would have been inconceivable were the object of her devotion a 'normal' man (that is, unless she was a courtesan or actress with no respectable reputation to lose).[43] In this respect, the 'unnatural' castrati were thought to provoke 'unnatural' behaviour in women who heard them sing and who met them in person. Castrati were even said to know the *'secret des Lesbiennes'* when it came to giving women sexual pleasure, cheerfully making up for their cruel loss with improvised dildoes made of wax.[44] There are distinct lesbian overtones in John Dryden's verdict upon women who found castrati erotic: 'There are those in soft eunuchs place their bliss | And shun the scrubbing of a bearded kiss.' According to the then poet laureate, women who found 'softness' appealing in castrati were perversely giving up their devotion to men, and the special form of bristling masculinity that they should have prized as the most virile and desirable. Simultaneously, of course, Dryden also playfully acknowledged the appealing sensuality of castrati compared to the brutishness of other members of his own sex—for who would willingly submit to 'scrubbing' for pleasure?[45]

Though such poetic musings provided the cultural commentary which framed people's reactions to castrati, this was more than just a literary conceit. Some eighteenth-century women relished an opportunity to express desire and affection for a male love-object, finding a loophole that was an escape from the sexual double standard. This remarkably long-lived principle meant it was deemed acceptable for men to be sexually experienced, while women were expected to remain virgins before marriage and chaste as wives, which normally kept such expressions in check.[46] In the generation after Tenducci, Rauzzini, 'a beautiful, animated, young man, with a sweet, clear, and flexible voice', was beloved of Louisa Harris, a well-born young woman, who wrote him love letters until she transferred her loyalty to another castrato. Miss Harris, observed Lady Clarges over tea with Lady Hales, 'is now quite *Notorious* with Pacchierotti... first with Rauzzini—then Pacchierotti—it's really being what I call quite common'.[47] When it came to castrati, respectable women could 'play the field', displaying their affections publicly and going from one man to another at their pleasure. Unlike common prostitutes, however, their virtue remained intact owing to the apparently undisputed sexual incapacity of their chosen love-objects. In heterosexual terms, castrati were as appealing, and as dangerous, as life-size dolls, colourfully dressed and flamboyant, safe for women to dress up, buy presents for, and play with, but pass over according to their whim. Like the giant Brobdingnag 'Maids of Honour' in *Gulliver's Travels,* who held the doll-like tiny Gulliver to their oversized bosoms, castrati were the ultimate in a rich woman's toy box, little better than a lap-dog to be cosseted and lavished with gifts without fear of jeopardizing their reputations.[48] This dynamic produced sentimental love relationships akin to romantic friendships between women of a kind which were especially fashionable in eighteenth-century literary circles.[49] 'I dare say we remember one another daily (I'm sure I do *you*)', wrote Catherine Talbot to Elizabeth Carter. Likewise, the 'Queen of the Blues', Elizabeth Montagu, pined at separation from her friend: 'how can my grief be childish when it is all that is not childish in me that weeps for the absence of Miss Carter!'[50]

Some castrati, like Pacchierotti, evidently reciprocated the adoration of their female admirers, and became embroiled in love affairs expressed through correspondence which was framed in similarly heightened and passionate language, which owed much to the conventions of the newly invented epistolary novel.[51] Susanna Burney recorded her great joy at hearing Pacchierotti's carriage arrive outside her father's house: 'Lord—I was so glad!' she enthused in her private letter-book.[52] On another occasion, she told the singer, 'You spoil me when you sing, Signor Pacchierotti, for everything else—before you begin I am occupied by thoughts of the pleasure I have to come, and after you sing everything is flat and insipid.' Pacchierotti reciprocated, telling Susanna with tear-filled eyes that 'I ought not to come too often because it makes it harder for me to leave you—Indeed I know it.'[53] Like romantic friends of the same sex, however, society expected that such friendships would be no more than a testing ground for expressions of heterosexual attraction that would be superseded when a suitable marriage partner came along.[54] The inclinations of the castrato's heart were therefore a matter of frivolity and ultimately therefore, according to society, did not 'count'. This inevitably brought tragic emotional and psychological consequences for castrati who held out frustrated hopes for a family life of their own. The famous castrato Gaetano Guadagni lived out his days in Padua playing with life-sized dolls, onto whom he could project the dramas of his own emotional life in much the same way as others, particularly the aristocratic women who had 'kept' him in riches, had done to him throughout his career.[55]

♪

Many women admired castrati on stage but never met them in person; their admiration was based upon their appreciation of these singers' talent. The emotions stirred deliberately in *opera seria* doubtless fed fantasy and admiration from afar, but there was seldom any question of this translating into an actual encounter with a castrato. Nevertheless, many eighteenth-century British men were vexed that Italian castrati inspired droves of women, if not to fall in love with them, then at least to express more than intellectual pleasure at hearing them sing. When the subject of castrati came up in conversation, a certain Mr Blakeney, an acquaintance of Fanny Burney, recalled, 'Why now, there was one of these fellows at Bath last season, a Mr. Rozzini [Rauzzini]— I vow I longed to cane him every day! Such a work made with him! All the *fair females* sighing for him! Enough to make a man sick!'[56] The vitriol that some male authors heaped upon castrati was a mocking check upon the spectacle of such publicly known expressions of female devotion. One satirist lampooned Frances Brooke, the female manager of one of the prime London venues for Italian opera, the King's Theatre, Haymarket, as the 'Queen of Quavers' for promoting uncontrolled 'quavering'—that is, an intoxicating and unaccountable love of Italian opera.[57] The nub of these anonymous male authors' complaints was that castrato singers 'can command our most enchanting females, especially those that are not yet initiated into the mysteries of the *naked truth*'.[58] In *The Ladies Lamentation for the Loss of Senesino* (1735) (Plate 11), an anonymous male author lampooned the grief of the castrato's female fans at the singer's departure from England for the Continent, nobles bowing before him, ladies weeping and trying to make him stay, with servants following and carrying hand-barrows loaded with 'Ready Money', the profits of his talent. As one female fan, a 'beautiful Creature' laments his loss, she admits her love is hopeless: 'Tis neither for Man, nor for Woman' that she is crying, her 'sweet Darling of fame', Senesino, 'Is a Shadow of something, a Sex without Name'.

In the same year that Tenducci was born, 1735, a semi-pornographic work, *The Happy Courtezan: Or, the Prude Demolish'd*, featured an imaginary love letter in verse from a notorious prostitute, Mrs Constantia Phillips, to Farinelli, lamenting their mutual suffering at the hands of men, and offering a mutually satisfactory arrangement whereby her sexual 'wants' can be supplied by a eunuch, without consequences. It was just a short step in the chain of responses from rendering a castrato into a *thing* to concluding, albeit in jest, that castration rendered a man less-than-human; being 'neither man nor woman', he was something 'betwixt the human species and the brute creation, like a monkey, and may be properly termed an outlaw of nature'.[59] Castrati were likened by some to 'exotick animals': for eighteenth-century Londoners, this would have recalled the imported wild beasts caged in the menageries at St James's Park and the Tower of London, which visitors paid to gawp at as part of the regular tourist trail for foreigners and provincial visitors to the capital.[60] But unlike other imported luxury commodities—from exotic beasts to porcelain cups—the castrato was human, and had emotional, perhaps even sexual, needs of his own.

Some male commentators satirized castrati as effeminate, with the intention of making them as powerless in social and political terms as women were supposed to be at this time. In theory at least, castrati were not allowed to desire women, nor were they thought to have any sexual feelings towards them. However, the eighteenth-century press enjoyed spreading rumours that castrati were not really what they purported to be. As far as gender went, many questioned they were men at all, but neither could they occupy some indeterminate sex or gender of their own. Society depended upon the binary division of man/woman, male/female, so castrati were routinely suspected of in fact being either biologically female, or 'intact' men fully in possession of their genitalia. Farinelli, for example, was at one time rumoured to be pregnant, and to be masquerading as male only to conceal his/her licentious sexual behaviour. The anonymous author of an obscene poem on this subject invited further fantasies: the author envisaged which groups in society would be most dismayed by the discovery that Farinelli was really a woman. In one camp was 'Clarinda', an archetypal frustrated female fan, who loved the castrato because he did not threaten her with pregnancy, and was therefore dismayed to find the object of her love was not in fact male ('Her lovely *Eunuch* to a Woman turn'd, | For whose secure Embrace so long she's burn'd!').[61] Such women who preferred castrati, the author suggested, 'refus'd a thousand filthy Men', because they did not have the stomach for a relationship with 'real' members of the opposite sex. Their only other options for physical gratification were with their 'beastly' lap-dogs, or with a lesbian lover (hence 'Clarinda' could 'only stroke her Parrots and her Cats, | Or else with Squire JENNY play at f—s [flats]', a coded reference to lesbian sex, which would have been well known to consumers of eighteenth-century erotica).[62] In the other camp of disappointed fans were decadent men like 'Lord Epicene', dedicated to sensual pleasures including lust for members of their own sex. The shock of Farinelli's alleged pregnancy was that these men had been lavishing presents, not upon a male beloved, but upon a 'girl'. Such men, of 'new-improv'd, uncommon Views', it was said 'Are fainting, dying at this fatal News'. Other commentators at the time may have accepted that Farinelli was not a woman, but neither was he regarded as fully male. In the face of so much female adoration, one male author wrote urging Farinelli: 'Exert thy *Reason* | like a *Man* appear'.[63]

In similar vein to Farinelli's suspected pregnancy, Senesino (Farinelli's contemporary) was rumoured not to have been castrated at all, but to have been an unscrupulous and fully functional Lothario who took advantage of his 'safe' reputation as a castrato to inveigle himself into private sexual liaisons with numerous women. Senesino, one author claimed, 'is no more an Eunuch than Sir *Robert Walpole*'. Warming to his theme, the author continued in gossipy fashion, 'nay, I am told, there are no less than four of the waiting Girls at the Opera now pregnant by him.'[64] These allegations regarding Senesino's connivance were complicated, as was so often the case, by xenophobia and anti-Catholic sentiment. The Pope used eunuchs to infiltrate British society and government, an idea which European potentates were supposed to have 'learn'd of the *Asians*', but with this difference, for 'in *Turkey* they [eunuchs] are real, in *Italy*, only nominal ... '.[65] Pretended Italian castrati, like French Jacobite spies, were not what they seemed to be. They posed a threat to society not just by secretly seducing women, but by promoting the Church of Rome, just as followers of the exiled Stuart

Pretenders were thought to be engaged in covert operations to over-throw the Protestant Hanoverian regime in Britain. Such rumours were symptomatic of the public debates evoked by the idea of the castrato. Satirically, and somewhat vindictively, they explored the limits of what was conventionally permissible for good British citizens of either sex, in ways which associated castrati not only with subverting normal relations between men and women, but with other political threats to the social order in terms of religion and foreign influence.

♪

Tenducci's career in London and other parts of the British Isles during the second half of the eighteenth century must therefore be understood within a context of a society in which the glamour and success of castrati had already accrued widespread and well-known social and cultural criticism. Castrati inevitably inspired debates about sex and gender in public commentaries and private encounters, and in turn these framed the way in which castrati were regarded in their personal and professional lives. Unlike previous generations, where some castrati were associated with homosexual relationships among the highest social élite of cardinals and royalty, the stereotyping of the castrato in the eighteenth century centred upon his heterosexual appeal to a wider audience of female fans, as well as to men who may or may not have found castrati erotically appealing. The question remains, however, regarding the castrato's own subjective experience, how Tenducci saw his own identity as a man, and as a lover. He was not an inanimate 'doll', the plaything of the rich and famous, but evidence of his private thoughts on these most personal of matters is very difficult to find. Unfortunately, we lack an account of his inner life in his own words. Music, not words, was his métier—even in his native tongue. A solitary, somewhat childishly written signature, possibly inscribed at the request of a fan, survives upon a copy of his *Six Italian Songs* (1778).

One of only two surviving letters[66] written by Tenducci himself is a note to one of his admirers, the musicologist Dr Charles Burney (Plate 12). The letter is written hastily and ungrammatically in a careless hand, in an era when fine expression and good penmanship were prized marks of accomplishment. After expressing his formal greetings and respect (*'Tenducci reverisce distintamente il Sig[no]re Dr. Burney'*), Tenducci asked the eminent musicologist for assistance regarding two little articles (*'due articoletti'*) on breathing techniques and the musical coda which Tenducci did not know how to express in English.[67] This letter suggests that even in the 1780s, after many years of living in English-speaking countries, Italian was his preferred language. This was a severe handicap to him at crucial times, such as his frequent brushes with the law. Once, when he was asked for two passes to admit some ladies to the opera in which he was appearing, he responded 'that he knew so little of English that he could not do even so trifling a thing', adding obligingly, 'if you will write the necessary words I will copy them'.[68] His spoken English was no doubt better, although certainly not fluent. Later in life, he was interrogated by persons who 'took advantage of his ignorance in the English language, by catching at his answers to questions, the meaning of which he misunderstood'.[69] Tenducci's letter to Charles Burney also highlights how, as a musical *virtuoso*, in some senses his education never ended. Throughout his life, he had to work hard to maintain the discipline demanded of an internationally renowned performer, and be constantly aware of the changing tastes in music. In the ensuing decades, as his career progressed, he was especially praised for developing his voice as it matured, and adapting his techniques of composition and performance as the public started to move away from the excessive ornamentation of Baroque and towards a more sincere and direct form of sentimental expression in music. It is unlikely that his spoken voice lacked charisma.

There are a very few, tantalizing suggestions in the archives which hint that Tenducci used some of the commonly held stereotypes about castrati to his own ends. In doing so, he actively fashioned his own masculinity in ways that varied according to his circumstances, social situations, and life-stage, and in this respect he was no different from any other man in history. Tenducci's sexual boasting—recorded by Passerini—that he was a woman's dream lover since he could give pleasure without consequences—echoed the erotic fantasies of the satirists, and perhaps those of many female admirers of castrati.[70] Since it was common for unmarried men to boast of their heterosexual conquests in all-male company, as a means of enhancing their reputation among their peer-group,[71] Passerini's recollection suggests that Tenducci took on board the reputation which castrati of the eighteenth century had for being popular with women and used it to his own ends. But was asserting that he 'could' very safely sleep with a woman a form of boast, or a statement of fact? Eventually, this point was to prove to be a matter of more than private concern. It is telling that, between men, in a moment of private conversation, the singer styled himself as a lady's man, a lover of women, and that this was part of his personal identity. It is similar to the boast of another castrato, Bartolomeo Sorlisi, who concocted the story of how his alter ego had suffered a wound on the thigh in battle which had rendered him infertile, but 'not entirely incapable of sexual congress', finding that 'he could at times nevertheless perceive the erection of the virile member'.[72]

Another indication of Tenducci's identity as a man took a more tangible form. The singer owned a fine *intaglio* or gem, an expensive and highly collectible item amongst Grand Tourists to Italy in the eighteenth century, which usually featured figures and beasts from classical mythology. A collector like Sir William Hamilton owned dozens of *intaglios* of various sizes and shapes which were displayed as a mark of connoisseurship for after-dinner scrutiny. Tenducci's lozenge-shaped gem, rather large in size at half an inch square, was probably set into a signet ring since it was used to seal correspondence, and may have been the same ring displayed prominently in the portrait that was mass produced as an engraving for his fans (Plate 7). Tenducci's trademark wax seal was the imprint of two near-naked human figures: a muscular man with a rippling physique worthy of a deity, entwined with the scantily clad form of a woman.[73] Tenducci used this imprint of seduction, permissible through its formal reference to the high ideals of classical art and learning, every time he wrote a letter, sealing his identity with an idea with which he was repeatedly associated throughout his adult life: that he was a lover of women both on- and off-stage. During the mid to late 1760s, having forged a successful career on the London stage, and just as he was on the cusp of European-wide fame, a chance meeting with one particular young woman brought an adventure in love, but it was one which also risked his total ruin, and which nearly cost him not only his career, but his life.

---

## Chapter Five

# A Dublin Scuffle

W hat is to be our mental picture of Dorothea Maunsell as she was in the year 1765, when she met Tenducci for the first time? We do not know what she looked like, whether she was fair-haired or dark, pretty or plain, but we do know that she was a lively and engaging girl of 14 or 15. She was the youngest of many siblings, and so perhaps she was the spoilt darling of the family, as is sometimes the case. Dorothea was certainly headstrong, fond of dressing fashionably, and was censorious of those less polite and cultivated than herself. A normally well-behaved young woman, she was singular in at least one regard: she discovered that she had a taste for music from a young age, and was eager to cultivate not only her appreciation and understanding of the art, but her considerable talent as a singer.[1] Her father, Thomas Maunsell, was a wealthy and influential barrister-at-law in Dublin. He was open to the idea that his daughter should receive private tutoring from a music teacher, among whom Italians were reputedly the best.

♪

The circumstances which led to the fateful meeting between Dorothea and Tenducci were these. Just before the summer of 1765, the singer had received an invitation from Henry Mossop, the manager of Smock Alley and Crow Street Theatres, to come to Dublin and perform operas in English, a winning formula which Thomas Arne had pioneered in *Artaxerxes* and which Arne repeated with *Amintas, or The Royal Shepherd* in 1764, with Tenducci playing the eponymous hero.[2] Tenducci's currency was high following his London triumphs. His reputation started to extend to the provinces. In August 1765 he made a star appearance at the celebrated Salisbury Musical Festival, which kept alive the 'immortal memory' of Handel.[3] For the Italian singer looking to cast his net still wider, Dublin was an attractive option for the following season, offering rich rewards in the form of benefit concerts and fees. Tenducci expressed his reluctance to leave his friends in London, but the promise of £150 for the first two months' work, plus the proceeds from a benefit concert, were too tempting.[4]

So Tenducci made the journey across the Irish Sea, arriving in Dublin in the autumn of 1765. From his first view as he came ashore at the docks, he would have seen that the city resembled one large building site. This was a sign of Dublin's new prosperity, but one which brought mixed fortunes, particularly among its poorer residents. Among the remarkable events noted by contemporary Dubliners was the massive expansion of the city in their lifetime: between 1711 and 1750, some 4,000 new dwellings had been built to house an extra 32,000 people.[5] Travel was made easier with the construction of the Queen's Bridge in the 1760s, and major new work was begun on a canal that looped around the city basin. The scale of ambition among the town planners was marked by the appearance of grand new Georgian streets and squares on the south side of the Liffey, at the heart of which lay the fashionable residences surrounding St Stephen's Green and Merrion Square. In the same period, the front-of-house buildings of Trinity College received a facelift, a neo-classical façade to impress upon passers-by that this was a venerable institution in the finest tradition of the ancient European universities.

Tenducci's arrival was therefore of a piece with Dublin's growing confidence and wider cultural ambitions. As its city boundaries spread, the new Georgian town staked its claim in bricks, stone, and mortar to being part of the 'urban renaissance' that was taking place throughout the British Isles, enlivened by the public culture of leisure that flourished upon the prosperity of the rising middle classes. The merchants, tradesmen, and professional men of Dublin, their wives and children bedecked in the latest fashions, made a show of parading in their very own Ranelagh, where they took tea and bread-and-butter in an ersatz Rotunda.[6] The city had a thriving print trade, fashionable shops to service the upwardly mobile, and numerous smoke-filled coffee houses, where buying and selling was the order of the day: everything from book auctions 'by the candle', to the latest news of the progress of foreign wars and the fortunes of merchant adventurers.[7] Dublin also had a darker reputation for crime, which left residents and visitors alike in constant fear of cut-throats and footpads in pursuit of their pocket-watches. For all its growing social pretensions, this was, fundamentally, a port town, and prostitutes were not difficult to find, particularly in the teeming streets around Smock Alley on the south side of the Liffey, just off the quays.

It was here in the Old City area of Temple Bar, in a music hall on Fishamble Street, that Handel's *Messiah* received its world premiere on 13 April 1742. Among the crowds hurrying to the concert through the narrow streets on that occasion had been a young Irish lawyer, Thomas Maunsell, who doubtless joined the rest of Dublin's fashionable society eager to take part in the musical event of the decade. The event brought universal acclaim and a boost to the cultural esteem of the town.[8] Since the early 1700s, the concentration of theatre-goers and music-lovers among the city's élite and growing middle-class population provided the market for plays, concerts, and operatic performances. The Dublin Academy of Music was founded in 1728, and in

1731 a new concert hall was opened 'for the practice of Italian Musick' under the direction of a Signor Arrigoni. The composer Geminiani, who is credited with having brought the *concerto* to England and popularizing it among British and Irish composers, performed in Dublin in 1733 under the patronage of Lord Tullamore, and lent his name to concert rooms in Dame Street. Dublin was also visited by the distinguished Baroque composer Domenico Scarlatti, and a host of less well-known Italian musicians, tutors, conductors, and impresarios.[9] In February 1746, Thomas Sheridan and the players of Smock Alley staged a production of Dryden's *All for Love* for the young gentlemen of the King's Inns; in 1758, a new theatre opened in Crow Street.[10] Italian singers appeared frequently at the Smock Alley Theatre, and an Italian, Nicolo Pasquali, conducted the musicians who provided the musical interludes and accompaniments for Sheridan's performances.

During the 1760s, the Smock Alley Theatre continued to be able to afford to lure well-known Italian singers away from London with the promise of large fees, a pattern which contradicts the notion that Handel's celebrated visit was followed by a rather lacklustre period of cultural stagnation.[11] It was here at the Smock Alley Theatre that Tenducci planned to stage his own English opera, *The Revenge of Athridates*, according to the successful formula pioneered by Thomas Arne. While Tenducci was a composer in his own right, in this instance he admitted that 'Some passages in this opera, and a few of the songs, are taken from an opera named *Pharnaces*'.[12] Ever-sensitive to his public reputation, Tenducci was more cautious than was usual among eighteenth-century authors and composers about the imputation of plagiarism, and considered it proper to acquaint his audiences with this detail, perhaps in anticipation of the ever-sharp quills of journalists and opera connoisseurs.[13] In these changing times, Georgian men and women were less likely to sue one another for public slander. Libel was another matter, however. This budding Italian opera star was learning how to manage both his private and professional reputation in the British press.[14]

♪

As a stranger newly arrived in Dublin, Tenducci looked up an old friend—an Irishman named Charles Baroe, whom he had met in Sardinia in 1750. Baroe had been an ensign in the King of Sardinia's marine regiment and met the young Tenducci when he had just graduated from the conservatory in Naples and was performing one of his first engagements to sing at the wedding of the King of Sardinia's son.[15] Baroe, who was a few years older than Tenducci, went on to pursue a living as a grocer in Dublin, and evidently was prosperous since he was used to travelling around town by coach. He and the singer were on very good terms: during the winter of 1765 they were fellow-lodgers in the house of Mr Cullen, the box-office keeper of the Smock Alley Theatre where Tenducci was engaged to perform. At Cullen's, Tenducci and Baroe had separate rooms, but they later doubled up in the spring of 1766 at new lodgings in Dirty Lane. Here, they slept in the same bed, as was common for male friends at this time, although the intimacy of this arrangement and the uncertain sexual reputation of castrati perhaps required the additional explanation later made by Baroe that there was 'but one spare room in the said house'.[16]

During the time that Baroe and Tenducci lodged together, the polite folk of Dublin opened their houses to this charismatic and fashionable Italian who brought with him the cachet of Italian manners and London celebrity. Among these was Thomas Maunsell. Described as 'an honest but a very dull man', Maunsell was now in his mid-fifties, and had risen through the ranks of his profession to become a powerful and successful barrister, a King's Counsellor in the Court of Exchequer.[17] Maunsell's family connections in Limerick enmeshed him in an influential network of Irish MPs, judges, and landowners. The Maunsells were an archetypal Elizabethan Protestant Ascendancy family, and as such had an equal measure of swaggering local importance and the siege mentality of a minority ruling élite. By the accession of

George I in 1714, they had only just begun to consider themselves as indigenous Irish rather than English colonial rulers in exile. This particular branch of the Maunsell family had strong connections with County Limerick, but claimed descent from a sea-captain who had helped defeat the Spanish Armada, and who later sold his English estate and moved to County Cork. They were granted lands in Counties Waterford and Limerick at the Restoration of Charles II as a reward for loyalty to the royalist cause during Cromwell's Protectorate. Two generations later, Thomas's father, Richard Maunsell, had been the fourth son of a colonel, and as such was the unexpected inheritor of the family's Irish estates after he was predeceased by three elder brothers, none of whom had male heirs. Richard Maunsell was Mayor of Limerick and represented the city in the Irish parliament for over two decades.[18] His political career enriched his family and their social prospects: one of Thomas Maunsell's sisters married an earl, another a colonel in the army. Thomas's mother, Margaret Twigg, was closely related to an archdeacon in the Church of Ireland. The Maunsells were therefore from good stock, affluent, and extremely well connected among the political and social élite of loyalist families in Ireland.

Unusually for the only son and heir, Thomas was destined for the law, and was sent to fulfil his eight terms in residence at the Middle Temple in London, since only the English Inns of Court had the power to admit lawyers to the bar at this time.[19] Having paid his £100 security, and eaten the requisite number of dinners whilst seated at the 'Irish side' of the great dining hall of the Middle Temple, Maunsell returned to Dublin, where he became a member of the King's Inns, the professional association of Irish barristers, in Michaelmas Term, 1741.[20] The Irish bar was in a state of decline in the 1740s and 1750s, to the extent that the King's Inns premises were scaled back in order to save money, and barristers ceased to dine there together.[21] The law-making powers of the Irish parliament were hamstrung by Poyning's Law by which Westminster retained a right of veto over any legislation passed in Dublin. However, Maunsell's connections were on the side of the ruling élite who kept a monopoly on power by ensuring only those who conformed to the Church of Ireland could practise law, hold office, or take out mortgages upon land and property.

Thomas's career as a barrister prospered, and he consolidated his own family connections with the county gentry by marrying well, choosing Dorothea, the daughter of Richard Waller of Castle Waller.[22] They had eight children who lived to adulthood, four girls and four boys. Richard, the eldest son, went to Trinity College, Dublin, at the age of 15 in 1749: he subsequently emigrated to America where he died unmarried. Thomas and Robert went on to found Maunsell's Bank in Limerick, and George pursued a successful career in the Church. In the early to mid-1760s, their daughters Blanche, Margaret, and Elizabeth fulfilled their parents' wishes by making suitable marriages: only the youngest, Dorothea, remained at home.[23]

♪

What happened next can be pieced together from Dorothea Maunsell's published account, the *True and Genuine Narrative ... in a Letter to a Friend at Bath* (1768) (Plate 13). In this 68-page booklet, Dorothea gave a detailed account of her relationship and subsequent elopement with Tenducci, and the immediate and catastrophic consequences which resulted from her marrying a castrato. The tone of the *True and Genuine Narrative*, in which Dorothea uses the rhetorical device of addressing an unnamed female correspondent, may be gauged from the opening sentence:

> As my dear friend has been kind enough to express some concern for the many misfortunes I have lately undergone, and to desire an account of my sufferings ... I shall fully inform her of every particular; and I assure her, that, notwithstanding my being so much interested in this affair, I shall relate the facts just as they happened, and without the smallest exaggeration.[24]

As with all forms of writing, published and unpublished, this was a form of self-fashioning and performance, with a specific aim in mind. Dorothea, writing in late August 1767 about events that had taken place since the autumn of 1765 (when she had first met Tenducci), wished to justify her actions in retrospect, and publicly to re-establish both her own good name, and Tenducci's. It is likely that there would have also been a financial motive for capitalizing upon what became a public scandal to her own advantage.[25] We cannot know for sure whether her version of events was fully accurate, or the true nature of her feelings for Tenducci. The publication was the prototype for teenage romantic fiction written by girls, for girls, perhaps the first ever example of its kind.[26] Its best-seller potential was increased since newspaper reports ensured that the story was publicly known to have at its core a narrative based upon actual events.[27] It was certainly penned with an eye to the entertainment value of the story, hence the playful promise to relate the facts 'just as they happened, and without the smallest exaggeration'. But could it really have been written and published by a teenage girl, perhaps no more than 16 years old?

The context of Dorothea's family history and other external sources of evidence suggest that the events described in the *True and Genuine Narrative* are fundamentally accurate. For generations, the men of the Maunsell family had helped to enforce English control of law and government in Ireland, and had enjoyed privilege and power in return for their loyalty to the monarch and spiritual allegiance to the Church of Ireland. The main job of their wives had always been to keep house, safeguard their sexual reputations, upon which the honour of the Protestant Ascendancy depended, and provide them with heirs. As a daughter of one of the most prominent families in Dublin, Dorothea had been raised with great care by her parents, who wanted her to be schooled in all the polite accomplishments: dancing, music-making, and the art of conversation. But none of her talents, including her evident flair for singing, was to be taken *too* seriously: her future was pre-ordained. In 1765, in order to mark her entry into adult womanhood, she had been launched into local society in Dublin and thus entered the marriage market like other girls of her rank and fortune. Amid the social round of tea-taking, assembly-going, and concert parties, her sole duty and concern ought to have been to make an advantageous match with a respectable young man of a similar background to her own.

Dorothea would have been schooled to understand that this was her destiny in life from an early age. Although we do not know the details of her education, good literacy skills (including the ability to write fluently and in a stylish hand) were of a piece with the curriculum for well-to-do girls.[28] Suitable reading matter for young girls was deemed to be conduct literature of a godly sort. The maxims of Protestant conduct writers such as the Puritan divine Richard Allestree were still being reprinted and widely read in Dorothea's generation. Many seventeenth-century conduct writers assumed that women had an unruly nature and were prone to passions that needed curbing with prayer and self-discipline: modesty in a girl would lead her to eschew 'all lightness of carriage, wanton glances, obscure discourse, things that show a woman weary of her honour that the next comer may reasonably expect a surrender'.[29] Unlike her female forebears, however, Dorothea's generation was exposed to new types of literature that transported them to a world of romantic love. Most girls of her age and social position participated in the craze for novels, with leading authors such as Samuel Richardson depending upon female readers for their livelihoods. Since Dublin was one of the main centres of the Georgian print trade, genteel and middle-class Irish girls, like their English counterparts, had easy access to a wide range of literature. Writing letters, reading, and taking part in consumer culture (of which attending musical concerts was just one example) broadened the horizons of young women of her generation as never before, moving them into 'a tantalizing world of apparent choice'.[30]

Reading encouraged independent thought and solicited ideas of unconventional behaviour, but the appearance of novels by women showed girls that it was not impossible to publish literary endeavours of their own. It is no coincidence that Dorothea's account of her relationship with Tenducci was expressed in the most popular format of the day. Written as a letter to a friend in Bath, the *True and Genuine Narrative* mirrored the epistolary novel popularized by Richardson in his most famous work, *Pamela* (1740), the best-selling novel of the eighteenth century. The conceit of Dorothea telling her story of her relationship with Tenducci by writing to a female friend in Bath was a way for Dorothea to claim genteel respectability, through reference to the most fashionable spa town in the British Isles. Even though it was most probably an entirely fictional conceit, the mention of Bath associated both author and reader with the milieu of the polite world, rather than the scurrilous outpourings of Grub Street.[31]

Some shrewd male authors, following Richardson's success, capitalized upon the popularity of the novel by writing under a female pseudonym, so it is not impossible that the author of the *True and Genuine Narrative* was not Dorothea, but a 'hidden hand' (most likely male). But there was considerable precedent for women writers to be published: female authors such as Aphra Behn, Delariviere Manley, Jane Barker, Eliza Haywood, and Mary Davys were popular in their own day, and were outnumbered by many more aspiring female novelists. Between 1692 and the end of the eighteenth century, more novels were published by women than by men, although few were so bold as to put their real names to the title page.[32] The principle of anonymity, to which Fanny Burney and other respectable English women writers were keen to provide lip service as an indication of their appropriate female modesty in spite of their transgression into the male literary sphere, was not followed by Dorothea: perhaps because her reputation needed mending, and she hoped to reinstate it by her own account, she took the bold step of publicly subscribing her own name. Though there is no external evidence to support the authenticity of the *True and Genuine Narrative* as Dorothea's actual first-hand account, in the context of widespread literacy among genteel girls, and the vogue of literary aspirations, it is not impossible that this was indeed her own version of events, penned originally in her own hand. A reminder of the popularity of female 'scriblers' at this time is contained in the public advertisement for Dorothea's *True and Genuine Narrative*, which was listed for sale in the *Gazetteer and London Daily Advertiser* for January 1768 alongside the two-volume *Memoirs of Miss D'Arville*.[33]

Whether Dorothea was inspired by reading novels to engage in her own romantic adventure with an unsuitable match we shall never know, but the story of the scandal that was published in her name and from her perspective was written in the style of a novel, the most fashionable and conventional literary idiom of the day. Novels did not usually provoke young women to sacrifice the broader interests of parental consent, economic prudence, and social prospects in their choice of marriage partner for the wilder shores of romantic love and sexual attraction.[34] It was however an age when the relative merits of marrying for love or duty were hotly debated in print, the very discussion of which unsettled churchmen and other guardians of public morality, and for good reason. Even if the novels them-selves, like Richardson's *Clarissa: or the History of a Young Lady*, whose fourth edition was published in Dublin in 1765, provided a suitably orthodox message about the importance of female virtue, they put ideas into girls' heads (so it was thought) about the tall handsome stranger, and the power of desire. Novels had begun to spread ideas about a new kind of femininity, where virtue, rather than unruly passions and sexual urges, was deemed to be at the core of a girl's being. Instead, a young woman's natural sentiments and impulses towards love sprang from her essentially sexless inno-cence.[35] The influence of this new interpretation of 'natural' fem-ininity explains the recurring insistence in Dorothea's *True and Genuine Narrative* that she was acting out of fidelity to her modest nature. She describes how, in the course of events, she and Tenducci were to have 'the liberty of our persons restrained, our property robbed, our lives endangered, and the sacred honour of my sex insulted, by those to whose care I was committed (with grief and horror I speak it) by my F[ather]'.[36] To the modern reader, this seems overblown and melodramatic, proof of the fictitious character of the story, but to the Georgian reading public it would have been understood as of a piece with pious feminine ideals of their day. In its insistence upon the modesty of its main protagonist, the *True and Genuine Narrative* featured Dorothea as a real-life version of the kind of fictional heroine who sacrificed all for love, for whom the female reading public in particular had demonstrated an astonishing appetite.

♪

Dorothea recalled that her first meeting with Tenducci occurred in the late summer or early autumn of 1765 at a gentleman's house outside Dublin.[37] Tenducci was known to be a castrato, and was fifteen years her senior. It was not love at first sight, but their rapport was established instantly through their mutual passion for music. They conversed freely together and enjoyed one another's company, to the extent that he soon started to provide instruction for her 'without fee or reward'.[38] Dorothea was later keen to show that during this time Tenducci had never received payment as her tutor, most likely because this would have implied a lessening of his status in relation to hers as an employee of her family.[39] She thereby also avoided the vexed territory of a teacher's moral obligation to safeguard the virtue of the pupil in his care. Dorothea wished to depict Tenducci as a man of honour, a suitor rather than a seducer. According to Dorothea, her family actively sought to cultivate Tenducci. She recalled that her father and mother, upon making his acquaintance, were very favourably disposed towards the singer and his encouragement of their daughter's musical talent. Evidence of this was that her parents sent invitations 'almost every day' to Tenducci to 'pass with us as many leisure hours as he could spare' and offers to dine with the family, a much-coveted favour which signified a particular mark of social acceptance among the best company in town.[40]

It is plausible that Dorothea's parents were quite willing to entertain an Italian castrato in their own home, considering the Maunsells' social ambitions. In 1765, the year of Tenducci's arrival in Dublin, the family had only recently moved from their previous house in York Street to Molesworth Street, a step which marked them out as people of fashion and part of Dublin's establishment.[41] Molesworth Street was a newly built terrace of two- and three-bay Georgian townhouses, a stone's throw from the palatial mansion of James FitzGerald, Earl of Kildare, later Duke of Leinster.[42] Viscount Molesworth and Sir Joshua Dawson were responsible for creating this part of town, the most fashionable suburb in Georgian Dublin, and home to members of the aristocracy, gentry, and professions, including the Anglican archbishops of Dublin.

It was here that Tenducci made his first personal call at Dorothea's house on Molesworth Street, stepping from a coach onto the newly laid granite pavement, walking a few steps past black iron railings to the front door of the house, with its imposing doorway designed to look for all the world like the entrance to a Roman temple.[43] As he stepped across the threshold of the Maunsells' imposing home, this son of an Italian servant, who by then was no stranger to palaces, would have been ushered upstairs by the butler to the decorous surroundings of the drawing room, a public saloon customarily on the first floor in genteel Dublin houses with long floor-to-ceiling sash windows, long mirrors, and ornamented ceilings, furnished in the height of good taste, where guests were entertained after dinner to music, dancing, and card games. This was, in effect, the teenage Dorothea's schoolroom. Here Tenducci helped her practise harpsichord-playing, singing, and developing the conversational skills deemed necessary in a young woman if she was to catch herself a husband of rank and fortune, and keep her spouse entertained thereafter. With Tenducci as her companion, Dorothea discussed foreign customs and his travels in Europe, which her parents encouraged since they thought it would provide their daughter with the kind of superficial polish much condemned by the early English feminist Mary Astell, who railed against a society that nurtured its young women to be like 'Tulips in a Garden, to make a fine *shew* and be good for nothing'.[44]

The visits were a success and continued on a regular basis, unsupervised. These meetings must have had a cosy intimacy as autumn turned into winter and the afternoons drew in. With their heads bent close to one another over a book, and hands brushing lightly on the keys of the harpsichord, Dorothea and Tenducci found delight in one another's friendship: she conveyed the naturalness of her developing affections by confessing, 'I began to feel a secret pleasure in his conversation and company', although at first she attributed this to no more than his 'fine singing, his pleasing manner', and the obliging attention he paid to her instruction.[45] By Christmas 1765, Dorothea recalled that 'tender sentiment' had arisen between the pair, with an intensity that was beyond the imagination of her parents. Doubtless the Maunsells had entrusted their virgin daughter's care to Tenducci in much the same way as the Grand Seignors of the Ottoman Empire yielded their harems to the supervision of eunuchs. Unmarried men and women of fortune were not usually permitted to have private one-to-one audiences unchaperoned unless they were at an advanced stage of courtship. The presumed lack of danger to Dorothea's honour in this case must have resulted from the assumption that castrati could not act upon sexual desires even if they experienced any such feelings. Counsellor Maunsell was later to relate that from his earliest encounter with Tenducci he knew him to be 'a public singer, of great eminence, and an eunuch'.[46] The implication was that he was reasonable in his assumption, as any other father might have been, that his daughter was in safe hands.

Towards the end of 1765, the Maunsells agreed to let their daughter spend Christmas as the house-guest of the same gentleman at whose residence she had met Tenducci earlier that year. There, together with a 'numerous party', Dorothea was treated to a month-long series of entertainments, music, dancing, and 'all kinds of mirth'. Tenducci also happened to be there among the house-guests. When she returned home, Dorothea realized that she had fallen in love: as she recalled, 'Music, that had always been before my greatest pleasure, was now become insipid, unless when accompanied by Tenducci's voice; neither did the conversation of my friends please me half as much as his.'[47]

Tenducci's fellow-lodger in Dublin, Charles Baroe, recalled that at this time the feelings on the singer's part towards Dorothea were mutual. In a private moment, during the time when he was a frequent visitor to Molesworth Street, the Italian confided to his room-mate that he had 'got most intimately acquainted with Miss Dorothea Maunsell, daughter of Counsellor Maunsell'.[48] Baroe recalled that during the winter of 1765 he witnessed the singer make his frequent visits to the Maunsell residence, and that Tenducci told him of his growing feelings towards Dorothea: 'with whom … Tenducci [said he] … was then in love', so much so that he was unwilling to leave her and go to London where he was engaged to sing. In following his heart and staying in Ireland to be with Dorothea, Tenducci incurred a hefty fine of £500 (a sum which would have sustained a gentry household in fine style for a year) payable to Mr Rich, the manager of Covent Garden Theatre, for reneging on his promise to appear there during the winter season in 1765.[49]

The teacher–pupil aspect of the relationship between Tenducci and Dorothea was clearly a problem. The reputation of singing and dancing masters was a trouble to many parents' consciences, owing to the unusually close, even tactile relationship that was required as a routine part of instruction. Though musical accomplishment and knowledge of dance-floor etiquette were now deemed 'polite arts' in society, there was an enduringly close association between the arts and libertinism, overlaid with the exotic mores that were imputed, rightly or wrongly, to the presence of a foreigner in the house, whether he was French or Italian. There were several scandalous cases reported in the press involving private tutors and their pupils. Even respectable women were not immune, as in the case of Dr Johnson's confidante Hester

Thrale. The widowed Mrs Thrale caused a scandal when she ran off to Italy with her daughters' dancing master, Signor Piozzi, a handsome younger man and her social inferior, with whom she was ever after exiled from polite society, albeit with some compensations.[50]

Later, when the story of his relationship with Dorothea became public knowledge, Tenducci was keen to correct the impression fostered by the Cork newspapers that he had been paid to teach Miss Maunsell. He placed an advertisement in the press in which he announced that the report that she had formerly been his pupil was 'entirely void of foundation' and that 'I never was entertained as a singing or music master by any person, or persons, since I had the honour to perform in this kingdom [of Ireland]; never taught the art of singing, and consequently never had a pupil'. Tenducci's trouble in placing this advertisement showed how greatly he was concerned not only for Dorothea but for his personal and professional reputation. In spite of the catastrophic chain of events in which he soon found himself enmeshed, he was eager to show his lasting regard for his paramour and her 'friends' (a word which also encompassed her family), 'whom I cannot mention but with the utmost respect', and thus publicly and categorically denied ever having been her 'teacher of music, or singing in any degree whatsoever'.[51]

Counsellor Maunsell's version of events was rather different. Dorothea's father later presented Tenducci as a highly manipulative person, a chancer who had turned up in Ireland 'in the character of a public singer, of great eminence', someone known to be 'an eunuch', who had preyed upon his daughter whilst providing her with musical instruction, exploiting her youthful inexperience and 'artfully insinuating himself' into her affections.[52] As a father of a girl of tender age responsible for protecting her honour, the tone of Maunsell's recollections suggests that he sought publicly to exculpate himself for failing spectacularly to do so, even though she was under his own roof at the time.

♪

Like the many other young girls who admired castrati, Dorothea's feelings for Tenducci may never have progressed beyond a harmless crush, had not her father decided in the early months of 1766 that it was time his daughter was married. Each year in the spring the Maunsells decamped to Cork for the local assizes, where Dorothea's father, as Chief Justice of the county, meted out punishment to sheep-stealers and petty larcenists. In the courtroom, Thomas Maunsell's verdict was decisive: upon his word, a man could be transported or hanged. In the privacy of his own household it was another matter, and he found that exercising his patriarchal authority was subject to female whim. In response to pressure, Dorothea would not capitulate: 'I persisted in refusing', she recalled, 'and [he] in tormenting me to comply'.[53] It transpired that his daughter found the man he had chosen to be her future husband 'perfectly disagreeable'. Though parental approval was desirable in a match, there was a long-standing precedent in English law that the consent of both parties was vital, since forced marriage was regarded as tyrannical.[54] At the higher end of society, among royalty and aristocrats, there was a long precedent for marriages to be little better than dynastic arrangements.[55] But at Dorothea's level of society, among the lesser gentry and middling professional families, there were growing expectations at this time that love, as well as duty, was a necessary ingredient in a marriage. The young girl certainly did not love her father's choice of spouse for her. Instead, Dorothea's hopes became increasingly focused upon her singing teacher, who was by then engaged by Mr Barry, the manager of the new Crow Street Playhouse in Dublin, to provide evening enter-tainments for the assize crowds at Cork once the main business of hanging and flogging had been decided during the day.[56] Faced with a loveless marriage, Dorothea must have watched Tenducci's luminous performances on stage with a thrill of secret knowledge that she alone out of the crowds of his adoring fans nurtured a special intimacy with her tutor. If she followed her father's wishes, a life of duty and drudgery lay ahead. While her father pressed his demand that she should marry the man of his choosing, she confessed that it brought her 'to a determination of marrying Tenducci, sooner than I otherwise should have done'.[57] She had to act quickly.

*Chapter Six*

# The Elopement

Shortly before the assizes were wound up in Cork in the summer of 1766, with her father trying to talk her into an arranged marriage, Dorothea told Tenducci that she wished to marry him, and fast. 'This design I immediately imparted to him,' Dorothea recalled, 'and ordered that every necessary preparation should be made with the greatest expedition.'[1] The bride therefore not only inverted the usual order of things in proposing to the groom, but in giving her prospective husband instructions, and telling him to be quick about it. From the moment these words were uttered, she must have known that her reputation would be in peril. Unmarried girls were not supposed to reveal their true intentions during courtship, nor were they permitted to defy their fathers and order men about in the general scheme of things. Perhaps Dorothea considered that the virtues of chastity and submission to paternal authority which were drummed into girls of her class from birth were now overtaken by the more fashionable view that romantic love justified rebellion in the face of parental cruelty. Perhaps, spurred on by antipathy to her father's wishes as well as her emotional attachment to Tenducci, she did not think at all. Her retrospective explanation to the public was that it was preferable to marry a castrato for whom she felt 'every tender sentiment' than submit to tyrannical patriarchal will, although she made it perfectly clear in doing so that she had acted rashly, and with 'thoughts of avoiding a marriage for which I had conceived the greatest horror' at the forefront of her mind.[2] She made no secret of the fact that she had used Tenducci as an escape route from an unwanted marriage, her fondness for him notwithstanding.

We cannot be privy to what discussion passed between Dorothea and Tenducci before their wedding, and lack even a formalized public version of what happened in the events leading up to their union from his point of view. Whether or not he had intended their relationship to be a courtship leading to marriage we simply do not know. What is plain is that the timing of events was not his, but Dorothea's.

♪

Dorothea and Tenducci hatched a plan. They intended to wed immediately, but not live together at first. She was to remain with her family and keep the fact of their marriage hidden until Tenducci had finished his singing engagements in Ireland, at which time they would escape together to England.

A full description of the wedding ceremony was provided by Mary Holland, a widow of Tuckey's Quay, who had been Tenducci's landlady while he had been staying in Cork to perform in the assize week concerts. Mrs Holland later recalled that, on the evening of 19 August 1766, Dorothea and Tenducci prevailed upon her to go with them to the northern suburbs of the town so that she could be a witness to their marriage.[3] That she was indeed present at the ceremony is made more likely by the specific details she recalled, such as the fact that the bride and groom travelled there in sedan chairs and were attended by Tenducci's manservants. When the party arrived at a certain private house, they were shown into a room, where Tenducci's landlady recalled 'an elderly infirm man lay in or near a bed'.[4] Mary Holland said that she had understood this man to be a Catholic priest, a man by the name of Patrick Egan, who proceeded to utter a ceremony 'not known or understood' by her. Mary stated that she believed the language to be Latin, as 'was the usual matrimonial ceremony of the Romish church'. Once the priest had finished muttering, Tenducci, the groom, slipped the old man some money, and the whole shady business was concluded.[5] Mary Holland was later keen to distance herself from her collusion in this clandestine union, since the circumstances were entirely dubious (it was after dark, the priest was senile, *hocus pocus* was muttered but the witness could not say what was promised or whether it was legal). Later, Dorothea's father also recalled that his daughter described her marriage to Tenducci at the priest Egan's house in Mallow Lane in similar detail. For Thomas Maunsell, and for Dorothea's family, this Catholic wedding was only ever a 'pretended ceremony of marriage'.[6]

In labelling it a 'pretend marriage', they had the backing of English law. The status of Catholic weddings was at best uncertain in Britain and Ireland at this time, highlighted in the case of Scrimshire v. Scrimshire (1752), in which the judge ruled that a marriage conducted by a Catholic priest according to the 'Romish' ceremony of marriage was not valid; only if the same priest converted to Protestantism and used the Anglican rites would the marriage be fully legitimate.[7] Moreover, Tenducci's secret wedding to Dorothea had many of the characteristics of clandestine marriage which had been outlawed by Harwicke's Marriage Act just over a decade earlier, in 1753. The minority of the bride, the lack of parental consent, and the fact that the ceremony was concluded at night by a priest of dubious credentials were irregularities which the Act had explicitly set out to eradicate in order to regularize lawful marriage ceremonies, after centuries of confusion between canon law and customary practice, and a more recent rise from the end of the 1700s in the number of couples forging clandestine unions.[8]

The couple's plan that their marriage would be hatched in secrecy and remain so was soon confounded, however. Within days, rumour of their affair was 'whispered every where'. The problem was not just that the groom was a castrato (though this was bad enough). The significance of the groom's Catholicism in the context of his elopement with an Irish Protestant girl of good fortune was another dimension to the marriage which would have shocked Anglo-Irish society. The Church of Ireland raised its children on a diet of anti-Popish rhetoric that was fundamental to their identity: whatever their level of personal devotion, in terms of political, familial, and cultural allegiance, to marry a Catholic was an act of extreme betrayal. In Dorothea's home county, Limerick, only about a tenth of the population was Protestant. But the town of Limerick itself, for which Dorothea's uncle Richard Maunsell had served as both mayor and a member of parliament, was regarded as a bastion of Protestantism.[9] Its cathedral on the King's Island was in sight of the citadel, where 1,000 soldiers were garrisoned to defend the port from invasion by European forces loyal to the Pope.[10] Neighbours were vigilant in case of Catholic infiltration and skulduggery, and were easily provoked into anxious credulity regarding the quasi-terrorist tactics of the Church in Rome, of which the errant behaviour of Italian singers would have been regarded as further proof positive.

Following their clandestine wedding, Dorothea wrote to Tenducci with the news that their secret was being reported in the neighbouring county. Fearing her father's anger, she asked him to meet her in Limerick the following Sunday. Dorothea made plans to go to her sister Elizabeth's house and, from there, to secure her escape route with Tenducci. She later wrote in great detail in the *True and Genuine Narrative* how this was achieved, in a manner which conveyed drama and fearful excitement in equal measure. It was the moment when Dorothea ceased to be a spectator and entered the stage in her own real-life drama of operatic proportions.

♪

Elizabeth, Dorothea's elder sister, had been married in 1765 to a man named Henry White, whose country estate was Greenhall in County Tipperary.[11] It was at Greenhall, on the designated night of 25/26 August 1766, that Dorothea put her daring plan into action. She had been in company with her family after dinner, but at about ten o'clock she made her excuses and retired on the pretext of writing a letter, taking with her a female friend who was privy to her scheme. Locking herself in the parlour, she recalled how she began in haste to write a letter of explanation to her family while she awaited the arrival of Tenducci, her husband. Her plot was nearly discovered when a servant came repeatedly to collect her letter for the post; only by taking this servant into her confidence was she able to keep her designs secret from the rest of the household. She had already secured a go-between in the form of her father's servant Jerry, who had delivered her letters to Tenducci, and returned with his instructions. Jerry was only a young lad, and uneasy in case he was conniving in some ill deed, but Dorothea reassured him 'of my resolution of going off with Tenducci as soon as he should arrive ... I told him, my resolution was already taken, that I was now Tenducci's wife, and could not live without him.'[12]

Finally, under cover of darkness, Tenducci arrived with his horses and a servant. He paced up and down outside with his horses, while Dorothea delayed and finished her farewell letter to her family. 'The thoughts of leaving my friends affected me so that I could not forbear tears,' she recalled, in testament to her finer feelings, 'but in other respects, I was extremely glad that Tenducci was coming according to my desire.' He meanwhile was fatigued so much with waiting for Dorothea that he 'lay down on a gravel walk to rest himself'. Eventually, she finished writing her letter, which she entrusted to her friend, and asked her to give it to the family the next day. Next came the heart-stopping part: her actual escape. Creeping out of the house unnoticed was no mean feat. Dorothea's faithful female servant 'stole softly into Mr. W[hite]'s bedchamber, and took the key of the hall door, which we attempted to open, but found it would make too great a noise'.

Gamely, the servant returned upstairs a second time to steal the back-door key from the host's bedroom. Finally, Dorothea exited from the rear of the house into Tenducci's waiting arms. With the loyal Jerry in tow, the pair were soon mounted on their horses and galloped off towards Cork, undiscovered.[13]

Through this minute-by-minute account, Dorothea's sense of excitement and adventure invited admiration from her readers at the bold measures she was taking for love. She justified her rebellion against her family by the fact of her already being married at the time of her escape. She was also keen to put her side of the case and show that her elopement with Tenducci was free and unforced, reiterating that he had come to carry her away 'according to my desire'. She showed her duty to her family by means of the letter she left explaining the circumstances to them. Even though these were extraordinary measures, Dorothea at least tried to pay lip service rhetorically to customary social expectations. She used to her own ends the convention that her duty to her husband now outweighed the duty to her father. Such was the fearful respect which she demonstrated towards the latter, who clearly had no compunction about trying to exert his rightful authority as a patriarch, that in spite of her rebellious elopement she made only veiled references to Maunsell as 'F.' ('he is my F[ather] and I will say no more than what the necessity of self defence extorts from me').[14]

Early the next day, Dorothea's close family discovered her bed empty and the girl gone. They sent word 'by an express from Green-hall' which reached Limerick by ten in the morning, informing Dorothea's father of what had happened, and delivering her letter to him. We do not know who was awarded the unenviable task of breaking the news to Chief Justice Maunsell that his daughter had run off with a castrato. The lawyer read his daughter's letter, signed 'Dorothea Tenducci', in disbelief, a reaction which was quickly followed by anger.[15]

♪

By eloping with Tenducci, Dorothea found herself at the centre of a real-life drama. Upon discovering his daughter's disappearance, Dorothea's desperate father sent messengers to find out where the couple had fled. By his own account, he 'immediately pursued them night and day to Cork; and, having there received intelligence of their place of lodging', he at once 'applied to the then mayor of Cork, for a warrant against . . . Tenducci'.[16] In the face of entirely predictable paternal anger, the fugitives might have been expected to hide, or at the very least put some distance between themselves and her family. In fact they remained in Cork, where they dined out just three days later on 28 August among 'numerous polite company', a strikingly bold and provocative action resulting either from extreme naïveté, or confidence in the lawfulness of their marriage and the unassailable quality of Tenducci's fame. In either case, they were severely deluded. Having secured his warrant for the singer's arrest, Maunsell's men moved in. On the way home that night, the lawyer recalled, he 'got possession of . . . Dorothea and brought her with him back to Greenhall'.[17]

Dorothea's version of events was rather different from her father's. According to her, she left the party that night before Tenducci and was making her way home, carried in a sedan chair, when she was suddenly ambushed by several men armed with cutlasses. Upon refusing to surrender their passenger, the chair-men were wounded, one of them receiving a cut to the head that bled profusely which 'distracted and terrified' Dorothea out of her senses.[18] She screamed, and was held at the point of a pistol upon pain of death if she spoke. This terrifying ordeal was supervised by 'a near relation of her own', one of her Waller cousins, who conveyed her by force to his house. In describing these events, Dorothea did not spare the dramatic detail. But in doing so, she justified speaking out, as all women who put pen to paper were customarily obliged to do, by describing how privileges which she could reasonably expect according to her sex and social position had been violated. By telling her version of events, she hoped to expose the want of 'tenderness and delicacy' on the part of her father and relations in subjecting her to such treatment, who showed no deference to her as a kinswoman or young girl of feeling.[19] Counsellor Maunsell, by contrast, rationalized his actions by stating that he was merely 'getting possession' again of what was rightfully his property: his daughter.[20]

The barrister stepped up his strong-arm tactics against the man who had run off with Dorothea. Her cousin led a group of Maunsell's henchmen, including a lawyer, a revenue officer, and a number of servants, to Tenducci's lodgings. Here, they broke down the door, threatened him with a blunderbuss, frisked him, and marched him into the street 'without allowing him time to put on his shoes, or his hat'.[21] His wife wanted the world to know that Tenducci's treatment at the hands of her relations had been as a criminal rather than a gentleman. The man who had graced the salons of princes and who had been celebrated on the grandest stages in Europe was thrown into the notorious common jail in Cork, 'a dungeon intended only for felons and murderers, cold, damp, highly offensive to the smell, and without a glimmering of light'. Here, the *virtuoso*'s finely tuned ears were treated to the 'lamentable cries and groans of despair' from other prisoners. He languished in jail until the end of August, when he was charged in Tholsel Court under threat of a £2,000 fine for alleged abduction.[22]

Meanwhile, Thomas Maunsell's desperate attempts to salvage his own reputation and that of his family intensified, as did Dorothea's efforts to secure her own freedom and have Tenducci released. Allies were marshalled on both sides. Dorothea demonstrated her initiative by writing to a relative in Cork, a well-to-do merchant whom she could trust and who agreed to side with her and Tenducci. Dorothea's relation agreed to pay the bond of £2,000 to have the singer released from jail, on the condition that he should leave Ireland, never to return to the stage there again.[23] Even Dorothea's allies had an eye to minimizing the perhaps irreparable damage to their family's reputation which she had caused by her scandalous marriage.

And so by the end of August, thanks to Dorothea's initiative, Tenducci had been released on bail, and thus received a temporary reprieve. However, Maunsell's allies were powerful, and the lawyer's determination was unrelenting. During the autumn of 1766, Thomas Maunsell took every measure at his disposal to break Tenducci. He wrote to the Lord Chief Justice of Ireland, Lord Annaly, successfully petitioning him to issue a further warrant for Tenducci's arrest.[24] In November, Maunsell took his case against Tenducci all the way to the King's Bench, the highest court in cases of *habeas corpus*, where writs were issued in cases of abduction and suspected forced marriage.[25] Dorothea's cousin Waller appeared in person and swore an affidavit to the effect that Dorothea had been abducted, but she (a lawyer's daughter, after all) challenged the legitimacy of his action, pointing out that her cousin was not her legal guardian. The Mayor of Cork, evidently in Maunsell's pocket, issued a summons via an alderman of the city to have Tenducci re-arrested and cross-examined in front of several justices of the peace, under oath 'in relation to an Act of Parliament against clandestine marriage' (meaning Hardwicke's Marriage Act).[26]

All this time, Dorothea assumed almost the role of Portia in the *Merchant of Venice*, by commenting upon the use of the law in a manner that was usually regarded as beyond the proper concern of women.[27] She made a direct appeal to the reading public as though they were the jury, and she defended herself, and her husband, by invoking the misuse of the law and violation of natural justice. She may have been emboldened to do this through her own courtroom observations as a senior barrister's daughter, even though she was excluded by virtue of her sex from a formal legal training. Her arguments were clearly made and at times quite technical. Dorothea argued in her own narrative of events that she had not been abducted but had eloped of her own free will, hence there was no case to answer. Since these protestations fell on deaf ears with her father, she pressed her defence further. Tenducci's cross-examination was illegal on two grounds, she argued, first, because her husband was under duress, and secondly because he could not understand English very well.[28] 'But surely our laws are not to be twisted, and tortured, to answer particular purposes', pleaded Dorothea, appealing to the public to issue 'the censure his persecutors deserve'.[29]

Female rhetoric was little use in this case, however. It took the intervention of Dorothea's sympathetic relative, another senior male member of the family with financial resources and social influence, to secure Tenducci's release from prison on bail for £2,000. Dorothea's husband was again a free man, but it was only a temporary hiatus from persecution by her father. Most dramatically of all, on 1 September, in the early hours of the morning, Thomas Maunsell went with Dorothea's uncle Richard and a posse of armed soldiers and made a forced entry into Tenducci's lodgings. Richard Maunsell threatened Tenducci's life with a cocked pistol, at which sight Dorothea pleaded with her father, insisting she had eloped of her own volition, 'and that he had better put an end first to my life, as I could not survive the loss of [Tenducci]'.[30] At this intervention, Thomas Maunsell changed tactics, attempting to plead with his daughter, using 'the most endearing expressions to get me to rise, and dress', which Dorothea eventually agreed to do. This moment illustrated how a 'darling daughter' could prove to be the 'achilles heel of patriarchy', reducing even the most authoritarian father to pleading and soft words.[31] While the exchange between father and daughter was taking place, the Maunsell menfolk ransacked the singer's private papers for evidence and had him escorted off to the bailiff's house under armed guard, and thence to prison once more.

These melodramatic events took place before a humiliating mob, who heard Dorothea protest that she would rather die than see Tenducci shot.[32] Following this very public denouement, the press got whiff of the breaking news. The very next day, the *Dublin Mercury*

117

reported: 'We hear the celebrated Mr. Tenducci was lately married at Corke to a young lady of family and fortune, *Mirabile dictu* [wonderful to relate].'[33] When the press lapsed into Latin, it was a sure sign of attempted witticism and usually drew attention to, rather than veiling, a subject unfit for explicit discussion in the vernacular. The *Dublin Courant* reported simultaneously from Limerick that 'an amiable young Lady has deserted her Parents and Friends and thrown herself away upon an Italian Singer; a most extraordinary Matter of Amazement, and no doubt great Distress to a very respectable Family'.[34] As they pored over the *Courant* in the coffee houses of Dublin, readers would have been drawn to reports of a murder trial in Limerick that was being prosecuted on behalf of the Crown by 'Mr Maunsell', the eminent attorney. But who among the keen-eyed reading public could have guessed that there was a connection between the two stories, that the father of the girl who had eloped, and the lawyer prosecuting the trial, were one and the same? Thomas Maunsell was a powerful figure in Irish society, and for this reason, perhaps, the newspaper editor dared not name him as the man whose daughter had scandalously absconded, but instead hinted at it by juxtaposing the two news items.

Within days, the *Dublin Mercury* published a report that Tenducci had been imprisoned:

> We can with pleasure assure the public, that the young Lady mentioned in our last to have been carried away by an Italian singer, was secured by her friends last Thursday, and the ruffian committed to the jail of Corke.[35]

By mid-September the news had been picked up in the London press, which was less circumspect about naming the parties involved. The *Public Advertiser* spread the reports from Cork that Tenducci had eloped with 'a young Lady of good Family and Fortune, who had lately been his pupil'. One month later, the public was informed of

her name 'Miss Mansell . . . Daughter to Counsellor Mansell, of Limerick . . . entitled to £2000 Fortune'. The *St James's Chronicle* verified the
details of Tenducci's arrest, release, and re-arrest at the hands of
Dorothea's father, and the firmness of Dorothea's resolution to stay
with her husband, in spite of opposition from her 'friends'.[36] The
scandal had made the national news.

The bitterness of Maunsell's attack upon Tenducci was made even
more public by the attempts on both sides to use the newspapers to
champion their cause. Dorothea's relations even took the extreme
measure of issuing her obituary, effectively signalling that she was
dead to them, in an effort to salvage the good name of their family.[37]
On the other side, Tenducci's use of the press to rebut the publicity
offensive waged by her family continued a habit he had begun in
London of using the media to promote his career and to put his
side of any controversies, personal or professional, in which he was
involved. Thus he wrote letters of protestation from prison, presenting
his story to the *Dublin Courant*, perhaps mindful of the fact that his
livelihood depended upon the goodwill of the public:

> Mr. Tenducci desires a Letter from his Confinement, as an Act of
> Justice to contradict the mention in our last, of his having been a
> Tutor to the young Lady whom he married.[38]

Tenducci's use of the media in this way is strikingly modern. The
private lives of public figures were already being lived out in the gossip
columns of the press. A new development was the deliberate attempt to
manipulate news items by rival parties. From the earliest days of the
mass media, individuals were already acting as their own publicists,
having realized how powerful newspapers had become as the bearers of
reputation.[39]

♪

Thomas Maunsell's reaction to his daughter's impetuous marriage was entirely predictable, more so given her singular choice of husband and the public humiliation of their family name in the national and local press. His writs against Tenducci amounted to accusations of seduction and kidnapping, and he used every means available to him as 'the grand figure' in his local community.[40] The unsuitability of Dorothea's choice was plain to all who read about it in the gossip columns of Dublin, Cork, Limerick, and London. She and Tenducci had broken sacred principles that were widely recognized by men and women of sense. But there is another dimension to understanding why such opprobrium was heaped upon them for marrying, a specifically Irish and local perspective to the list of taboos over which the Tenducci marriage rode roughshod. If we are fully to understand the reaction of the Maunsell family, particularly Dorothea's father, to the monumental scandal of her elopement, we need to consider more closely the peculiar circumstances of Irish Protestant families in the 1760s and the dynamics of local power politics. For the plain fact is that the abduction of girls was regarded by the squireens of Limerick, Dorothea's home county, as a broadly acceptable way of securing a wife. In the 1740s, in a notorious case, Frances Ingoldsby, a Limerick heiress, was abducted by the man who eventually became her new husband, Hugh Fitzjohn Massy. Toby Barnard, the leading historian of eighteenth-century Ireland, identifies this abduction as part of a general pattern in the south of Ireland, one which marked a certain ambivalence among leading Protestant families towards the law and its enforcement. Though some have seen this as the mark of a remote and backward people, when viewed from the perspective of the impoverished sons on the fringes of landed society who were would-be abductors, the kidnap of rich women could be regarded as their only rational course of action.[41] This pattern of marriage-making, one that circumvented the usual niceties of courtship, is observable among the pages of eighteenth-century newspaper reports from Counties Cork, Kilkenny, Limerick, and Tipperary. There was sufficient public outcry to warrant legal measures against abduction in the Dublin parliament, especially in the wake of one particularly violent case just a few years before Dorothea's disappearance, when Mary Anne Knox from County Londonderry died whilst being stolen away by John McNaghten, who was subsequently hanged.[42]

Notwithstanding the alarm and scandal attached to such cases, the abduction of an heiress was for many men a successful strategy, leading to a legitimate marriage, although it did entail risk if the enterprise failed, and Irish courts were exceptionally zealous. Irish Protestant families with polite ambitions would have wished to disassociate themselves from thuggery, but even those who were otherwise law-abiding could occasionally collude in such activities. A man like Hugh Massy risked the noose by such bold action, but success brought dividends, since he not only increased his fortunes by securing an heiress for a bride, but strengthened his local standing by increasing the mutual ties of obligation and patronage among his neighbours. By forging a fresh alliance through forced marriage, Massy increased his political and economic power in what were often partisan local struggles in Limerick and its neighbouring counties to nominate a sheriff and elect municipal or parliamentary representatives. The Protestant ascendancy, re-established notoriously under Cromwell and secured from the 1690s onwards by the military power of King Billy's troops, produced an enduringly combustible mix of factionalism stirred up by differences of ethnicity, religion, and employment.[43]

As a pre-eminent member of the legal profession, Thomas Maunsell was intimately connected both personally and politically with the intrigues of leading families in County Limerick, such as the Ingoldsbys of Westmeath and the Hassets of Riddlestown. In the preceding generation, there had even been a direct personal connection between Frances Ingoldsby and the Maunsell family: before her abduction, the young heiress had lodged under the supervision of her guardian Arthur Hasset at the home of his political ally, Alderman Richard Maunsell, who stood as MP for Limerick earlier in the century.[44] Thomas

Maunsell must have known that his daughter's elopement was quite different from Frances Ingoldsby's case, since there was no evidence that Dorothea had gone off with Tenducci against her will, and many protests on her part to the contrary. But the force of Maunsell's actions suggest that he *wanted* what was in reality a free choice to be interpreted as an abduction, since that would be a commonly understood phenomenon in his neighbourhood among his fellow-gentry. It was not simply that the law offered a route that would ensure his daughter's safe return to her family: his issuing of numerous writs and incarceration of Tenducci was a very public means of trying to reassert his own honour in response to their marriage.

In the light of these local power struggles and customary marriage practices, Dorothea's account of her father's violent reaction not only against Tenducci but against his own daughter is entirely plausible. When he could not continue with the public pretence that she had been abducted, Maunsell had her effectively imprisoned under house arrest, jeopardizing her reputation still further by entrusting her to the care of social inferiors, including a gang of men. For three days she was interrogated 'to persuade me to swear falsehoods against my husband, with an intent to hang him if possible'. When she proved too stubborn to relent, Dorothea recalled, 'I was dragged down the stairs, and forced into a post-chaise, under the guard of my uncle, and two armed men.' She was moved first to Tipperary, to her sister's house, where she was briefly reunited with her mother. 'I trembled at the thoughts of seeing my M[other],' she recalled, 'whom I always loved and respected.' It is significant that at the point where Thomas Maunsell's arsenal was exhausted, the distaff side of the family, in the form of her mother, sister, and aunt, was brought in to try and see whether they could succeed where patriarchal authority had failed to bring Dorothea back into line. Her sister, Dorothea recalled, treated her 'in a very disagreeable manner'. Her aunt 'reasoned a great deal with me, represented Tenducci in the worst light that it was possible, [and] related many circumstances much to his disadvantage'. Her mother (also named

Dorothea) meanwhile received her 'with the greatest tenderness and affection, and lamented what she thought my misfortunes'.[45] Dorothea, however, was intractable. Her father soon returned with increasingly violent threats against Tenducci: he 'talked a vast deal of having him pillory'd, transported, and made use of many other such threats'. Maunsell even implied that he would exert his influence to ensure that the singer would be denied legal representation ('that Tenducci should not have one Barrister to plead his cause'), and that he would see him hanged for his alleged crime.[46] Dorothea's tactic in response was silence, 'well knowing that what I had to say was far from being agreeable to him', which exposed Maunsell's ultimate impotence to do anything further to cajole or threaten her into submission.

At his wits' end and in a passionate rage, Dorothea's father gave orders 'that I should be fed on bread and water, and confined in a garret; and, to terrify me further, sent to let me know, that I should soon be removed to [a]... private mad-house, near Dublin, where I should remain for life, if I did not comply'. This was no idle threat, but a real possibility. Though relatively rare, there were well-known cases of 'bad' rather than mad eighteenth-century women who rebelled against their families who as a result were confined indefinitely and against their will to local asylums.[47] In one case, a husband had his wife falsely imprisoned and chained to the floor; in another, an unruly wife was confined to a madhouse by her husband, and praised by a judge for doing so, even though the wife had successfully petitioned for her own release.[48] So notorious were these cases that parliament eventually intervened and in 1774 passed an Act to prevent the worst abuses— but this would have been too late to protect Dorothea, had her father been true to his word.

Eventually, Dorothea's parents presented her with one final ultimatum: as she recalled, she was told to give up Tenducci, or 'be confined in a remote mountain, for the remainder of my days, and never see any human creature, but an old Hag, who should be left to attend me'.[49] Since Dorothea declared she would rather die than give up her husband, her parents followed through with their threat. In their subsequent course of action, Dorothea was effectively stripped of her identity as their daughter. First, she had her gentlewoman's wardrobe confiscated, leaving only the 'rags' she was wearing and some highly functional clothing such as a pair of 'coarse leather shoes' and black worsted stockings, without 'one shilling to procure others'. Dorothea appealed to her readers particularly to empathize with her plight at this moment ('Only think what was my situation, well knowing it was my F[ather]'s intention to imprison me for life, and not knowing where I was to be confined').[50] She was taken in stormy autumnal weather, travelling day and night, across 'a great tract of barren country'. Her destination was the far west of Ireland, a remote and derelict farm-house in County Clare. Here, her father carried out his threat to abandon her with an 'old Hag' for company who was 'the only female in the house'. The elderly woman of his choosing was the only line of defence against the three strange men with whom Dorothea was now confined under the same roof: the woman's husband, her nameless brother, and 'Jacky', her unmarried grown-up son. A girl called 'Miss Jenny' Dorothea took by her poor apparel to be the kitchen maid, but turned out to be the daughter of the house.[51]

Dorothea described her living conditions in this alien household where she spent several months against her will in great detail. She was in the unique position of cohabiting across a class divide in much the manner of an accidental tourist on a holiday from hell. It says much about the prurience of polite Georgian readers that Dorothea's account of being forced to live intimately with a family of much lower social status provided an engrossing, if horrific, window for them, as it had done for her, into another world.[52] Doubtless much of the description of the 'shocking manner' of the country people among whom she was forced to reside was embellished to satisfy the prejudices of the literate, urban élite who were her usual company. According to Dorothea's grotesque description, the house where she was now an effective prisoner was filthy: the table linen was dirty, and the family ate with their hands. She complained of the meagre diet, even though her captors supplied her with oaten bread and tea, while they made do with potatoes and sour milk. The shocking dimension of these details was that her parents knew of the conditions under which she was kept, since her mother sent additional decencies, such as a dress of rough fustian cloth. Otherwise, she was deliberately deprived of the luxuries she had enjoyed in her father's house with the intention of destroying her wilful spirit. But Dorothea was made of stern stuff, and it would take more than menaces, drab clothes, and a high-fibre diet to make her relent.

The threat of rape hangs over the later part of Dorothea's *True and Genuine Narrative*, a violent substitution for the act which Tenducci her husband supposedly could not supply. The danger to her virtue was presented by the son of the house, who Dorothea complained 'took very great liberties with me' with his 'professions of love' and 'conversation so indecent and shocking, as terrified me out of my senses'.[53] One anecdote related by Dorothea was particularly menacing. In the face of his constant solicitations she demanded a bible so that she could swear she would never marry him. She also requested a prayer book in this godless house, whereupon her suitor instead showed her *Memoirs of a Woman of Pleasure*, John Cleland's notoriously pornographic work more commonly known as *Fanny Hill* (1748–9), which she threw on the fire as a mark of honourable contempt and resistance to his sexual advances.[54] Later, in the form of a letter from Tenducci, Dorothea confronted her father directly with the danger to which she had been subjected from this man: 'he [Jacky] surprised her very often in bed in the morning, came in his shirt, and lay on the bed, to endeavour to succeed in his horrid purpose, and closed her in his arms to force her'.[55] The novelistic device of a woman's virtue being tested was familiar to eighteenth-century readers, but this does not mean that she made up her story.[56] The circumstances which Dorothea described were entirely plausible: they happened all too often in the close confines of eighteenth-century households with female lodgers or servants as the victims, as the harrowing evidence from actual rape trials from the Old Bailey during this period testifies.[57] Unsurprisingly, the cumulative effect of these constant unwanted sexual advances, insults, and degrading conditions left Dorothea feeling suicidal.[58]

All of this time, the servant Jerry had continued to act as a go-between for Dorothea and Tenducci to exchange their letters. During the long hard winter of 1766–7 she contrived with her husband to escape, her spirit unbroken in spite of the fact that she was worn down by lack of sleep, the 'badness of the weather, and the itch' (a skin condition caught from her unwashed jailers). Though she said little about how she eventually gave her captors the slip, sometime in the spring of early 1767 she seized her opportunity and escaped across country to County Waterford. Here, she made her way to a house of an acquaintance where she hoped Tenducci would be staying. Alas, she was a month too late: her husband had already left for Dublin. At least she was able here to ascertain with relief that Tenducci's recent obituary, planted maliciously in the newspapers by the Maunsells, was inaccurate.[59]

In December 1766, Tenducci had written to Dorothea's father, warning him that 'all further attempts to injure or distress me can only serve, as heretofore, to subject to vulgar tongues the name of a lady that ought to be dear to all her friends'. He undertook to preserve Dorothea's name from 'scandal and calumny' by submitting to any more of Maunsell's 'oppressive measures that have been taken hitherto to crush me', and that he would do all that was necessary to make his wife, and her friends, happy.[60] As his wife later testified, Tenducci's concerns for her wellbeing during her period of forced confinement were heartfelt ('You cannot conceive his concern and astonishment at the miserable situation I was in').[61]

By the end of January 1767 the Maunsell family had finally realized the futility of further attempts to persuade or force their daughter to relent. By all accounts, Dorothea arrived back in Dublin in a parlous state, her health ruined by her travails, her nerves shredded by the need constantly to defend her honour.[62] Her family had symbolically cast her out from their ranks, but perhaps at this point they realized the consequences of their actions. Via a mediator, Tenducci agreed that he would leave Ireland as soon as his contractual obligations to perform for the last time in Dublin were fulfilled. Furthermore, he promised that he and Dorothea would not live together in Dublin (thus sparing her parents further embarrassment on Maunsell's home turf) and that Dorothea would never appear on the stage in public, a promise which he later failed to keep.[63] At last, Dorothea and Tenducci were reunited, both drained by their incarcerations, but determined to stay together. Counsellor Maunsell at length agreed to drop the charges against Tenducci. By the summer of 1767, his daughter joyously recorded that she and her husband were 'once more restored to the free enjoyment of our liberty, of which, by means of the various prosecutions formed against us, we were long deprived'.[64]

♪

Tenducci thereafter tried, somewhat unsuccessfully, to make himself acceptable to his new in-laws. The press announced his renunciation of the 'Errors of Popery' and reception into the Protestant religion in the parish church of St Bridget, Dublin, on 4 July 1767.[65] This was followed a week later by their remarriage in a Protestant ceremony by special licence from the Bishop of Waterford and Lismore.[66] Dorothea wrote 'we have since been Married (or rather RE-married)' as a happy 'Postscript' to her account of the affair.[67] All parties, including the groom and his gentlemen witnesses, John Power and Lawrence Keating, swore under oath that they knew not of any impediments to the marriage. The bishop's clerk went ahead with issuing the licence, secured by the bond of £200 put up by Tenducci as a mark of his honesty in the proceedings.[68] But of course there *were* obvious impediments to the marriage, had anyone in the bishop's registry bothered to enquire. In addition to the most poignant fact of the groom's status as castrato, their disparate age, wealth, and social positions, was the added problem of the lack of parental consent. It was a long-established principle in English law that parents did not have the right to coerce their children into marriage. At the same time, permission of the father was considered highly desirable in an age when the social order rested upon male authority within the household, shored up in principle by the fiats of Church and State. Those over the age of 21 were generally freer to dispose of themselves as they pleased, but in this case Dorothea's tender age would have increased the desirability of securing her father's permission. On this issue, Tenducci's sworn statement on the Protestant marriage licence that both parties in the marriage had obtained 'the express Consent of their Parents' was an outright falsehood. There is no evidence that Counsellor Maunsell ever accepted his daughter's choice of husband, and, to the contrary, over the course of an entire year, from their elopement in August 1766 to their remarriage in July 1767, he had exercised his 'persecuting genius' to the utmost to try to prevent them living together.[69]

♪

Two marriage ceremonies, both of dubious legitimacy, one Catholic, one Protestant. The honour of a powerful father, and entire family, brought into disrepute. A public scandal reported in the press, both in Ireland, and across England via the London papers transmitted first in the capital, then in provincial towns hungry for news of metropolitan shenanigans. From these inauspicious beginnings, the Tenduccis, Giusto Ferdinando and Dorothea his wife, were finally free to pursue their married life together from the late summer of 1767. Their partnership was never likely to be lived in the quietness and ease for which most eighteenth-century married couples yearned. But a more fundamental question remained. What future did Tenducci foresee in his role as a husband? And what were Dorothea's expectations in her transition from her cosseted life as the youngest daughter in a financially and socially secure household, to her itinerant and precarious living on the road, at the side of her glamorous husband of uncertain means? Though they had succeeded in twice performing the rituals of a wedding ceremony, was it a marriage, if society refused to recognize it as such? Given that the groom was unlikely to be able to consummate the union, was it a marriage at all?

## Chapter Seven

# Married Life

The unconventionality of the marriage between Tenducci and Dorothea illustrates in the breach many of the prevailing norms that existed in the eighteenth century regarding how best to choose a spouse and establish a marriage that was respected by society. In addition to the extraordinary fact that the groom was a castrato, there were other dimensions to the match that confounded propriety. Ideally, conventional wisdom advised that marriage partners ought to be of similar age, social status, and wealth, and have the same religious convictions.[1] With regard to religion, Tenducci renounced his Catholicism and became a Protestant, and was even prepared to remarry in a Protestant church, perhaps in a vain attempt to appease his vengeful in-laws. As for social status, Dorothea's background was solidly upper middle class, bordering on gentry: she was closely related to the landed Irish élite on both sides of her family, and her father and close kin were professional men. By contrast, Tenducci was a servant's son, for which his celebrity status was hardly compensation. In spite of his ability to command extraordinarily large fees, Tenducci's was a financially precarious vocation, and he had already served time in prison for debt when he married. As for age, Tenducci was born in or around the year 1735, and so, although we do not have his exact date of birth, he would have been around 30 years old when he and Dorothea first met. His bride's exact age is also uncertain. An entry in the official Registry of the Archbishop of Canterbury noted that in April 1773 she was a 'Minor of the Age of twenty year and upwards but under the Age of twenty one Years', who had turned 21 by 17 September that year.[2] This means that Dorothea was just short of 15 when she met Tenducci (allowing for a late birthday), and was not yet 16 when they married. To the many insults and calumnies which were levelled at the castrato in the course of his life, the modern ignominious label of paedophile was never applied, since until 1875 the age of consent in English law was 12. In practice marriage at such a young age was extremely rare, in most cases confined to royal houses, where dynastic unions were made between pre-pubescents who did not live together until they were much older.[3] At 15 or 16, Dorothea was several years younger when she married than was common for girls of her rank. Some observers, particularly her family, blamed her reckless conduct upon her youthful inexperience. But for the press and public at large, their censure was not tempered by consideration of her young age. From the time that a girl-child reached an age of reason and understanding, it was instilled in her that virtue was everything.[4] The axe consequently fell upon Dorothea in the press for her scandalous conduct. A stern critic in the *St James's Chronicle* reflected that the most appropriate punishment for her would be to allow her to live with her choice of husband, with the (inaccurate) prediction that 'she will never be taken Notice of' by other suitors.[5]

The cause and extent of the scandal that Tenducci's marriage to Dorothea caused was reflected in the publication of an epigram in the *Dublin Mercury* shortly after news of the elopement broke in September 1766, one which would have doubtless horrified the Maunsell family:

> Unhappy maid, By what ill star misled,
> Cou'd you admit a singer to your bed;

By some false daemon, you were sure possest,
To please one sense, you needs must cheat the rest.[6]

The public joke was that the only conceivable pleasure Dorothea could gain from marrying a castrato would be to hear him sing: all other sensory gratification would have to be denied. The theme of sexual disappointment that would inevitably result from getting wed to an 'Italian singer' (a synonym for a castrato) was played upon in the press both in Dublin and London. There was much speculation about whether the Tenducci union would be consummated. One town wit writing in the guise of a 'Cob[b]ler of Walbrooke', a ward in the city of London populated with small businesses, offered to judge the character of public persons by their shoes, and asked readers to send a shoe belonging 'to the Lady who is lately married to Signor Tenducci, the Italian Singer at Dublin [*sic*]'. The author promised salaciously that 'what some People may have expected to have happened since the Marriage shall be cleared up to entire Satisfaction'.[7] Though the chattering middle classes could snigger, the problem with the Tenducci marriage, which came down to the question of whether the husband was capable of consummating the union, could only be mentioned explicitly in print in the character of someone lacking in polite finesse.

Evidence for the truth of what happened when the couple married, and whether they ever had a sexual relationship of any kind, is limited. Dorothea made it plain in her account that she and her new husband spent the night together after the first wedding ceremony. She also let it be known for the record that she and Tenducci had been in bed together, and that she was undressed, when her father and uncle had forced their way into their bedroom, dragging Tenducci off to prison at gunpoint.[8] On the first night which they passed together as man and wife, like most Georgian couples, Dorothea and Giusto probably went to 'naked bed' in their night shifts, total nudity being thought to be both unhealthy and immodest.[9] Whether Dorothea knew what to expect from 'normal' sexual relations between men and women is another matter. She wrote in the letter to her father just before she eloped, and so before she had spent the night with Tenducci, that 'she considered the said Tenducci, her husband, in the sight of God'.[10] This may have implied that Dorothea knew that the marriage would never be consummated.

Her lawyer father picked up on this phrase and recounted it many years later. He did so in order to play upon the legal ambiguity surrounding the customary practice of some couples making promises of marriage in the present 'before God' (so-called *de praesenti* promises). This kind of marriage bond had been the cause of much controversy since pre-Reformation times. It left considerable legal ambiguity for the church courts to resolve if one party subsequently withdrew their promise of marriage, if consummation did not follow, or if the female party was then seduced and abandoned.[11] Though these kinds of marriage promise had effectively been outlawed by Hardwicke's Marriage Act in 1753, changes in popular attitudes and behaviour took longer to effect. As one historian has commented shrewdly, 'Hasty words breathed in a moment of private passion might create a marriage "in the sight of God" but if either reneged on the contract it would be impossible to prove it as a matter of law.'[12] Though the first Tenducci marriage ceremony was not, by all accounts, a *de praesenti* promise of marriage (since it was before witnesses and conducted with some form of priestly intervention, albeit a questionable one), it had echoes of the marriage promises whose legitimacy 'before God' was not sufficiently robust to withstand a legal challenge. But this was of course a retrospective judgement, recalled *after* Dorothea had lived with her husband for some years. At the time, she insisted Tenducci was her lawful spouse and that the marriage was both consensual and valid.

The rudiments of male anatomy cannot have escaped even a well-brought-up young woman, although it is likely that Dorothea's knowledge of the mechanics of sex and conception were probably hazy.[13]

Since she had married unusually young for a girl from her background, a sexual relationship and children of her own were less likely to have been matters of immediate concern. Barely out of the schoolroom, Dorothea surely fantasized that choosing Tenducci would not only be an escape from marrying the man her father had selected, but of itself an exciting adventure with a kindred spirit, maybe even a route to a stage career of her own. But the reality of her choice must have been only too plain when the bedroom doors closed for the first time upon Dorothea and her husband. It would have been the first time she had been alone and in such an intimate situation with a grown man. At the moment when most newlyweds got down to the business of consummation, what did the Tenduccis *do*? For now, we must patiently wait in the same state of speculation as those who relied upon the reports in the newspapers of the day.

♪

The Tenducci marriage did not meet with unalloyed public mockery, in part due to Dorothea's clever publicity offensive in publishing her version of events. The *Monthly Review*'s response to Dorothea's *True and Genuine Narrative*, which the anonymous reviewer did not doubt was her own composition ('Mrs. Tenducci herself is the writer'), was broadly sympathetic. The *Review* presented her story as 'an affecting one', and opined that any polite reader who read the details of the 'severe persecution which she and her husband have met with from her enraged parents &c.' could not fail to be moved. Indeed, the verdict was that Dorothea's family had been 'shocking to humanity'.[14] There was particular empathy with her husband: 'poor *Tenducci* . . . appears to have gained nothing but trouble and distress, by this his most unaccountable connection'. There were limits to their understanding, however. The *Review* called the marriage 'unaccountable' because it involved 'so *peculiar* a husband', rather than because they judged Tenducci to have made a bad choice of wife and in-laws. Even the sympathetic *Monthly Review* had to acknowledge that the wedding was a surprise, since 'We always understood Signior Tenducci, the celebrated opera-singer, to be an *eunuch*'. With a wink towards the knowledge that the couple were now living together as man and wife, presumably sharing the intimacies of bed and board, the author reflected that it was more strange that Dorothea's affection for her husband 'hath not suffered any diminution, from her better acquaintance with him, after more than a year's cohabitation'. This raised an interesting but unsettling reflection upon the institution of marriage among the readers of the *Monthly Review*. Never mind sex, it might be sufficient for a woman to be happy married to a companionable husband whom she loved 'for his fine singing and agreeable behaviour'.[15] In an era when rising notions of sensibility were becoming culturally fashionable, society may well have been more receptive to this idea than in preceding generations. In Shakespeare's day, women's putative weakness and irrationality was thought to derive from their inherently sinful nature (as daughters of Eve) and susceptibility to brute carnal passion. During the sixteenth and seventeenth centuries, women were believed to be prone to lust since their bodies were thought to crave the heat-releasing quality of sexual intercourse to balance out their naturally cold and moist dispositions.[16] By the mid-eighteenth century, however, new rationales for female second-class citizenship emerged from scientific discoveries that were interpreted as proof of women's delicacy and susceptibility to nervous emotion.[17] It was not long before Mary Wollstonecraft challenged the notion of female sensibility since it promoted the idea that the fair sex was 'unstable' and 'troublesome'.[18] Such debates sowed the seeds of new ideas about women's ability to exercise reason, and articulated a demand for marriage to be reconsidered, not as a patriarchal institution ordered by God according to the principle of male mastery and female subordination, but a contractual relationship based upon mutual respect, intellectual compatibility, and the equality of both partners. In this sense, Dorothea was ahead of her time in choosing the ultimate companionate husband.[19]

The influential novelist and literary critic Tobias Smollett was another person who read and reviewed Dorothea's *True and Genuine Narrative*. It prompted Smollett to write a short piece on the historical and literary precedents for castrato marriage, a tactic which at once made consideration of the subject 'respectable', and distanced the author from any accusations of being a Grub Street hack dealing in mere society gossip:

> Juvenal some where mentions the passion which many of the Roman ladies entertained for eunuchs, without entering into any physical disquisition, we have always considered the charge as the overflowing of the satirist's gall, and as having no foundation in truth or nature. Mr. Wycherley introduces upon the stage a character, which we cannot now think to be improbable, and which is known to every one who has read his Country Wife.[20]

The Roman satirist Juvenal had indeed observed in his famous *Satires* that 'There are some women who take a delight in . . . eunuchs | With their girlish kisses and beardless faces (another advantage: | They do not necessitate drugs to procure abortions)'.[21] Such was the decadence of one Roman matron, he alleged, she had a handsome servant castrated to pleasure her without consequences ('He will do no damage').[22] Smollett's parallel with Wycherley was more complicated. *The Country Wife* (1675) was a play featuring a male protagonist, Horner, who only pretended to be a 'eunuch' by spreading a rumour that he had been the victim of an accident and the hand of an 'English-French chirurgeon [surgeon]'. In this case, Horner feigned a 'coldness or averson to the [female] sex', merely as a ruse to secure the confidence, and love, of women.[23] Though these literary representations of eunuchs and pretend eunuchs were of questionable relevance to the Tenducci marriage, they illustrated the cultural familiarity of the subject to eighteenth-century readers, and an attempt to find points of reference that would make the story of Dorothea's elopement with a castrato intelligible. A recurring theme among Georgian commentators drawn from literature and history was the broad recognition of the proverbial attractiveness of castrati to women. People had heard of the widely recognized, if singular, phenomenon of women falling in love with eunuchs; what was 'unnatural', by contrast, was the cruel behaviour of Dorothea's family towards their own daughter. Like the critic in the *Monthly Review*, Smollett concluded that Dorothea's narrative 'is penned in a most affecting manner, and every page of it seems to contain the most genuine effusions of conjugal love, in the most distressful situations'. Dorothea's prediction that her account would appeal to 'the natural love of justice which shews itself in every breast' found some confirmation, at least if the response of some of the leading critics of the day is an accurate gauge of public opinion.[24]

These sympathetic responses in the press did not hide the fact that Tenducci was widely censured 'for marrying when he was sensible of his Incapacity', since he was unable to father children.[25] But by his actions the singer was taking advantage (whether knowingly or not is uncertain) of the difficulties of English law. It was simply unprecedented for a castrato to marry in this way, since no one had thought to outlaw it, and no previous case had come before the church courts. In Italy, it was a different matter. Castrati had been expressly forbidden from marrying since the late 1500s by Pope Sixtus V, on pain of excommunication, and even capital punishment.[26] Canon law was applied across Europe in Catholic countries, but its precepts were often challenged in Protestant nations after the Reformation. Since Tenducci and Dorothea were married in Ireland (which at this time was under the rule of English law) their case was unique and of uncertain legal status. This was not to say that the idea of a castrato marriage had not been considered in England. Earlier in the century, a lengthy work on the subject, *Eunuchism Display'd* (1718), had been published by Edmund Curll, one of Grub Street's most prolific and notorious hacks.[27] An English translation by Robert Samber of the Huguenot lawyer Charles Ancillon's *Traité des Eunuqes* (1707), the conceit of this book was that it was written in the form of advice, addressed to the male relative of a woman to whom the famous castrato Nicolini had made a proposal of marriage. It ran to over two hundred pages, and managed to be both scholarly and scurrilous (or, as the author had it, both 'Instructive [and] . . . Diverting').[28] It was typical of a certain kind of popular literature that circulated in the late Stuart and early Georgian period, which appealed widely to the tastes of the metropolitan gentry, and to middling readers with autodidactic ambitions. *Eunuchism Display'd* was primarily aimed at men with a classical education, and upwardly mobile autodidacts. It made no apologies for its frank handling of the delicate subjects of sexual relations and the rudiments of male anatomy. The Preface contained a nod to preserving the modesty of the fair sex who might happen to come across the book. The author claimed that at certain moments, when referring to the 'naked Truth' of the subject, he would resort to the familiar strategy of using Latin, 'a Language they [women] are generally unacquainted with'.[29] Though it claimed to distance itself from works such as the *Priapeia* (a semi-pornographic compendium of classical poems dedicated to the phallic god Priapus), the potential for *Eunuchism Display'd* to be read as erotica must not be entirely discounted.[30] Daniel Defoe condemned its 'verbal Lewdness' (which surely would have increased sales), but in a bid for respectability the text was larded with scholarly references to Roman law, scripture, the Church Fathers, and 'modern' authors ('The whole confirm'd by the Authority of Civil, Canon, and Common Law, and illustrated with many remarkable Cases by way of Precedent').[31] It started with a consideration of the origins and causes of male castration, and progressed to a discourse upon 'whether they [eunuchs] are capable of Marriage, and if they ought to be suffer'd to enter into that State'.[32] The rumour of Nicolini's marriage proposal to a 'young LADY of a considerable Fortune' was evidently enjoyed by the author as an opportunity to engage widely with a thorny moral, theological, and philosophical dilemma. In doing so, the author clearly intended to profit from the fashionability of Italian opera at the time, and the public stir caused by some of the earliest encounters of Italian castrati with English society at large.

*Eunuchism Display'd* was a significant publication, since it placed in the public domain a discussion of what constituted lawful marriage, and the expectations that marriage placed upon husbands. People in the eighteenth century, as in preceding generations, acknowledged that marriage was a fundamental building-block of society. The new debates which had emerged from the political crisis of the mid-seventeenth century, precipitated by the English Civil Wars, had had consequences in the long term for the family and for men's roles within it. The family was a form of government in microcosm, a 'little commonwealth' of which the male head of household was the ruler. He was sanctioned by religion, law, and custom to exert patriarchal authority over his wife, and probably children and servants. Questions about the government of the country could also therefore, by extension, be applied to who had authority in marriage. Some commentators favoured a Hobbesian model of patriarchy as benign oligarchy, with the husband exerting absolute authority as the prince in his private domain (with all the potential for tyranny that this entailed). However, from the late 1700s onwards, other models for male authority were inspired, notably by the political philosophy of John Locke. These developments eventually raised questions over whether marriage was not a divinely ordained institution, but a form of civil contract in which men still held the reins of authority, but on the basis that they were naturally the more 'rational' of the two sexes, not because God had ordained it so.[33] These debates took many decades, if not centuries, to develop into the concept of marriage that exists in modern times as an equal partnership bound by a contract that can be broken. (Divorce, for example, only became accessible to non-élite members of society from the mid-nineteenth century onwards, and was not common until the second half of the twentieth century.)[34] But the seeds of these arguments are to be found in *Eunuchism Display'd* since it was published at a moment of transition in the history of marriage, when old and new ideas about the nature of the institution were coming into conflict. The idea of eunuchs, and the real presence of castrati in eighteenth-century society, acted as a catalyst for exploring some of the major issues relating to the renegotiation of men's and women's roles within marriage that were to continue over the course of the following two centuries.

The author of *Eunuchism Display'd* claimed to be conservative in his outlook, 'Marriage being', he reminded his readers 'the Gift of God, and his Work who has united thereby the two Sexes ... and commanded them both to *Increase* and *Multiply*'.[35] On one hand, he seemed to be promoting only certain kinds of marriages, ones that were 'Chast, Religious, and Holy, full of Piety and heavenly Benediction, having for its end only to execute the Command of God, who is its Author and Protector'. All other kinds of sexual relationship, such as 'unchaste' marriages (such as those where husband and wife had sex for pleasure rather than procreation), and those involving castrati, were to be condemned 'with a general Hatred and Contempt, and are even the aversion and horror of all Good men'. At the core of his argument was his rejection of the eunuch's right to marry, due to his inability to propagate the human race. The eighteenth-century castrati, like the eunuchs of antiquity, were deemed incapable of personal relationships that met with 'public Favour and Applause'.[36]

Overall, Tenducci and his fellow-castrati would have found little comfort had they read *Eunuchism Display'd*. There was a small glimmer of hope, however. In discussing the existence of precedents for eunuchs to both desire and enact heterosexual relationships with women that sometimes led to marriage, the author of *Eunuchism Diplay'd* publicized the fact that alternative possibilities existed to the status quo in marriage. Even though he refuted arguments which were raised in favour of allowing castrati to marry, he first articulated the views of those who evidently might support such a position.

Thus, he argued, one rationale for allowing eunuchs to marry might be that not all castrated men were physiologically the same. He gave recognition, therefore, to the idea that 'there are some capable to satisfy the Desires of a Woman' (that is, some eunuchs were able to have sex without being able to father children). The author repeatedly highlighted that procreation was one of the primary ends of marriage, according to biblical precedent and divine injunction. Though he did not accept that sex without at least the *potential* for procreation was sufficient to make a marriage legitimate, it raised the possibility that such an arrangement might be considered by some to be feasible, and perhaps even desirable.

*Eunuchism Display'd* also aired a rational and humanist view of marriage, one that would become increasingly important during the latter years of the eighteenth-century Enlightenment: 'That Marriage is a civil Contract, and therefore lawful for every Body to engage in it, and consequently Eunuchs.'[37] This was essentially a secular argument, made in an age still dominated by religious injunction, where marriages were made, and marital law was administered, by the church courts. Although the author of *Eunuchism Display'd* claimed that he did not agree with this view, he aired the intellectual case for those who argued that if a eunuch could fulfil all other 'Duties of Marriage', that is, all the social responsibilities expected of a husband, except fathering children, then this might be an acceptable basis for a marriage. The opinion that 'it is the Consent of Parties, not Bedding, makes a Marriage' was rejected on the grounds that child-rearing was essential to the social role of being a married man. But the fact of the debate is evidence of the emergent rift in the eighteenth century between what would become an essentially secular, modern view of marriage, based upon love and a companionate relationship between husband and wife, and an older pre-Reformation model of marriage that gave primary importance to the divine injunction to 'be fruitful and multiply'.[38]

*Eunuchism Display'd* left no aspect of the subject of castrato marriage untested. Most pertinently from Dorothea's perspective, it considered the legal maxim of '*Volenti non fit Injuria*' ['there is no Injury to those that are willing'] in relation to a hypothetical scenario of a woman who married a castrato. The implications of this legal principle could be that if a woman agreed to marry a eunuch, and was fully aware of the implications, then she might do so because she consented to such a match.[39] It was a scenario which the author of *Eunuchism Display'd* dismissed, on the grounds that it was most implausible that such a match would ever occur.

♪

Of course, it was not just castrati who were unable to consummate marriages in the eyes of the law. It was not uncommon for men to marry in pre-modern times with some form of anatomical or psychological problem that prevented them (or made them averse to) having sex with their wives. It was a long-established principle in canon law that a marriage could only be legitimized by consummation, that is, penetrative sex leading to male ejaculation with a procreative potential. Lawyers and theologians throughout the centuries, and in different countries across Europe, had debated the legitimacy of marriages in which a husband proved impotent, that is, unable to obtain or sustain an erection leading to ejaculation. Other problems with male reproductive function, such as male infertility, were poorly understood and difficult to diagnose before the advent of modern medical science.[40] In Roman law, a husband's sexual impotence, like insanity, was grounds for a wife to divorce him.[41] Later, in the early medieval period, Catholic theologians argued that there was some precedence for a husband and wife to live together without engaging in sexual relations, although this usually applied to couples later in life when the business of child-rearing was over.[42] Such arguments tended to recede during times of economic crisis or warfare when there were anxieties about producing enough men to sustain and defend the population.[43] It is not a coincidence that, at such times, society actively encouraged large families, and punished those who took measures to prevent or limit conception. At such times the persecution of non-procreative sexual activity, notably homosexual sex between men, also increased.[44]

On the whole, marriage annulments tended to be rare. Consanguinity, or marrying within the degrees of prohibition (that is, marriage to a close family member) were usually given as reasons for petitioning in cases of marriage annulment.[45] This was especially true in England after the all-too-infamous precedent set by Henry VIII, who (contrary to popular wisdom) never divorced, but had his marriages terminated either by annulment or execution.[46] By the eighteenth century, male impotence was still one of the few grounds upon which a wife could secure an annulment of marriage. It was still the case that comparatively few marriages were actually ended on these grounds, however, since it was difficult to prove. Notoriously, it had traditionally required the intervention of several sturdy midwives sent by the court to see whether the husband's penis would respond to manual stimulation (a scenario which was surely enough to make any man wither at the prospect).[47] Such practices were effectively obsolete by the Georgian period, though the press enjoyed speculating about their revival, and publicizing the few cases that went to trial. One unhappy wife, Catherine Weld, published the proceedings of her own libel against her husband Edward in the Court of Arches (the church court under the jurisdiction of the Archbishop of Canterbury dealing with marriage annulment cases) in the *Cases of Impotency and Virginity fully Discuss'd* (1732). As it was usually humiliating for a man to admit to impotence, it frequently remained a secret, exposed only, as in this instance, if his wife took umbrage at her lack of sexual fulfilment or childlessness, or if neighbourhood gossips enquired into the abilities of the husband in the bedroom, and made the shame of the situation untenable. The difference in the Tenducci case was that the castrato's inability to father children was public knowledge, although whether he could still have penetrative sex was a matter of some uncertainty. Some modern scientists believe that if the operation was performed just at the onset of puberty (as was the case with Tenducci) some form of erectile function may have been possible.[48] Regardless of this speculation, unless a man could produce semen, whatever else he could do did not 'count' as sex in terms of social or legal recognition in Tenducci's day. Dorothea might as well have married a woman, since nothing Tenducci did in bed would count as consummation in law, meaning that she was technically still a virgin and free to marry someone else, should her marriage to Tenducci be formally annulled.[49]

The main reason for this was that in the early modern imagination sex and procreation were inextricably linked, much more than in modern times. Since the 1960s, sexual pleasure without the possibility of conception, or indeed the fear of contracting a venereal disease, has been an option available to many couples in the Western world. Reaching back to earlier attitudes towards sex is often difficult. One illustration of this is that the distinction between the capacity to consummate and the capacity to impregnate was an invalid one in English law: the two were one and the same. Castrati had the reputation of being timid, since bravery was something which was long associated in the European imagination literally with *cojones*, an idea preserved in the modern sense of having 'balls'. This was the reason why mothers in the Basque region of Spain fed their sons ram's testicles in soup to ensure they would have the physical strength and courage required of men of honour.[50] Likewise eighteenth-century English erotica celebrated not only the virility of the penis, but the reproductive power of the 'nutmegs' belonging to Britain's vigorous and fertile youth, in contrast to the shrivelled specimens allegedly found in other nations.[51] Charles Burney, anticipating the 'common assertion' that castrati 'are all cowards', was at pains to assert the historical precedents for bravery among the eunuchs of antiquity, and among the castrato singers whom he knew personally.[52]

By his marriage, Tenducci made a trial of his manhood, exposing his reputation to public censure or approbation in a manner which required particular bravery, especially in Italy, his native land, where marriage could have incurred the death penalty for the castrato. But, unlike other husbands who could never be biological fathers, he could not keep the fact of his incapacity hidden. Since the state was not in control of marriage law in this period and did not initiate prosecutions in this realm of private life, and the church courts (who retained jurisdiction over marital disputes) were in relative decline,[53] the question was: would Dorothea wish to continue with the situation in which she found herself, with a castrato as a husband?

♪

Relations between Dorothea and Tenducci started out on a romantic footing, and it is evident from events after their marriage that they remained exceptionally close companions, with the singer taking steps actively to promote her musical vocation and protect her personal reputation. Though we lack first-hand accounts penned by either of the Tenduccis about their married life, which would have afforded a deeper insight into their personal motivations and experiences, there are written records left by those who became acquainted with them from the time that they effectively began their married life together in the summer of 1767 which make it possible to reconstruct their geographical movements, and the impressions they made upon those whom they met.

The first remarkable feature of the Tenduccis' life together as husband and wife is that the marriage appears to have made little or no impact upon Tenducci's continuing professional success. Neither is there evidence that the notoriety of his elopement with Dorothea actively promoted his fame. It was as though in the public imagination he was merely fulfilling the same kind of unconventional personal life that was expected of any eighteenth-century celebrity. His uncertain social status as a man of obscure and foreign origins, and stage occupation, placed him beyond the censure of the bourgeois, who continued to flock to his concerts. Among the aristocracy and nobility,

who were his leading patrons, such incidents were of little consequence, especially considering their own distinctive patterns of personal morality.[54] For Dorothea, the consequences were more severe.
As a genteel young woman, she would have had to get used to the
social ostracism from polite society that came with the territory she had
chosen for herself. This was documented in the reaction of one of her
former music tutors, Josiah Passerini, who instructed his nephew
Stephen not to call upon the Tenduccis, 'saying, that . . . Tenducci was
a vile man for having seduced Counsellor Maunsell's daughter . . . and
having inveigled her into a marriage'.[55] Cut off from her family and
friends, she faced a future in which those around her, particularly
women, would think twice about befriending her, particularly when it
came to invitations to private functions. Though she was presumed to
be still a virgin, her reputation had been sullied by the public scandal
she had caused. Tenducci's employment, though glamorous, brought
her into the social milieu of actresses and female singers, who were
widely thought to be no better than prostitutes. She had sacrificed
much in choosing freedom from her father's tyrannical control.

At first, the couple lodged together at Portobello near Dublin, and
then moved into the city, to a house in Dame Street, where they stayed
for about six weeks.[56] In the autumn of 1767, Tenducci made one last
appearance in Limerick alongside Cremonini, an Italian soprano. It
was reported that both singers appeared 'with their Consorts', though
no further details were provided about Dorothea, or Signora Cremonini's companion.[57] The Tenduccis finally considered leaving Ireland
in accordance with her father's wishes. Unsurprisingly, given the dis-
tractions of his personal life, Tenducci was again in need of funds, and
for this reason he chose to bypass London, where his creditors lay in
wait. Instead, between the autumn of 1767 and spring of 1768, he
went to England alone and undertook a number of concert engagements in provincial towns. In Worcester, he was paid the considerable
sum of 50 guineas for a performance at the annual 'Meeting of the
Three Choirs' across three counties. Tenducci took umbrage when the

PLATE 1    The rooftops of Monte San Savino, the Tuscan hill town where Giusto Ferdinando Tenducci lived as a boy. The bell tower of the church of Sant'Agostino is in the foreground.

PLATE 2    Michele Foschini, *Interior of the Teatro di San Carlo, Naples*, c. 1762. Oil on Canvas. Museo Certosa di San Martino, Naples, 23908.

PLATE 3    Attributed to John Vanderbank, *Portrait of Senesino, Cuzzoni and Berenstadt*, c. 1723. Etching and engraving (214 x 262mm). Handel House Collections Trust, London. English audiences flocked to hear performances by castrati but their bodies were the subject of much cruel satire.

PLATE 4
Charles Townley after Richard Cosway, *Portrait of Elizabeth, 1st Baroness Lyttelton*, undated. Etching. Tenducci was implicated in her separation from George, 1st Baron Lyttelton.

PLATE 5    Francsco Bartolozzi
after Giovanni Battista Cipriani,
*Ticket for Tenducci's benefit concert*,
1786.  Etching and engraving (128
x 116mm). Yale Center for British
Art. B1978.43.743. Tickets were
saved as souvenirs by fans as mementos of an expensive night out.
For the Georgians, patronage of
Italian music was a mark of taste.

PLATE 6
Title page, Thomas Arne, *The
Winter's Amusement*, c. 1762.
Beinecke Library, Yale University. Ma31 Ar6 S81. Through his
performances of popular songs
in English Tenducci succeeded in
building a fan base beyond the
opera houses.

PLATE 7    John Finlayson after J. Bruscett, *Giusto Ferdinando Tenducci*, 1770. Mezzotint (346 x 251mm). British Museum, Department of Prints and Drawings, 1889.0603.289. A slender Tenducci holds a copy of 'Water Parted From the Sea', the aria from Thomas Arne's *Artaxerxes* (1762) which made him famous.

PLATE 8    Anon., *Fitz-Giggo* or, *the New English Uproar*, 1763. Etching (190 x 265mm). British Museum, Department of Prints and Drawings, 1868.0808.4276. Tenducci (centre), Peretti, and the soprano Charlotte Brent, are interrupted by rioters during a performance of *Artaxerxes*. The diminiutive male figure on stage is the composer Thomas Arne, appealing (unsuccessfully) for calm.

Thomas Gainsborough, *Portrait of Giusto Ferdinando Tenducci*, c.1773-75. Oil on canvas (766 x 640 mm). Barber Institute of Fine Art, University of Birmingham, 44.3. Tenducci as a man of sensibility exercising his most seductive talent—his voice.

John Nixon, *Signor Tenducci*, 1796. Engraving (192 x 126 mm). Holburne Museum of Art, Bath, FB41. In contrast to the society portraits which focus upon his character and taste, here Tenducci's identity centres upon the 'lack' in his breeches.

PLATE 11
Anon., *The Ladies Lamentation for the Loss of Senesino*, 1737-8. Etching and engraving (328 x 202 mm). British Museum Department of Prints and Drawings, 1868,0808.3506. Castrati had the reputation of attracting crowds of female admirers from their first appearance in London.

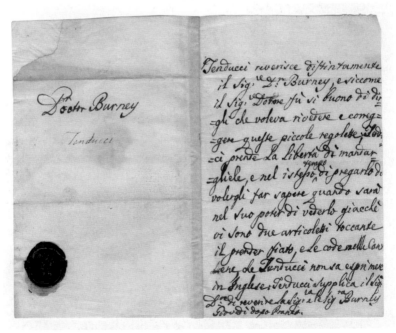

PLATE 12   Letter from Giusto Ferdinando Tenducci to Dr. Charles Burney, undated. Beinecke Library, Yale University OSB MSS 3. A rare surviving example of Tenducci's handwriting, the singer seeks advice from the eminent musicologist on vocal technique and composition.

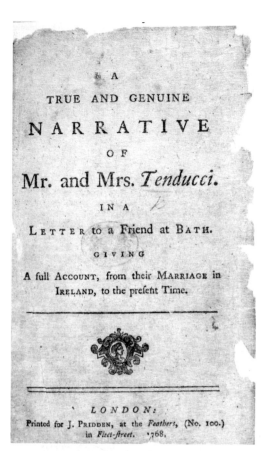

### A
### TRUE AND GENUINE
# NARRATIVE
OF
# Mr. and Mrs. *Tenducci.*
IN A

LETTER to a Friend at BATH.

GIVING

A full ACCOUNT, from their MARRIAGE in
IRELAND, to the prefent Time.

*LONDON:*
Printed for J. PRIDDEN, at the *Feathers,* (No. 100.)
in *Fleet-ftreet.* 1768.

PLATE 13
Frontispiece to *A True and
Genuine Narrative of Mr.
and Mrs. Tenducci*, 1768.
Dorothea Maunsell's teenage
account of her elopement
with the castrato Giusto
Ferdinando Tenducci.

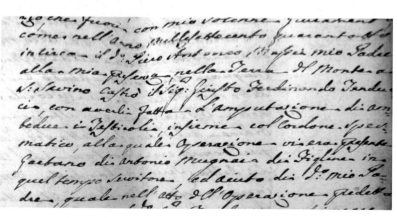

PLATE 14   Extract from the London Consistory Court archive, LMA/DL/C/558/21,
of the original Italian deposition by Tomasso Massi, taken down in Florence on 23
October, 1775 (For full details and translation, see Appendix).

PLATE 15
Valentine Green after Maria Cosway, *Maria, Baroness Cosway*, 1787. Mezzotint (460 x 330mm). British Museum, Department of Prints and Drawings, 1941.1011.65. A concert impresario fluent in five languages, the Baroness was a friend of Tenducci during the later stages of his career.

PLATE 16
Thomas Beach, *Giusto Ferdinando Tenducci*, early 1780s. Oil on canvas (749 x 610mm). Garrick Club, London, G0796. Tenducci as an eminent tutor and composer in his later years. His rich suit of clothing and solidly respectable appearance belied his recurrent problems with debt.

stewards of the music festival requested a receipt to confirm he had
been paid. The townsfolk remembered that the Italian responded with
a temper tantrum, saying 'that he should be sent for to sing at all the
*horse-races and cock-fightings* in the kingdom', and that, rather than
provide a receipt, 'he would rather give his performance'.[58] Though his
diva-like behaviour was by all accounts fairly moderate compared to
some other eighteenth-century opera stars, here Tenducci's ego was
bruised by the implication that he was not a gentleman whose word
alone was his bond. The meaning of his retort (in reference to horse-
races and cock-fights) was that it was a coarser, provincial sort of person
who demanded receipts, someone who might be familiar with the
entertainments beloved of the masses, but not the sophisticated international milieu of opera. The fact, of course, was that the world in
which he moved was full of skulduggery, but his disassociation from the
cautious bourgeois habits of his patrons in Worcester is telling about
the singer's own attitudes towards money, and his self-perception as an
artist more used to being treated as beyond the pecuniary concerns of
other mortals.

The irony was also that, in spite of his lofty attitude towards mercenary matters, Tenducci needed to raise money since his Irish travails
had severely depleted his fortune.[59] He received an offer from the
Edinburgh Musical Society to accept employment as their star soloist
for the following season, which he accepted. Financially, it was a
shrewd decision. Georgian Edinburgh was populated by a concentration of wealthy professional and genteel patrons with town residences
who sustained the cultural life of the town, attracting actors and vocal
performers from across the British Isles. By the 1760s, Scotland's
capital was flourishing as one of the leading centres of the European
Enlightenment, its university at the forefront of advancements in
medical science, philosophy, and political thought. Its architecturally
magnificent New Town took shape during the 1760s, linked to the
medieval Old Town by the New Bridge, which opened in 1763.[60] The
new Theatre Royal in Shakespeare Square opened in 1769, another

example of the city's new-found cultural confidence.[61] In May and June 1768, at the time that Tenducci and Dorothea established themselves in the town, the printer Alexander Donaldson issued the *Edinburgh Advertiser* bi-weekly from his print shop near the Castle. Its pages give some sense of the extraordinary extent to which Edinburgh's citizens were actively engaged with the news and politics, trade, ideas, and fashions of not only Europe but North America. Among the high-water times for the Leith, Donaldson printed news of the arrival of cargoes of Virginia tobacco on the Clyde in early June, which were to be auctioned at Forrests and the Exchange coffee houses. The unfolding news from London that month was of the trial of John Wilkes at the King's Bench. Across the Atlantic, ill-omened reports were received from Boston regarding newly imposed trade embargoes. Later that same month, Sir Laurence Dundas, MP for the City of Edinburgh, gave 'a very sumptuous dinner in the Assembly-hall, to the Magistrates and Town-council, and to around 70 other gentleman of the city'. Meanwhile, the university awarded Doctor of Physic degrees to 'Mr. Benjamin Rush of Philadelphia', and 'Gustavus Richard Brown of Maryland'. Readers of Edinburgh's newspapers could keep up with essays by Voltaire and the complete works of Henry Fielding, and keep an eye on the fluctuating price of oatmeal.[62] They were altogether more urbane than the good citizens of Worcester, and had a particular fondness for European, especially Italian, music.[63]

And so Tenducci arrived in the city in May 1768 as a guest of the Edinburgh Musical Society.[64] This prestigious organization had been founded in 1728 by a group of élite men who were also amateur musicians. By 1762, the Society had opened its own concert venue, St Cecilia's Hall, and paid large sums each year to bring the best professional vocalists and musicians to Edinburgh to perform in concerts and oratorios.[65] Its members included the Earls of Aberdeen, Glasgow, and Elgin, the Lord Chief Baron of the Exchequer, numerous baronets, senior advocates, politicians and members of the judiciary, merchants, army and naval officers, physicians, and 'Mr Adam

Ferguson, Professor of Philosophy'.[66] Tenducci was employed by the Society as their principal singer from June 1768 until the end of 1769. Their treasurer, William Douglas, had negotiated a fee of £150 for him on behalf of the Society's directors, in return for which Tenducci agreed to play the harpsichord and sing at concerts and oratorios for a year. The Society's minutes recorded that

> as Mr. Tenducci had his family to bring from Ireland for which purpose he was obliged to go there but proposed being in Edin[bu]r[gh] again about the 20[th] of June, he therefore begged he might be advanced Forty pounds sterling in part of his sallary which Willm. Douglas has done accordingly, all which the meeting approved of.[67]

Tenducci's reference to Dorothea as his 'family' was significant, and evidently raised no objections among the leading citizens of Edinburgh. The singer went to Dublin to retrieve his wife, and began his concerts on 17 June, appearing at almost every concert date subsequently until July the following year. So began a long association which was to shape Tenducci's vocal style and repertoire, bringing him lasting fame, for his new venture north of the Border was as a performer of Scottish ballads. His timing could not have been better. Scotland was undergoing a revival in nationalist pride following what many Scots had regarded as the humiliating Union in 1707 (as a result of which Scotland lost its own parliament) and the defeat of the Highland clans in the ultimate and calamitous Jacobite rebellion. The aftermath of the '45 had been as much about the eradication of Scottish cultural pride and identity as it had been about tactical military defeat.[68] Highland clans (or rather, what remained of them) were absorbed into the British army, and there were active attempts to eradicate Gaelic and the Scots dialect.

By the 1760s, however, there was a nascent revival in Scottish national pride. One manifestation of this was the interest in traditional Scottish music, of which the ballad tradition (in many cases re-invented) was a leading example. During the 1720s and

149

1730s, Allen Ramsay's *Tea-Table Miscellanies* had led the way in publishing early Scottish texts, ensuring their survival and encouraging the revival of a Scottish literary and musical tradition. From 1726, these had included volumes of airs for domestic performance, with a simple musical score that could be played for entertainment in polite households. Of more immediate influence during the 1760s was the publication in 1759 of James Macpherson's *Fragments of Ancient Poetry*. Macpherson had supposedly rediscovered ancient manuscripts containing a Scottish bardic epic comparable to the *Iliad*, which, though entirely fictitious, prepared the ground for a new interest in Scottish national culture, as well as an early inspiration for the rise of the Romantic movement in the British Isles.[69]

Tenducci had learned in London that singing in a language which the audience could understand was a highly popular move. Scottish ballads suited his vocal range, and his preference for a direct and more sincere style of performance, both of which were ideally suited to the fashionable taste of his audience. His Edinburgh concerts had the additional benefit of not requiring the same kinds of capital investment and elaborate stage settings as classic Italian *opera seria*. One of the leading collectors of Scottish ballads, George Thomson, who was a close acquaintance of Robert Burns, recalled that it was after hearing Tenducci sing 'a number of our songs so charmingly' that he conceived the idea of gathering and arranging 'all our best melodies and songs, and ... obtaining accompaniments to them worthy of their merit'. 'If I were to live ever so long,' recalled Thomson of Tenducci, 'I could not forget the effect of his performance of "Roslin Castle", "Lochaber", or "The Braes of Ballenden"'.[70] The irony that it took an Italian to reveal the beauty of Scottish song to Thomson was not lost on his biographer, J. Cuthbert Hadden. Such was Tenducci's popularity that in March 1769 he renegotiated a contract with the Edinburgh Musical Society for the following year of £250, an increase of £100, but with a penalty of £500 attached for non-completion of the contract.[71]

It was in Edinburgh that Tenducci also re-established his reputation as a fashionable music teacher among the social élite, charging half a guinea a time for a lesson. Significantly, his liaison with Dorothea does not seem to have stopped families from sending him pupils, including unmarried girls. He taught the lute to Christian Fullerton, who in 1772 married Henry Erskine, a future Fellow of the Edinburgh Musical Society.[72] Another of Tenducci's Scottish students, John Campbell, went on to a successful career as Precentor in Canongate Church.[73] Campbell recalled that Tenducci had been particularly kind to him as a talented boy of limited means (his father had been a carpenter). Tenducci taught the young John and his brother for half price, and was perhaps sympathetic to them both due to his own humble origins. Later, Campbell benefited from his tutor's network of illustrious patrons, who included 'the witty Duchess of Gordon, the volatile Lady Wallace, the Earl of Hopetoun, Sir John Halket, and other equally distinguished persons'.[74] Tenducci evidently was successful in establishing his reputation among the highest tiers of Scottish society, and was generous in his willingness to promote younger protégés. Campbell only discovered many years later that the Italian had written in secret to wealthy patrons in order to promote his young pupil's career.

It was in Edinburgh that Dorothea began to appear in public performances alongside her husband, contrary to her father's explicit wishes. Such was her success as a soprano that, when Tenducci left to go to London for two or three weeks in November 1769, Dorothea wrote to the directors asking that she might sing in his place so that the contract would continue. The Edinburgh Musical Society showed remarkable forbearance towards the *virtuoso*. News reached them of his departure just the day before the concert season was due to start, but such was their desire to retain his talent that they agreed to the arrangement, with Dorothea drawing upon Tenducci's salary and performing in his place, until Christmas 1769.[75] This was further proof that Tenducci's wife had been harbouring artistic ambitions of her own, and demonstrates her considerable mettle, and talent, in her own right.

It was never Tenducci's intention to return to Edinburgh for the remainder of the season. His long-anticipated return to the metropolis was reported widely in the press, and was marked with a new production of *Amintas*, an adaptation of *The Royal Shepherd* by George Rush, sung in English, with 'music selected from the best composers and adapted by Mr. Tenducci'.[76] *Lloyd's Evening Post and British Chronicle* raked over the past, reminding the public that Tenducci was 'distinguished for his misfortunes', and implying that he had returned to perform in London 'in consequence of his having incurred the resentment of a great family in Ireland'. Even this ill-disposed press was forced to acknowledge that Tenducci was also distinguished 'for his abilities as a vocal Performer'.[77] Other press commentators made the connection between Tenducci's marital status, and his new-found productivity on the stage. A notice in the *St James's Chronicle* in December 1769 made reference to the publication of *Amintas*, calling it his 'dramatick Bantling' (that is, the artistic equivalent of Tenducci producing a wailing infant—the word was also synonymous with 'bastard'). But there was another reason why Dorothea had remained in Edinburgh, and why the press was issuing puns about the singer's fecundity. Some time during 1769, Dorothea was rumoured to have given birth to a child, and Tenducci was said to have issued an affidavit claiming to be the father.[78]

The idea that a man could claim paternity of a child if he owned the child to be his had some precedent in English law. A fourteenth-century test case had offered the rationale of 'whoso bulleth my cow, the calf is mine', that is, if a husband discovered that his wife had been unfaithful but chose to adopt the illegitimate offspring as his legal heir, then he could do so.[79] This precedent was seldom used in the subsequent three hundred years, however, since it was counteracted by other social injunctions which shamed men who had been publicly cuckolded by their wives. It may be that Tenducci's idea of paternity was a remarkably modern one, based on the idea that if he was willing to accept the social role of father to Dorothea's baby, then society at large ought to acknowledge him as the legitimate parent. It is also likely that Tenducci wished above all to protect what was left of Dorothea's reputation in continuing publicly to call her his wife, and claiming paternity of her child.

This was not without precedent in the history of European castrati. Men like Tenducci had been known to execute elaborate plans in order to secure an heir. It is not impossible that, having discussed the possibility of children, Tenducci consented to allow Dorothea to find a suitable man to fulfil this role.[80] Alternatively (and this is the more likely possibility given subsequent events), perhaps even before their move to Edinburgh, Dorothea had met and fallen in love with another man. In either scenario, it is evident that Tenducci was highly tolerant of the situation, and that he wished to continue to protect Dorothea as far as he could from public shame by acknowledging her child as his own.

Strikingly, the Tenduccis had not long been able to live together peacefully as man and wife before a third party entered the scene. It was only a matter of months from the summer of 1767, when they were left in peace by Dorothea's father, to the spring of 1768, which could have been the approximate time that Dorothea gave birth. It may be that, once the element of persecution of their match had been removed, they found there was little else binding them together. That she was pregnant, or gave birth, around the time that her *True and Genuine Narrative* was published is even more intriguing. Was the man who fathered her baby the amanuensis behind the publication, someone with whom she had worked closely in order to tell her story?

♪

Tenducci appeared occasionally at Covent Garden in the winter of 1769–70, and performed at the oratorios sung in the King's Theatre in 1770. By the spring of 1770, Dorothea had rejoined her husband in London and they lived together in lodgings at a smart address in New Bond Street, as recalled by Charles Baroe, Tenducci's former room-mate. Around this time, Baroe was surprised to see Tenducci appearing at Almack's concert, where, he recalled, 'after some discourse, [Tenducci] asked . . . if he had seen Doro?' upon which the singer presented his wife and her female companion.[81] Tenducci's pet name for his wife ('Doro') gives the impression of continuing intimacy between the pair. In April 1770, Dorothea took the part of Thamiris in a performance of *Amintas*, with Tenducci as the leading man, at the Theatre Royal, Haymarket. She was billed as 'a YOUNG LADY Scholar of Mr TENDUCCI'.[82] Though the newspapers were silent regarding the critics' judgement of Dorothea's singing, the production evidently generated a great deal of public interest and boosted ticket sales, to the extent that the theatre managers issued an advertisement humbly requesting that ladies and gentlemen who had pre-bought tickets should 'send their servants to keep places in time, in order to prevent confusion'.[83] Tenducci's career was further consolidated the following month with favourable reviews, and top billing in a concert that was one of a famous series organized by Bach and Abel.[84] Even *Lloyd's Evening Post* (which often gave castrati an unfavourable press) praised Tenducci for singing in 'masterly' fashion, so 'that words can but faintly express the satisfaction the audience appeared to receive from the exertion of his astonishing talents'.[85]

Tenducci's most prestigious engagement in 1770 was undoubtedly his royal command performance in August that year to celebrate the birthday of Queen Charlotte's brother. Tenducci made a star appearance performing a new ode set to music by his friend, J. C. Bach. The event pleased the royal family so much, it was noted, that George III himself 'honoured Mr. Tenducci so far as to request him to sing some Songs from Handel's Oratorios and other favourite Pieces', and their party stayed up until after midnight.[86] The newspapers reported that, having had his fill of special requests, the king 'was graciously pleased to express his satisfaction in ordering [Tenducci]... the liberal bounty of 100 guineas'.[87] Tenducci's star was in the ascendant.

In early September 1770, Tenducci was engaged to sing at the Winchester Music Festival, in advance of the famous annual Salisbury Music Festival, which began on 3 October. Elizabeth Harris was the genteel wife of the gentleman philosopher, composer, and musician James Harris, who was instrumental in organizing the Salisbury Festival each year. She sent word by letter to her son James Jr., who was then travelling abroad in Spain, about the Tenduccis' arrival in their home town:

> Tenducci is already arriv'd [;] had he come alone we could have made some use of him in having him here to sing, but as he has brought Mrs. Tenducci I can have but little to do with him.[88]

The Harris family were extremely well connected. James Harris was a man of private means and Fellow of the Royal Society. He was closely related to the earls of Shaftesbury, and later forged a successful career in parliament, eventually rising to become a private secretary to Queen Charlotte.[89] He and his wife had been on friendly terms with Tenducci since the early 1760s, when he had first performed one of Harris's own compositions, *Daphnis and Amaryllis*, at the Salisbury Music Festival.[90] Elizabeth Harris's comment that she could not receive Dorothea at home is suggestive of how Mrs Tenducci was regarded as a social pariah, fit for the stage, but not for domestic sociability in polite company. Nevertheless, she was an object of curiosity. The Harrises' youngest daughter Louisa was at that time a keen amateur vocalist, and wrote excitedly to her brother James about the preparations for the festival that year. 'We begin already to be in a great bustle', she reported, adding whimsically, 'though the Saint does not arrive 'till this day I seem already to feel her approach[;] some of her votaries are

come[,] viz Tenducci, & Norris'. Louisa's reference to the arrival of the
'Saint' was meant figuratively in reference to St Cecilia, patron saint of
music, after whom the festival was named. She continued in gossipy
vein to her brother:

> The former [Tenducci] has brought his wife with him, she dined with
> us yesterday and we all think her a pretty [well] behaved kind of
> woman[;] she does not by any means possess the assurance which
> usually accompany's [sic] her Irish country-women; she was so
> obliging as to sing two duets (with her husband) and one song[,] all
> of which she performed exceedingly well, and as to him he is more
> improved than any one could imagine both in voice and manner.[91]

Evidently Louisa's mother had recanted her severe injunction against
Dorothea's company and invited the Tenduccis to a private dinner,
where both husband and wife provided the entertainment. They were
well received by those who judged themselves to be musical connoisseurs. Louisa's acquaintance with the couple deepened, to the extent
that she risked performing publicly alongside them. She told her
brother how, the next day:

> we had the Griesdales and Earls and a few more of the great genius's
> [sic] of the place to meet the Tenducci's[,] who were so good as to
> sing a great many fine songs & duets; Charlotte Lee play'd a harpsi-
> chord concerto & I sung two or three songs[,] but in such a grievous
> fright as to scarce articulate a word[.] However they were very candid
> & made me many flattering speeches & to day Mr & Mrs Tenducci &
> myself are to sing a trio.[92]

Even Louisa's mother was won over by Dorothea, and the charming
conduct of the Tenduccis as husband and wife. 'Tenducci has been here
ten days,' Elizabeth Harris told her son, '& is very entertaining to us[;]
his wife is a genteel[,] well behav'd young woman & many people here
take great notice of them.'[93] Just a week later, Dorothea had been so

successful at integrating herself into Salisbury society that she was invited to dinner again at the Harrises' house, together with 'all the professors [of music]' who were rehearsing for the festival. Elizabeth Harris, ever conscious of propriety, complained that 'we ladies were oblig'd to assist at the dinner as Mrs Tenducci[,] Mrs and Miss Lindley were of the party'. Her letter buzzed with the excitement of activity ('The music that morning began here at ten in the morning and never ceas'd till three. We eat [ate], drank, drest and went to the oratorio of Hercules which went charmingly'). Again, she could not fail to notice the improvement in Tenducci's voice: 'Tenducci is amazingly improv'd. In his part the old Handelian songs were left out & some fine Italian ones were smug[g]led in, in their place.' Later that week, she recorded, the soprano Elizabeth Linley and Tenducci sang Pergolesi's *Stabat Mater* 'like two devine beings'.[94] The striking development of Tenducci's voice, and his eagerness to gratify his hosts in Salisbury ('he will sing as much as you please', noted Elizabeth Harris), ensured his appearance was a social and critical triumph ('You may guess we took care to have our share [of Tenducci] during his stay', she told her son, with considerable satisfaction).[95]

It is not surprising that Dorothea, a carefully raised young woman, had winning manners. Her notorious reputation preceded her, but she confounded the prejudices of polite hosts with her modest demeanour and gentility. It is not inconceivable that the Harris family, and others of their social milieu, were unaware of Dorothea's motherhood. It was highly likely that the baby had been sent to a wet nurse, since this customary practice was especially adhered to when the imputation of illegitimacy made it especially important to conceal a child. Elizabeth Harris's change of heart regarding Dorothea's acceptance at her dining table and the tacit social approval which this implied was another matter. The niceties of social conformity and rigid moral codes which trammelled all social interactions among the professional and élite classes were portrayed in the novels of Jane Austen. In this sense, her novels may be viewed as minutely recorded and accurate anthropological observations of the social mores of her time. There were well-known stories of society women and the merely genteel who were ostracized or virtually imprisoned by their own families for even the suspicion of sexual impropriety.[96] That there was such tolerance and recognition given to Tenducci's unconventional marriage may in many ways appear surprising in a world which produced so many real-life Lady Catherine de Bourghs, fearsome matriarchs who policed the correct deportment, class, and gender distinctions in their own petty corners of provincial life.[97] A similar tolerance could be found elsewhere among musical circles in England at the time. Like the Harrises in Salisbury, the impresario and organizer of the Chichester Music Festival, John Marsh, could sweep aside social convention when presented with musical talent, provided the individual concerned was a person of 'sense' who understood the requirements of correct dress and deportment in company. At local assemblies in Romsey, where he was appointed master of ceremonies, Marsh permitted Mr Day, who was 'something of a Beau & always fashionably dress'd & a very well behav'd Man' to subscribe in the winter of 1770–1, even though Day had been excluded from the public balls in the neighbourhood, '[he] being Organist & ranking in their opinion with Tradespeople'.[98] Marsh's guardian, Mrs Daman, was 'surprized to hear that Day the Shoemaker's Son (as she call'd him)' had been allowed to subscribe, and said that she feared all the shoemakers and cobblers would now be admitted to the Romsey assemblies. 'As I told Mrs D.,' recorded Marsh in his diary, 'what.. . had [we] to do with the Son's Pedigree, who was only known in general as Organist Music Master in which profession he had always acquitted himself perfectly well.'[99] Though Dorothea and Tenducci's relationship represented a highly unique and unusual marriage, the favourable treatment they received in Salisbury was just one of many small signs that, in the long term, English society was becoming, in artistic circles at least, more favourably disposed to the idea of meritocracy in an era of capitalist expansion, mass celebrity culture nourished by the print trade, and increasing social mobility. Where fashion led, the rest of society eventually followed, for better or worse.

♪

It is significant that the Edinburgh Musical Society minuted Tenducci's reference to Dorothea as his 'family', and recognized Dorothea's right as his wife to honour the contract of employment issued in Tenducci's name. Similarly, the Harris family in Salisbury repeatedly referred to Tenducci and Dorothea as a married couple: he was her 'husband', Dorothea was 'Mrs. Tenducci'. This recognition of their marriage by men and women of good reputation in private correspondence and upon public social occasions was in spite of the reservations about the Tenducci marriage expressed elsewhere, especially in the press. Though responses ranged from mockery to sympathetic understanding, particularly in the light of the unnaturally harsh response of Dorothea's family to their elopement, the pair were described as husband and wife in a way which mirrored their own use of these labels in social introductions, in situations where it was safe to do so. Lorenzo Lombardi, Tenducci's former landlord near the Haymarket Theatre in London, recalled that he visited Tenducci in Dublin in 1767, shortly after the couple had ceased being persecuted by Dorothea's father. There, Lombardi was 'introduced . . . to [Tenducci's] wife, (as he called her)'.[100] The music master Francis Passerini recalled that when Tenducci was lodging at Portobello near Dublin, the singer invited him 'to see him and his . . . wife; (meaning . . . Miss Maunsell)'.[101] Further evidence that Tenducci referred to Dorothea as his wife is found in an extraordinary account of a meeting that took place between the Tenduccis and Giacomo Casanova, the infamous seducer. Casanova recalled that, sometime in the late 1760s or early 1770s (he did not record the exact date), 'I took [my friends] to Covent Garden, where the castrato Tenducci surprised me by introducing his wife to me'. Casanova, a man not easily shocked, continued:

I thought he was joking, but it was true. He had married her and having already had two children he laughed at those who said that being a castrato, he could not have any. He said that a third testicular gland which had been left him, was enough to prove his virility, and that the children could not but be legitimate since he recognised them as such.[102]

It seems unlikely that, sometime before the summer of 1771, Dorothea had given birth to a second child. This is the only surviving reference from this period to her having two children, and was most likely a misrecollection on Casanova's part. But Tenducci's side of the conversation with Casanova is highly illuminating. It gives the impression of a confident man prepared to make light of his bodily affliction, willing to engage in sexualized banter with a fellow-countryman and well-known seducer of women. Though his reference to having a third, unamputated testicle must have been a joke (given the facts that were soon to emerge about Tenducci's body), the singer played upon widespread suspicions that castrati had hidden powers. It was known that some men who reached puberty suffered from undescended, or partially descended testicles. Some authors and medical commentators therefore reasoned that certain castrati, like some biologically intersex (or 'hermaphrodite') people, were in possession of an additional 'secret' testicle, or anatomically uncertain generative organ hidden within their bodies (hence, perhaps, Tenducci's playful reference to a third 'testicular gland').[103] Tenducci's affidavit that Dorothea's first child was his own, like his post-performance banter with Casanova, took advantage of the suspicion surrounding the physiological status of castrati, and tested the plausibility that he could be the biological father. The doubts persisted over whether castrati really were intact men masquerading as something else, or whether for individual men their castration had been botched in some way, allowing them to function as 'normal' men sexually. In his meeting with Casanova, and on several different occasions, Tenducci boldly played upon the simultaneous

160

state of public knowledge and uncertainty about his body. He may have wanted to be a father, and in recognizing Dorothea's child as his own had found a way of securing an heir.

♪

By early 1771, Tenducci was again under contract to perform, by now as first man at the King's Theatre, in confirmation of his vocal ability, royal mark of favour, and popular acclaim.[104] His celebrity status in London was confirmed by the popularity of a Mr Palmer, who specialized in impersonating Tenducci on stage (suggesting that this would only have been entertaining if the public at large recognized the original), and by the mention of the singer, and his wife, in the equivalent of gossip columns relating to well-known society figures. In a laboured pun on Tenducci's employment as first man in *opera seria*, a wag of the town wrote this snippet:

> "Serious Thoughts on the Decrease of Population."
> FIRST *serious Man*, Signior Tenducci.
> A young Woman, genteelly educated, is willing—
> A Captain on [of?] the Irish Establishment would be glad to.[105]

The gossip hinted at the well-known presence of a shadowy third person in the Tenducci marriage.

Tenducci undertook a number of engagements in the early months of 1771, including performing at a concert for his friend J. C. Bach, and an appearance in an oratorio at Covent Garden.[106] But he was not in the best of health, or at least was suffering from some 'indisposition' which necessitated his sudden withdrawal from a production of *Semiramide*.[107] On 11 March, news had been reported that 'a celebrated Italian singer, it is said, was waiting for a fair wind at Dover to embark for the continent, when he was overtaken by his creditors'. More details emerged: that the same 'Celebrated Italian Singer (with his Wife and *her* Child) had absconded, having previously contracted Debts to the amount of £1000 and fooled the English out of £5000 more; with which, it is supposed, they are gone to Italy, to spend the Remainder of their Lives like Persons of Quality'.[108] Though these sums were doubtless exaggerated, as one historian has observed, 'Tenducci's financial circumstances were never happy'. While still in Edinburgh, he had made numerous applications to the Musical Society for advances on his salary. The directors had allowed the treasurer to give him 'twenty or thirty pounds on his receipt', even though he had never repaid a previous debt of £40 paid in advance to cover his travel expenses. His request for money in September 1769 had been granted 'in consideration of his being yet a stranger in the place and had not got so many scholars as he would get in winter', but their tolerance was further tested by several subsequent petitions by Tenducci for more pay.[109] The singer eventually defaulted on two successive contractual obligations, first to the Edinburgh Musical Society, and then to the King's Theatre. Though the latter breach of contract was probably due to an unforeseen physical illness or mental breakdown, the former was quite deliberate, and incurred the wrath of Lord Kellie, the deputy governor of the Edinburgh Musical Society. Kellie put it on record that Tenducci had tried to exculpate himself via Dorothea, to no avail: he 'produced a letter from his wife aldegeing [*sic*] he had leave of the Directors to stay away for a year ... [which] was intirely false as he had gone off without their knowledge and contrary to his contract'.[110] Tenducci's own version of events, recalled many years later, was that the reason for his departure was because he was invited by the director of the Teatro di Argentina in Rome to return to Italy and 'accept the office of First Singer in that Theatre'. Tenducci recalled that he left London with 'infinite regret'.[111]

The newspapers made reference to the couple fleeing the country with only one child, which suggests that Casanova's recollection that the Tenduccis had two children was a mistake. What is certain is that, as he had done earlier in his career, Tenducci needed to escape his creditors for fear of imprisonment. And so again, in March 1771, this time taking his wife and her child, he fled to Italy. As they crossed the Channel at Dover in haste in order to escape their creditors and make the arduous journey south across the European continent, Giusto and Dorothea were forced to leave everything behind them, including their identity as husband and wife.

*Chapter Eight*

# The Trial

Tenducci's return to Italy in 1771 came at a time when he was maturing as an artist. Now aged about 36, he was emerging as one of the leading singers of his generation and a star in demand among the salons of the rich and powerful, and as a *primo uomo* of the great opera houses of Europe. Such an improvement in vocal quality often comes with experience and maturity to opera singers as the vocal chords thicken with age. The change in Tenducci's voice had been remarked upon by Elizabeth Harris, and was also noted by Charles Burney, who found him 'so much improved, during his residence in Scotland and Ireland, as not only to be well received as first man on our stage [in London], but, afterwards, in all the great theatres of Italy'.[1] Sir Horace Mann wrote to Horace Walpole from Pisa in November 1771 that the Duke of Gloucester had gone specifically to Florence 'to hear an opera where Tenducci, whom you have despised so long in England, shines most extraordinarily, and intends upon this recruit of reputation to return to England for double the pay he had before'.[2] The source of Tenducci being 'despised' could have been the bad press he had received, not only for his scandalous personal life, but for his problems with debt. Mann's usual hyperbole may also have been his way of expressing his opinion that the quality of Tenducci's voice had not been fully appreciated by his fellow-countrymen.

But just as his professional career was reaching new heights, Tenducci's personal freedoms became more restricted. From the moment of their arrival in his native country, his marriage to Dorothea was effectively closeted. Charles Baroe, Tenducci's former room-mate, recalled that in the 'different places of Italy' during the times when Tenducci and Dorothea were together, Tenducci 'never... passed the said Miss Maunsell as his wife; but, on the contrary... at such times [he] passed the said Miss Maunsell as an English young lady, put under his tuition as a scholar, to be instructed in singing and music'. Baroe's explanation for this was that Tenducci knew that 'an eunuch or castrated person is strictly forbidden to marry under penalty of death' by 'certain laws in Italy'.[3] The difficulty in sustaining this arrangement must have become increasingly apparent.

In June 1771, Giusto and Dorothea had travelled together to Siena, where he performed at the opera house. By August, they had returned to Florence, and spent some time together at a country estate outside the city, where they received visitors.[4] Come the autumn, Tenducci was engaged at an opera house back in Florence, performing the role of Orpheus in a production of Gluck's *Orpheo*.[5] As Tenducci himself later recalled (not without a little hubris):

> The Grand Duke of Tuscany was pleased to make a point of it that my first performance as a Singer in Italy should be in the Theatre of my own country [i.e. in Tuscany, since Tenducci was a native of Siena]. He himself selected the Opera of Orpheus, in which he chose that I should sing. The effect of this performance, I must be permitted to say, was great, as can be attested by the many English people of distinction, who were present.[6]

The choice of Gluck's *Orpheo*, and the patronage of the Grand Duke of Tuscany, were significant developments for Tenducci. Gluck's new style of *opera seria*, with its simplicity of plot and lyrically expressive music, appealed to the changing tastes of the era. It was a departure from the 'cold' formality of ornamental Baroque music, and allowed Tenducci to pour into the role of Orpheus the warmth, passion, and direct expressions of emotion that he had developed in his repertoire of Scottish songs.[7] Tenducci was given the chance to play the romantic male lead as never before. With his ripened voice of seductive richness, he was transformed on stage into Orpheus, the husband who is motivated by love to follow his wife beyond the grave into the underworld.[8]

It seems especially poignant that just as he was being fêted in the salons of the Florentine nobility for his ability to convey the sensibilities of a heroic husband, off-stage his performance as a married man was effectively cancelled. Masquerading once more as his pupil, Dorothea was installed with Tenducci's mother and sister at his house in Florence.[9] All this while, Dorothea and Giusto evidently remained on good terms. They performed together as late as the autumn of 1771, to widespread critical acclaim. Back in London, it was reported:

> Mrs. Tenducci, who left this kingdom the latter end of last season, with her *husband* Signor Tenducci, has lately made her appearance at the Opera House in Turin, and it is said, is in high favour with the King of Sardinia, who, it is well known, is a great encourager of musical talents.[10]

From the late autumn of 1771, Tenducci embarked upon a gruelling round of engagements, appearing in Rome for the carnival, returning briefly to Florence, and then departing for Venice to sing for the Feast of the Ascension. Since much of Tenducci's time had been taken up with numerous performances, it may have been that Dorothea, now effectively demoted from the status of wife to pupil once more, had begun to feel neglected by him. She had the opportunity while in Florence to forge a relationship with another man.

In November 1771, about ten days after Tenducci had left Dorothea to go to Rome, his wife absconded for a second time. She departed from Florence in a post-chaise and headed south towards Naples, accompanied by a female servant of her own, and a male servant belonging to an Englishman by the name of William Long Kingsman.[11]

♪

In 1771, William Long Kingsman was aged about 23, and was therefore just a few years older than Dorothea.[12] He was described in the Florentine press as *'Cavaliere Inglese'* (an 'English knight'), although this courtesy title was something of an exaggeration.[13] Born in 1748 to a family from Kent, William was sent to Lincoln's Inn, where he was admitted in 1762.[14] He transferred to Magdalen College, Oxford just three years later in 1765, at the age of 17. Unlike most of the young gentlemen who passed through the portals of England's ancient universities at this time, Kingsman succeeded in gaining his master's degree, in June 1768.[15] But his prospects suggested that he would never have to earn his living as a barrister or scholar. William was the nephew and heir of Robert Long, a former 'Admiral in his Majesty's Navy'.[16] Long was also a well-to-do property-owner and resident of Marylebone, an area which is now part of central London but in the mid-eighteenth century was a prosperous parish in Middlesex, surrounded by fields.[17] Like many other men, including the never-married, childless widowers, those who could not father children (like Tenducci), or whose children had predeceased them, Robert Long had no male heir. Since there was no mention of a wife in his will, most likely this was because he was among the high proportion of eighteenth-century Londoners who never married.[18] William Kingsman had therefore taken his uncle's surname as his middle name in order to signify that he was his heir, as was common in families where a wealthy relative was without male children, and was probably brought up in his uncle's household since he was described as 'William Long Kingsman of St Marylebone' when he was admitted to Lincoln's Inn at the age of about 14.[19] Robert Long was a man of considerable means who owned his own 'Chariot and horses', a 'chariot', or carriage, being a sure sign of gentility, or at least genteel aspirations. He bequeathed William the rights to his rents and annuities, and ownership of his leasehold estates, which his nephew claimed provided him with an income of 'upwards of fifteen hundred Pounds a Year'.[20] He also left William £20 in cash, a gold watch and seal, and all his plate and household goods, including his furniture and linen.

When Robert Long died in, or shortly before, 1771, William Long Kingsman was an executor of his uncle's will and the main beneficiary.[21] The transfer of property from uncle to nephew was consistent with the system of primogeniture in England at the time by which property was handed down through the generations to the eldest male relative. Following the customary wording, Robert Long's will specified that the 'heirs of the body' of William Long Kingsman would enjoy the benefits from his property in perpetuity, provided they were 'lawfully begotten' (that is, conceived within marriage).[22] Unlike Tenducci, Kingsman enjoyed the full privileges of a male householder, including the right to marry, vote, hold property, and bequeath it to his children.[23] William's fortunes rose in the world, and he now had a claim to being a gentleman, considering his income was now partly from rents on land.[24] The timing of Dorothea's decision to leave Tenducci coincided with the period after Kingsman had inherited his uncle's fortune and could support a wife and family.

As for personality, character, and interests, further information about Kingsman is elusive. A tantalizing reference in the *Gazzetta Toscana*, almost a year after he and Dorothea had first begun to live together, mentions Kingsman acting as a host for a musical concert in Florence, attended by 'numerous distinguished foreigners and local nobility' ('*molto distinti Forestieri, è Nobilità Nazionale*').[25] This report suggests that, although he was not a professional musician himself,

Kingsman undoubtedly had an amateur interest in music, moved in the same social circles as Tenducci, and had a similar patronage network involving *virtuoso* musicians and vocalists, and their rich sponsors. Following his inheritance, he could entertain in grand style, and evidently became a respected member of the close-knit expatriate community in Florence.[26]

Tracing the origins of their relationship is more problematic. It is not impossible that Kingsman had met Dorothea as far back as Dublin while he was still a student at Oxford, that they fell in love, and he followed her and Tenducci on their travels to Edinburgh and London, during which time they consummated their relationship. For Dorothea, marriage to William Long Kingsman offered a belated attempt at respectability and the chance to legitimize her child by him.[27] Dorothea's voice, her version of her relationship with Kingsman in her own words, was not recorded for posterity, but her contrition, and attempt to undergo a radical change in circumstances, is evident from her actions. According to her father, she wrote to him from Naples 'that she was truly sorry for what had happened between her and... Tenducci, and that her misfortunes, in that respect, had been owing to her inexperience and tender age'. She blamed youthful infatuation for her rash conduct, and was now grateful 'that it had pleased God to restore her to a better understanding'. She still had not yet reached the age of majority, and she now had to make a performance of returning to the mode of a dutiful daughter, in order to assume the role of a lawful wife. Dorothea's change of heart, said her father, had made her realize 'that what had passed in the matrimonial way, between her and... Tenducci, was not binding in the sight of God'.[28] She begged her parents and friends for forgiveness, and asked to be readmitted to her family's protection. This rather formulaic account of Dorothea's penitential return to the Maunsell fold may not have been a true representation of her genuine feelings. Evidently Thomas Maunsell was delighted at his daughter's repentance, and immediately sent £200 to Naples to pay for her safe passage home. A hasty marriage ceremony took place in April 1772 between Dorothea and William Long Kingsman, conducted in a private house in Rome by an Anglican priest, Revd Sandys Clark, with the full consent of the bride's father.[29]

But a private ceremony abroad was not ideal. Since Dorothea was still under the age of 21 when she married in Rome, she and Kingsman needed to take part in a further marriage ceremony in public in order 'to obviate all doubts that have arisen or may arise touching or concerning the Validity or Legality of the ... Marriage'.[30] By the late summer of 1773, William and Dorothea had returned to England, where preparations could be made for what was, in effect, Dorothea's fourth wedding ceremony, but the first one to be conducted with paternal consent under the normal formalities of the Church of England.

♪

The Register of Marriages in the Parish Church of St George, Hanover Square, records that William Long Kingsman married Dorothea Kingsman, previously Maunsell, on 8 September 1773.[31] To be married amid the splendour of St George's, Hanover Square was a mark of social prestige in the eighteenth century, and for genteel families with a strong musical association there was no more appropriate place for a wedding. Handel had been appointed organist there in 1725, it was the venue for many of the most prestigious concerts of sacred music in the capital, and parishioners consisted 'chiefly of persons of rank and fortune'.[32] The ceremony, presided over by Revd Waring Willett, curate of St George's, was conducted fully in accordance with the rites and ceremonies of the Anglican Church. This solemnization of marriage was made with the consent of the bride's father, Thomas Maunsell, who was present as a witness, together with the deputy parish clerk, Caleb Greville.[33] When the assembled congregation was invited to declare whether they knew of any lawful impediment to the union according to the form of wording in the Book of Common Prayer, no one spoke out in protest.

The groom, William Long Kingsman, had petitioned the Archbishop of Canterbury's Office of Faculties for the grant of a marriage licence, an expensive dispensation permitting a couple to be married at any convenient time and location which was originally issued in very small numbers, and only to 'quality', often so that they could marry in fashionable churches.[34] In order to secure this, he appeared in person and swore under oath before the Archbishop's Surrogate, Peter Calvert, and the Registrar, Robert Jubb, that there were no lawful impediments to his marriage in England's established Church. He swore that no child had been born since he had married Dorothea in Rome, perhaps in order to imply that there were no illegitimate children from their union. If so, then this was a misleading piece of legal sophistry. Dorothea may not have been pregnant or given birth between her first marriage to Kingsman in April 1772 and her remarriage to him in September 1773, but, as we have seen, there are several sources which suggest that she had already given birth before leaving London with Tenducci in March 1771. The groom also swore that there were no other legal impediments, such as consanguinity, to hinder the marriage, and that Dorothea had now turned 21. Everything seemed in order, and the marriage licence was granted.

Except there was just one problem: Dorothea was still technically married to Tenducci when she married William Long Kingsman, both times. At some point the irregularity of this situation needed tidying up, perhaps at the behest of the bride's father, whose legal background may have foreseen some difficulties should any authority care to scrutinize the situation more carefully. Doubtless all parties on the Maunsell/Kingsman side were so sure that Dorothea's first marriage was invalid and would be considered so by the courts that they hastened her marriage to Kingsman, choosing pragmatism over due process. The dubious legitimacy of children fathered by Kingsman would also have been a powerful incentive to their marrying as soon as possible. Kingsman failed to disclose their offspring, and lied explicitly about there not being any lawful impediments to his marriage to Dorothea. Another curious feature of the conduct of Dorothea's remarriage was the fact that Kingsman appeared in person in the Registry at Lambeth Palace, the Archbishop of Canterbury's official residence, to petition for a marriage licence on 17 September 1773, nine days *after* the wedding had taken place at St George's, Hanover Square.[35]

This was a minor irregularity, however, in relation to the outstanding problem of the legal status of Dorothea's first marriage to Tenducci. In theory, the singer could have sued his wife for bigamy, which in the eighteenth century was a felony.[36] In order to restore the Maunsell family's reputation, and remove any possible threat of legal action on Tenducci's part, Dorothea's first marriage had to be erased from the record. An annulment would mean that her marriage to Tenducci had never existed, and that she had effectively been a spinster when she married William Kingsman. In English law, church courts reserved the power to redefine what had hitherto been a consensual marital relationship recognized in law so that the bride could remarry. Before the nineteenth century, marital suits were usually reserved for the higher ecclesiastical courts, the bishops' consistory courts, which ruled on whether marriage promises were valid or not, forced spouses to live together (or apart, with separations from 'bed and board'), and annulled marriages on the grounds of 'consanguinity, affinity, prior marriage and non-consummation'.[37] About one hundred and thirty matrimonial causes were brought before the London Consistory Court between the years 1770 and 1779. Historically, disputes over promises of marriage represented by far the largest cause of grievance brought before the church courts. In this period the number of petitions for marital separation was rising as an alternative to expensive divorces by an Act of Parliament, which was available only to the very rich, and only on the specific grounds of a wife's adultery.[38] Petitions for marriage annulment due to male impotence were highly unusual, with as few as thirty-two cases brought to court in the entire eighteenth century.[39] The specific circumstances of the Tenducci marriage annulment were absolutely unique in English law.

Almost eighteen months elapsed between Dorothea and Kingsman's marriage in London in September 1773 and the start of the formal legal proceedings towards the annulment of her first marriage in May 1775. In order for the marriage to be annulled, the 'Party proponent' bringing the case, 'Dorothea Kingsman, formerly Maunsell, falsely called Tenducci', issued a libel against Giusto Ferdinando Tenducci in the London Consistory Court, the ecclesiastical court within the jurisdiction of the Bishop of London. The libel, which contained sixteen articles, outlined the circumstances of the case. A bundle of documents presenting preliminary evidence in the form of exhibits were brought in to the court and presented before Dr John Bettesworth, 'Doctor of Laws, Vicar General and the Official Principal of the Consistorial and Episcopal Court', at Doctors' Commons on 24 May 1775.[40] These contained evidence relating to Dorothea's first marriage to Tenducci, and her second marriage to Kingsman, as well as a copy of the will of Robert Long, in order to establish William Long Kingsman's identity, and that he was a man of honour and credit.[41]

The case may have seemed relatively straightforward, since Tenducci was, as the libel emphasized repeatedly, 'universally deemed and reputed to be an Eunuch', including by his own admission.[42] But the level of proof for the annulment to be granted required actual evidence of the fact that his castration had been full and complete, and that he was therefore 'rendered totally incapable of the Act of Generation or procreation of children and consequently of consummating Marriage'.[43] It was necessary to establish beyond doubt that Tenducci was not only a castrato by reputation, but that there were eyewitnesses who had seen his body, including a medical doctor who could confirm he had been castrated before he eloped with Dorothea. Crucial witnesses would have to be found not only in England but in Italy as well, which would take time. A special hearing had to be convened at a court in Florence in order to take statements from people who had known

Tenducci personally. These depositions, in Italian and Latin, then had to be translated and presented as exhibits to the London Consistory Court together with the testimonies of witnesses in London. Meanwhile, a letter was sent by the court under the authority of the Bishop of London to the Bishop of Cork and Ross in Ireland, requesting eyewitness statements concerning the case, and documentary verification of the circumstances of Dorothea and Tenducci's nuptials in 1766 and 1767.

These convoluted proceedings would have been extremely expensive. In the early eighteenth century, even a straightforward case of marital separation from 'bed and board' could cost upwards of £20, with regular costs of £40 awarded if a suit was successful, which together amounted to the average annual income of a middling household. A case requiring multiple witness statements procured abroad would have incurred much higher costs, amounting perhaps to several hundred pounds, which would have deterred anyone but the gentry and nobility from litigation.[44] But Dorothea's new husband, William Long Kingsman, and her father, the barrister Thomas Maunsell, were undeterred. By the autumn of 1773, Kingsman had appointed an agent, Roger Wilbraham, to find proof that would satisfy the court that Tenducci was indeed a castrato.

We do not know where Roger Wilbraham's journey originated, but it is likely that he embarked upon his mission to Italy from London. Travelling on the European continent with relative freedom was still possible for an Englishman in the decades leading up to the French Revolutionary Wars of the 1790s, provided he had the right patronage and letters of recommendation.[45] Wilbraham would have taken the route followed by many youthful English noblemen embarking fresh-faced on their Grand Tour, most likely to Calais by boat and then overland to Italy via Germany. English travellers of a more modest social rank followed a well-established route, staying at inns where they lodged alongside their fellow-citizens, where the language was familiar and where English diets and customs were followed.[46] While gentlemen were there to gather antiquities and adventures, Wilbraham was on business: his journey would have taken weeks rather than the lingering months or even years which a leisured traveller could take on the Grand Tour.

His destination was Florence, since it was the location of the house in which Tenducci's mother and Dorothea had lived. Such was Tenducci's close association with what had been one of the great centres of Renaissance art, that he was even known posthumously as 'Florentinus', a Florentine.[47] When Wilbraham arrived in Florence, however, the city was well past its heyday.[48] A hub of European finance and trade during the fifteenth and sixteenth centuries, the focus of money markets had long since passed away from Florence northwards to Amsterdam and London. By the second half of the eighteenth century, the city revolved around the court of Pietro Leopoldo, the ninth Grand Duke of Tuscany, a Habsburg from the Lorraine branch of the family of Holy Roman Emperors, who also claimed the titles of Archduke of Austria and Prince Royal of Hungary. The Grand Duke's arrival in 1765 ushered in an era of reform that attempted to reverse the decline of the city and the Florentine state that seemed inexorably to follow the end of the tyrannical glory of the Medici. Pietro Leopoldo was a man of vision and strong Enlightenment principles who sought to re-establish Florence as a seat of culture in the visual arts, philosophy, and science. In the 1770s, he set about remodelling the Pitti Palace in neo-classical splendour, and a salon in the Uffizi Palace in similarly ambitious style to house his collection of classical marble sculptures brought from the Villa Medici in Rome. He eventually established an *Accademi di Belle Arte* in emulation of the Royal Academy of Arts in London and the *Academie des Sciences* in Paris. Drawn to Florence by the Grand Duke's interests in the arts and sciences, royalty and nobility were again on hand to provide important patronage to the visual and performing arts.

Though the benefits of the Grand Duke's efforts proved short-lived once Napoleon's forces arrived to occupy Florence in 1799, during a brief period in the 1770s there were rich rewards for the artists, singers, and musicians who gathered at his court.

Since the Grand Duke was a figure of international importance on the European stage, the Florentine court had exceptionally strong diplomatic ties with England, which in the early part of the decade were represented by George III's Envoy Extraordinary, Sir Horace Mann, the erstwhile friend and correspondent of Horace Walpole, who was so acclimatized to Italian manners and customs that he was reputed in England to have degenerated into effeminacy.[49] Mann's seal of approval was crucial in confirming the identity and correct procedure of the court officials who presided over taking witness statements in Florence. So although the Tenducci marriage annulment case was unprecedented in English law, there were diplomatic mechanisms that made it possible to secure witness statements abroad that would be recognized as legitimate in an English church court, provided the necessary procedures were followed correctly and the identities and accurate testimonies of witnesses were confirmed under oath, with the countersignature of His Majesty's Envoy guaranteeing the identity and authority of the signatories.

Acting on behalf of William Long Kingsman, during the months leading up to the hearing in October 1775, Wilbraham recruited the help of Ansano Rossi. Rossi was a surgeon by occupation, who usually resided at the Haymarket in London (the location where Tenducci had lodged and taken part in operatic performances). He had known the singer for many years, from the time he had first arrived in England in 1758.[50] Since he was able to speak Italian, and knew Tenducci's personal history, being 'well acquainted with him', Rossi took charge of summoning witnesses in Florence.[51] His brief was to procure people who had known Tenducci personally and who could testify to his status as a castrato.

The logical place to search for people who had known Tenducci was the city's theatres. One late eighteenth-century map of Florence shows no fewer than eight public theatres, added to which were the numerous venues provided for musical entertainment and theatrical performances within private palaces and noble apartments.[52] Just north of the famous *duomo* of Santa Maria del Fiore, directly opposite the towering edifice of Brunelleschi's famous cathedral dome, is the Via Ricasoli, which until the mid-nineteenth century was known as the Via del Cocomero. At the corner of the street nearest the Piazza del Duomo is the Teatro Niccolino, renamed in modern times after a hero of the Italian Risorgimento. Since 1648 this has been the site of a theatre, originally called the Teatro di Cocomero.[53] It was here in the 1770–1 season that Tenducci had performed in the critically acclaimed (though much embellished) production of Gluck's *Orpheo*. Ansano Rossi, acting via Roger Wilbraham on behalf of William Kingsman, found some colourful characters at the Teatro di Cocomero who claimed to know Tenducci personally, with varying degrees of intimacy. Among these were Luigi Bernardo Rossi, described as a Doctor of Law and Procurator of the Theatre; Gio Batto Brocchi, a 'Citizen of Florence'; Guiseppe Faleri, Giovanno Rossi, Gio Senti Ciotta, and 'Mr Fernando Maineiro [*sic*] Inventor of the Fashions of this Theatre'. Other sources of evidence make it possible to verify the existence of several of these witnesses, and their identities. Ferdinando Mainero, for example, is named in contracts issued during the 1770s by the *Accademia degli Infuocati*, the board of directors who supervised productions at the Teatro di Cocomero, charging him with organizing the annual carnival festivities, and procuring scenery and costumes.[54] Mainero and his colleagues were prepared to swear that they knew Tenducci personally, and that to their knowledge he was not then present in any of the Grand Duke of Tuscany's dominions.[55]

A key witness from the Teatro di Cocomero was Nicolo Tassi. Tassi described himself as a 'Poet and Master of Languages' and wrote *libretti* on commission for 'Dramatic Pieces' in the theatre. Tassi's identity can be verified since his name appears as the librettist for opera performances given at the King's Theatre in London during the 1770s.[56] The poet was crucial as a witness since he had known Tenducci's mother, who had told him details about where the family had lived, and who had performed the surgery upon her son. Through this lead, Ansano Rossi was able to trace the singer's early life in Monte San Savino, and the identity of the man who had performed Tenducci's castration. Tassi himself was to give a long and detailed testimony with all the theatrical *brio* that might be expected of a dramatist.

Eighteenth-century scandal sheets appealed to the prurience of their readers, highlighting words such as 'adultery' in their titles, and promising edification in the form of *Anecdotes, Bon Mots, Traits, Stratagems and Biographical Sketches of the Most Remarkable... Swindlers and Other Daring Adventurers... Collected and Comprised, so as to Render the Whole Both Cautionary and Entertaining; and as Much An Object of Wonder as of Pity!*[57] It is difficult not to feel similarly prurient when reading the details that emerge in the witness statements that were taken down in Florence, required as legal proof for the annulment of the Tenduccis' marriage. But they have left posterity with a unique and touching account of how Tenducci's fate was determined, and specific details which shed new light upon the secret history of the castration industry that affected hundreds, if not thousands, of boys like Tenducci and their families, during the seventeenth and eighteenth centuries, but about which so little has previously been known. Since he had dared to marry, English law required proof of the 'truth' of Tenducci's body. For all his efforts to dedicate his life to the art of music, it was the inescapable reality of his biological impairment that came to be of more than private concern.[58]

♪

The court session to take down witness statements relevant to the annulment of the Tenducci marriage was convened in October 1775, within the imposing walls of the Uffizi Palace, the legal and administrative nerve centre of Florentine government. Just a few years earlier, in 1771, the Enlightenment prince, Pietro Leopoldo, Grand Duke of Tuscany, wrote his own first-hand account of touring the administrative offices of the Uffizi and the busy corridors containing the offices of the proconsul. He described the impressive effect of the three courtrooms under the proconsul's jurisdiction on the first floor of this labyrinthine building.[59] It was most likely in one of these 'good-sized and well-lit' rooms, or an anteroom in this part of the Uffizi, that the witness statements relevant to the Tenducci marriage annulment case were taken down.[60]

Witnesses were called one by one over a period of two days on 23 and 24 October. Each made a statement upon oath in the presence of Judge Cosmus Gigliolini, the Florentine public notary. The words of the witnesses were written down by a clerk, Lorenzo Rossi. They then made a further oath with their hand upon a bible declaring that they had been telling the truth, and signed (or made their mark if they could not write) at the bottom of the testimony.[61] In addition to the public notary and procurator, the hearing was legitimized by the presence of a priest, Guiseppe Setti, clerk curate of the parish church of St Felici in Piazza.[62] In order to make sure that the witness statements were not fabricated, the authority and identity of the public notary, Judge Cosmus Gigliolini, was confirmed by Joseph Maria Mulatio, the senior proconsul (*Signorimus Proconsul*). A further validation of the statements was provided by Sir Horace Mann, who subscribed his name to the senior proconsul's endorsement.[63] Emblazoned with the necessary signatures and official insignia, these documents containing witness statements were admissible in the London Consistory Court with the force of legal evidence.

The first witness to be called to the Uffizi Palace to appear before the imposing presence of the Florentine public notary on the morning of 23 October 1775 was Tomasso Massi, described as a 40-year-old surgeon from 'Figlini'.[64] Tomasso was the son of Pietro Antonio

Massi of Norcia, the pig-breeding area known for its castration expertise, and he gave his account of Tenducci's boyhood castration. Massi was then cross-examined by Ansano Rossi, as to whether 'he did clearly recollect all what he had set forth and deposed', to which Massi replied, 'I do recollect very well when my ... Father ... Castrated ... Mr Giusto Ferdinando Tenducci', that 'I do clearly recollect that the ... Operation of Castrating was performed by Order of the said Tenducci's Father who was then Servant of the Commissary of [Monte San Savino]' (Plate 14 and Appendix). Pressed further by Rossi regarding 'for what reason and in what manner [were you] ... present[?]', Massi replied: 'My Father brought me up to the Profession of a Surgeon which I exercise at present and used to take me with him to all his Operations [so] that I might practice.'[65]

Why was it possible for Tomasso to tell the story of Tenducci's castration, with such candour, contrary to the normal secrecy surrounding these operations? A clue is in the opening witness statement, which begins 'I Tomasso Massi Son of the late Pietro Antonio Massi'.[66] The fact that the man who performed the operation upon Tenducci in 1748 had died by 1775 and was therefore beyond prosecution was significant: it allowed his son to speak without fear of retribution. The level of proof demanded by the London Consistory Court was to make sure that the castration was a full and complete one, and that it took place before Tenducci eloped with Dorothea, hence the revelation of such specific details. Tomasso therefore proceeded under further interrogation to provide exact details of the operation: 'I do clearly recollect that my Father Castrated the said Tenducci of both parts by making the usual Incisions in the Groin and of having Executed and cut out his Two Testicles and the Spermatick Ducts.'[67]

The next person to take the stand was the poet from the Teatro di Cocomero, Nicolo Tassi. Tassi told the court that he had been 'frequently at the House of Ferdinando Tenducci Soprano Musician during the time of Residence in Florence'. He had become acquainted with the singer after he had been sent for 'to compose him a Dramatic

Piece'. Tassi said he was 'informd by [Tenducci]... and his Mother how and in what manner... [he] was Castrated at a Place calld Terra Di Monte a San Savino'. Tassi recalled that Tenducci and his mother had told him 'that the Operation was done to him by Pietro Antonio Massi of Norcia now residing at Figlini who made it his Practice to go from Place to place to make those Chirurgical [surgical] Operations when ever he was calld upon and so requird'.[68] Tassi gave a vivid account of the operation as related by Tenducci's mother:

> I have... heard his Mother say that she had not Courage sufficient to be present at the Castrating of her... Son, but that she was in a passage next the Room where the Operation was done, and when she heard him Cry out, Ayi My Mama, which was in the very Instant of the Operation, she thought to have Died of the pain she felt at that Instant and I have often times heard her repeat the same.[69]

The next statement was deposed by the only other surviving eyewitness to Tenducci's castration, the surgeon Pietro Massi's assistant and servant, Gaetano Mugni. The 50-year-old Mugni, who was now a bookseller in Figlini, vividly recalled the events that had taken place over a quarter of a century earlier, including holding the boy fast during the operation, and seeing his amputated testicles on a dish.[70] The testimonies of Tomasso Massi and Gaetano Mugni, together with the anecdotal evidence of Nicolo Tassi, appeared conclusive. But Roger Wilbraham deemed it necessary to secure the additional testimony of a medical doctor in Italy, so that there could be no doubt as to the veracity of Tenducci's castration. The next witness, Antonio Frascani, was a 'Doctor of Phisic and Surgeon at this City of Florence'. Dr Frascani deposed that he had visited Tenducci and that, upon conducting a physical examination, he found that the singer 'had been Effectually Castrated... I found him wanting of his two Testicles and the Spermatick Ducts.' Crucially, since it was important to prove that the operation had been performed before 1766, the year that Tenducci eloped with Dorothea, the doctor added that the two scars about his 'Vacancies' indicated that the operation had been performed many years earlier 'when he was Eleven years of Age'.[71] Under cross-examination, however, Dr Frascani modified his story slightly, saying that, instead of paying the singer a visit in Florence, Tenducci had instead come to see him frequently at his home in 'Cuseiano', specifically 'in order that I might take some opportunity to Examine his private parts as soon as Convenient'. Oddly, perhaps to inject a note of decorum, the doctor added that he took the chance to examine Tenducci's body only when the singer happened 'to be one day in a profound Sleep'.[72] Dr Frascani admitted that he had known beforehand that Tenducci was a castrato, 'Tenducci having Confessed it oftentimes to me in the way of discourse and my having Interrogated his Mother with respect thereto she told me Candidly and without reserve the truth', which was 'that her . . . son was Castrated of both his Genitals at the Village of Monte St Savino when he was a boy'.[73]

Tomasso Massi made it clear under interrogation that the responsibility for the castration came from Tenducci's own father ('I do clearly recollect that the said Operation of Castrating was performed by Order of the said Tenducci's Father who was then Servant of the Commissary').[74] This evidence confirms for the first time long-held suspicions that parents were complicit in the castration of their sons. It may have been a coincidence that in or about the year 1748 the surgeon Pietro Massi just happened to be passing through Monte San Savino when he met Tenducci's father, and the idea occurred to him to have his lad Giusto operated upon.[75] Neither is it impossible that Tenducci's father (with or without the knowledge of his local priest) actually summoned the surgeon to perform the operation upon his son. No definite answer to these questions emerges from the surviving evidence. If money changed hands, from priest to father, unsurprisingly it was not recorded. If this was indeed the case, then Tenducci's father did not pass any financial benefit on to the man who performed the operation. A half-century earlier, the going rate for the services of *un norcino* was fifty *lire*, as paid in secret by the cathedral treasury in Siena for the castration of Francesco Bernardi.[76] The surgeon Pietro Massi who castrated Tenducci complained that he never received an adequate fee for his services from Tenducci's father, who kept putting him off when he demanded full reimbursement by saying 'that he must have patience and consider that he made the Operation on the Son of a Poor servant'.[77] Perhaps it was not so crude: maybe the Church did not provide a pay-off to the parents of boys procured for castration; maybe the promise of future riches was temptation enough to secure the family's permission. Bernardi's father, a barber by trade, gave up not one but two sons for castration. While the younger son, Francesco, became Senesino and an international opera star, his elder brother remained in obscurity, singing in a local church.[78] There may therefore have been a moral or even spiritual justification to giving up a son for castration if the procedure resulted in this type of divine service.

It was in Tenducci's generation that such attitudes began to change, as Enlightenment authors began to mount a public challenge to the collusion of fathers in the vicious and unnatural castration of their sons. The French philosopher Charles de Blainville, who heard castrati sing in Italy in the 1740s, blamed the boys' parents: 'It is known to everyone that these poor Fellows did not *cease to be men* with their own Consent, but merely thro' the Avarice of their Parents, who reduced them to that Condition, at an Age so tender.'[79] Voltaire and Rousseau added their voices to the denunciation of castrati, the latter reserving particular criticism towards 'fathers so cruel as to sacrifice nature to fortune, and . . . submit their children to this operation, that they may gratify the pleasure of the voluptuous and the inhuman'.[80] The singing teacher Giambattista Mancini (who specialized in the training of castrati) capitulated to growing public concerns by advising fathers only to have their sons castrated if they were really talented.[81] But these changes in social attitude did not come soon enough to save Tenducci.

It seems almost impossible in modern times to imagine how Tenducci's father as a parent could have consented to his son's castration, while the boy's mother stood outside in a hallway, listening and suffering as she heard her child cry out in pain. The recent fashion among historians writing about the history of the family has been to stress the historical constants of family life, such as the timeless quality of affection between parents and children.[82] The secret history of castration revealed here is a timely jolt out of complacently attributing our own modern sensibilities and values to the long-dead.

The personal ramifications for Tenducci in being surrendered by his own father for castration are also almost impossible to imagine. Nothing is said explicitly in the archives about Tenducci's subsequent relationship with the father who was responsible for his emasculation. A modern psychoanalytic response to Tenducci's case would be to suggest that the Oedipal scenario (in which the son wishes to murder his father so that he can supplant him and marry his mother) was dramatically reversed, so that the father committed violence against his son by brutally having him castrated. Tenducci's father pre-empted the Oedipal threat before his son became a man, and thus preserved his own manhood and status within the household.[83]

But there is another, rather more pragmatic explanation of why Tenducci's castration took place. In addition to the perennial depredations of living in a poor household with many mouths to feed, further research has revealed that, during the 1740s, there were additional pressures upon the Tenducci family purse. The everyday patterns of life in the palace of the *Commissario*, the grandest household in Monte San Savino, where Tenducci's father was employed as a servant, were interrupted by politics. In 1737, Florence had passed from the last of the Medicis to the House of Lorraine, cousins of the Holy Roman Emperors, Habsburgs who ushered in a new era of agricultural and administrative reform throughout Tuscany. Overseeing this transition in 1747 and 1748 were the two successive Florentine *Commissari*, Filippo di Lorenzo di Domenico Pissi and Giacomo Lorenzo di Giovanni Filippo di Lorenzo Gamucci.[84] In 1748, Tenducci's father was employed by either Pissi or Gamucci. In the same year, for the first time in its history, Monte San Savino's local officials surrendered their power and accepted the jurisdiction of Florentine lawyers and administrators under Austrian rule. The subsequent loss of status for the local *Commissario* could conceivably have led to a retrenchment in the size of his retinue, or at least a sense that these were leaner times. Could a sense of job insecurity or impending financial hardship have led Tenducci's father to take drastic measures to gain a little additional income by giving up his son for castration?

In contrast to the actions of Tenducci's father, his mother was presented as having genuine compassion for her boy, as Nicolo Tassi recalled. Contemporaries would have understood the psychic bond between mother and son, and the plausibility of his mother's sympathy manifesting in her own physical suffering at the moment he went under the knife.[85] Tenducci evidently maintained a close relationship in adult life with his mother. She knew his circle of friends and fellow-artists in Florence when he performed at the Teatro di Cocomero during the early 1770s, she was his housekeeper, and had chaperoned Dorothea when she moved to Italy masquerading as Tenducci's pupil. The fact that Tenducci's mother was not living with her husband in the early 1770s suggests that she was by then a widow. If so, it was she, and not her mercenary husband, who lived to enjoy the fruits of their son's costly success. Her protests that she suffered as much as her son did at the moment of his castration may be met with the observation that she, as much as his father, apparently colluded in that they did nothing to prevent it.

♪

By the end of October 1775, via Ansano Rossi and Roger Wilbraham's efforts in Florence, Dorothea's second husband, William Long Kingsman, had secured as much evidence on the Continent as he could. The hearing in Florence was over: in London, the trial for the annulment of Dorothea's marriage to Tenducci could now proceed to completion. In Ireland, depositions had been taken first at the 'usual place of judicature', the Consistory Court of the Diocese of Waterford and Lismore, and then, by virtue of an adjournment, in the more convivial surroundings of the Royal Oak Tavern in Waterford.[86] The deponents were Mary Holland, who was witness to Dorothea and Tenducci's clandestine union by the 'Romish priest', Patrick Egan; Samuel Griffith, clerk of the parish church in Shanrahan in Tipperary where the second Tenducci marriage had taken place; his daughter Joanna Green, a weaver's wife, who had witnessed the ceremony; and Simon Preston, the public notary to the Consistory Court of Waterford and Lismore, who confirmed Tenducci had applied for a marriage licence in Tipperary in 1767.[87]

After these depositions had been gathered in Ireland, in November 1775, further evidence was gathered in the Consistory Court in London. On 6 November, Charles Baroe, Tenducci's former room-mate and bedfellow in Dublin, made his deposition. As his bedfellow, Baroe had seen Tenducci in a state of undress. Overcome by curiosity, back in the winter of 1765, Baroe reported that he had asked Tenducci some questions about his castration, and 'he thereupon unbuttoned his breeches and shewed ... the cicatrice or scar of the said operation, which [I] ... clearly viewed, a little above the scrotum or testical bag'. But there was more that Baroe wished to tell. Later, in May 1767, he recalled that they were lodging together again at Mr Barry's house in Dirty Lane, Dublin. Baroe told the court how one day, 'upon ... Tenducci's changing some thing, from one pair of breeches to another', he had observed the singer taking 'a red velvet purse out of one pair of his breeches, to put into another'. Baroe was struck by the remarkable nature of the bag and asked Tenducci what he had got in there, thinking it was a relic, to which Tenducci replied, 'No; I have got my testicles preserved in this purse, and have had them there since my castration.'[88] Baroe had little to gain by adding this Baroque detail, which is not as far-fetched as first appears.

The Catholic practice of preserving relics was part of Tenducci's cultural tradition, and the expensive pouch of velvet, in a royal colour, was a mark of reverence for the pieces of once-living tissue that it contained. There is another source of contemporary evidence that this practice was not unknown. The eighteenth-century German traveller Archenholz, who made extensive enquiries in Naples about castrati, noted that the Church of Rome required only those who had not been 'mutilated [that is, castrated]' to take part in the Mass. Critical of what he saw as the sophistry of certain aspects of Catholicism, Archenholz noted that some 'have thought it sufficient for . . . a [castrated] priest to have his amputated genitals in his pocket, when he approaches the altar'.[89] Though this anecdote has been dismissed as a story invented by the Neapolitans to fool gullible tourists,[90] the evidence presented to the London Consistory Court by Charles Baroe suggests that castrati like Tenducci may indeed have kept their testicles as relics, perhaps in order to be allowed to take communion. The physical weight of the bag within his breeches may also have been comforting, providing a psychological boost to Tenducci's self-esteem. As a grown man, he was belatedly, if symbolically, able to safeguard his lost manhood in a way he had been unable to do as a vulnerable boy.

Other deponents stepped forward after Baroe. Lorenzo Lombardi, Tenducci's former landlord in the Haymarket, gave a similar testimony, confirming the intimate details that only someone who had seen Tenducci undress could confirm. Though he did not mention the bag in his breeches, Lombardi swore that Tenducci's penis 'was like a person's little finger', that he had seen that his scrotum was empty, and he had very little pubic hair. Within the context of eighteenth-century medical science, these details were necessary since they would have further confirmed Tenducci's infertility (although in the published account, the word 'penis' was printed as 'p–s' to protect public sensibilities).[91] The following day, 7 November 1775, Dorothea's father and mother, Thomas and Dorothea Maunsell, appeared in court to record their testimonies regarding the circumstances of Tenducci's elopement with their daughter. The Maunsells' personal contribution to the trial was a further indication that they were willing to go to some lengths to put right Dorothea's marital arrangements and to accept her back into the family, thus restoring her reputation, and theirs.[92]

A little over a month later, two further depositions were produced at Doctors' Commons towards the case of 'Kingsman, formerly Maunsell, falsely called Tenducci, v. Tenducci'. On 12 December 1775, there appeared Peter Crawford, one of the proprietors of the King's Theatre in the Haymarket, who had known Tenducci for the previous fifteen years, and Ansano Rossi, now returned from Florence. Though Rossi's evidence restated much of what had already been deposed in Italy, Crawford's deposition highlighted one extra fact that had previously been overlooked, but which would have been evident to any operagoer: Tenducci was a soprano, able to sing parts for 'the highest pitch of Voice that the human Voice can express', which he could not have done 'had he not been an Eunuch or Castrato...deprived of his Virility'.[93]

♪

Of course, matters would have been simpler if Tenducci had been willing to appear in person and undergo a medical examination. From the time of Dorothea's elopement, his career had continued to flourish. His critical acclaim was high: by reputation he was now known as 'always the most distinguished [singer] at the Teatro di Roma' ('*Sempre più si distingue nel Teatro Di Roma*'), where he had caused a sensation with his performance as Montezuma, King of the Aztecs.[94] He was honoured with a diploma for his efforts, and had pleased the Duke of Tuscany so much with his performance as Orpheus that he brought him under his direct patronage and ennobled him with the title of Count Palatine.[95] In terms of court procedure, Tenducci was given multiple opportunities to present his own side of the case. In relation to other trials for male impotence that appeared in the church courts, it was highly unusual for a husband not to counter a wife's allegation of impotence by issuing a libel of his own and appearing personally in order to mount a defence of his reputation. For example, in 1677, Edmund Syler had countered an accusation by his wife Elizabeth that he was frigid. Instead he issued his own libel against her, claiming that, contrary to her accusations, he was a physically 'perfect man', and that he was 'in all parts ready and able to perform the duty of a Husband'. Earlier, in 1662, Samuel Collins counter-libelled his wife Mary by saying that he would have had sex with her more often if she had not told him that once or twice a week was enough: Mary's failure to conceive a child was due not to his incapacity, but to her ill health, and the interference of her mother.[96] This pattern continued into the eighteenth century, though the church courts were in overall decline in the long term. Edward Weld issued a counter-libel in response to his wife Catherine's libel claiming he was impotent in a trial involving the Dorset gentry that attracted much publicity in the 1730s.[97]

Tenducci's failure to issue a counter-libel was in itself a mark of the hopelessness of his defence. Moreover, as the court case proceeded in Florence, Tenducci's name was 'call'd forth with a loud and audible voice', the clerk recorded, 'according to the custom and practice of England', but he did not appear.[98] There was no legal mechanism in existence at the time for Tenducci to be extradited to England, nor was there any likelihood of him voluntarily appearing before the court in person in Florence, specifically to be subjected to interrogation and most likely a humiliating examination of his body. Likewise his name was called three times at the consistory court in London ('Ferdinando Tenducci having been duly and legally cited thrice publickly called long and sufficiently'), but he did not appear. At the end of the trial, in passing sentence, the judge was especially critical of Tenducci for 'contumaciously absenting himself' from the proceedings.[99]

Neither did the other party in the case appear in person. Dorothea herself was not summoned as a witness in the annulment trial, but was represented by her lawyer, who prosecuted the case on her behalf. Her testimony would have been biased since she had a vested interest in securing the annulment in order to legitimize her first marriage, and in any case would have been protected by her family from having to articulate the most intimate secrets of the bedchamber in a public hearing, with society reporters waiting to take down the details for eager newsreaders. There was inevitable press interest in cases of marital annulment, which, like divorces on the grounds of adultery, were extremely rare at this time. When they did occur, extracts were transcribed by journalists in court and attracted widespread public attention, particularly when they involved the rich and famous. Printed in book form to elicit popular interest, titles such as the multi-volume bestselling *Trials for Adultery* promised 'A complete history of the PRIVATE LIFE, INTRIGUES, and AMOURS of many Characters in the most elevated Sphere, every Scene and Transaction, however ridiculous, whimsical, or extraordinary, being fairly represented, as becomes a faithful Historian, who is fully determined not to sacrifice *Truth* at the Shrine of *Guilt* and *Folly*'.[100]

On 28 February 1776, Dr Bettesworth issued his 'Definitive Sentence or final Decree in this Cause', having 'heard seen and understood and fully and maturely discussed the Merits and Circumstances of a certain Cause of Nullity of Marriage by reason of Impotency now depending before Us in Judgement'.[101] His verdict was that the two marriage ceremonies conducted in Ireland were but 'pretended Marriages or rather Effigies of Marriages... solemnized or rather prophaned between the said Ferdinando Tenducci and Dorothea Maunsell now

Kingsman Wife of William Long Kingsman Esquire'. The reason for these being 'pretended Marriages', he ruled, was that they were 'solemnized while . . . Ferdinando Tenducci was an Eunuch or a castrated Person and without generative Faculties and totally impotent'. His verdict had retrospective force, since he judged that the ceremonies joining Dorothea and Tenducci in marriage 'were from the beginning and are absolutely null and void to all Intents and purposes whatsoever by reason of the Impotency of . . . Ferdinando Tenducci'. The judge pronounced that Dorothea 'was and is free from all Bond of Marriage with . . . Ferdinando Tenducci and had full Liberty to contract and solemnize Marriage with any other Person', a critical ruling which instantly gave full legitimacy to her marriage to Kingsman, and to their offspring.[102] Furthermore, he ruled that Tenducci 'ought to be condemned in the lawful Costs made and to be made in this Cause on the part and behalf of . . . Dorothea Kingsman to be paid to her or her Proctor', and that he should pay not only her costs, but all legal expenses incurred in bringing the case. Nearly two and a half years after she had married William Long Kingsman in London, Dorothea's marriage to Tenducci was officially annulled.

♪

The press followed the news of how Tenducci's marriage ended and reported the events as they unfolded with alacrity. At the time that Dorothea eloped with Kingsman, one account from Rome reported that 'Mr. Tenducci was inconsolable for the loss of his wife', and planned to seek her, 'being determined, like his vocal predecessor Orpheus, to pursue his Eurydice to the shades below, rather than not recover her'.[103] The comparison of Tenducci's personal loss with his on-stage persona as Orpheus the grieving husband was simultaneously bathetic and insulting. Though it was easy for the press to caricature Tenducci as a celebrity, a heroic stage character with no personal feelings, the emotional impact of the annulment of his marriage to

Dorothea undoubtedly affected him. In a private conversation with Ansano Rossi over dinner at the house of Signor Vannini in Florence, in August 1773, Tenducci told Rossi that 'he had lost his Wife, calling her his Dorothea, and that she had married one Mr. Kingsman at Rome and that they were gone to England'.[104] Tenducci's comments indicate that in his mind, and in spite of the fact that he evidently knew the law was against him, she was still his wife, 'his Dorothea'. The law pronounced otherwise. But the cause of his greatest grief was doubtless that Dorothea herself had deserted him for another man.

## Chapter Nine

# Legacy

Regarding the story of the ill-fated marriage of Dorothea Maunsell and Giusto Ferdinando Tenducci, what was excised from the official record is almost as interesting as what was left to posterity to puzzle together. The original libel issued in Dorothea's name and presented to Dr Bettesworth at the London Consistory Court in petition for the marriage to be annulled is riddled with crossings-out. This suggests, not that it was presented by a shoddy clerk whose penmanship left much to be desired, but that certain unfortunate details relating to the case had to be omitted from the record. These included drawing a line through all references to Dorothea as 'Wife of . . . William Long Kingsman' some time before or after the libel was brought in. If the record was changed after the libel was presented, this may have been because the court may have insisted upon retaining its right to determine (albeit retrospectively) whether or not her second marriage was lawful.[1] A few still-legible and tantalizing details of Dorothea and William's courtship may also have been struck off the record by order of the judge, or by Dorothea's advisors. Item nine of the libel originally submitted that the pair had met at Florence when Tenducci arrived there in October 1772, and that Kingsman 'made his Addresses and Courtship to her in the way of Marriage', which she accepted, agreeing to go to Rome with him to be married on 22 April 1773. At this time, William was said to be a bachelor of the age of 25, and Dorothea a 'Spinster of the Age of twenty one years ... free also from all Matrimoniall Contracts', except her 'Effigy' of a marriage to Tenducci. Yet this contradicts the claim that Dorothea's remarriage to Kingsman in London was necessary because she was not yet 21 years old when she married him in Rome. Furthermore, if these details were true, then more than one report of Dorothea meeting another man and giving birth to a child before leaving England in the spring of 1771 were entirely fabricated. Dorothea and her second husband were constructive with the truth when they presented their court libel to have her first marriage annulled. For the purposes of the trial, these inconsistencies had to be smoothed over so that the marital arrangements of the parties concerned could be presented in a manner that conformed to the expectations of the church court. Meanwhile, the press reported none of these discrepancies. An edited version of the trial was published as a seamless narrative, with Tenducci the unambiguously culpable party.[2]

♪

Dorothea's change of heart was crucial to the annulment of her first marriage. Though she was undoubtedly fond of Tenducci, her elopement with him had been an expedient means, in the first instance, of escaping marriage to a man of her father's choosing and, in the long run, ensuring she could marry again once a better offer came along. Though Dorothea's reaction to the verdict went unrecorded, we must assume that in the end she got what she wanted. After her marriage to Tenducci was formally annulled, of Dorothea herself there is no further mention in the archives, nor in the press. Having caused her family so much trouble early in her life, thereafter she effectively disappeared silently into history. Dorothea's ultimate conformity to the expectations of her gender and class meant that she not only effaced her first marriage from the historical record, but herself from the attention of posterity. It was a situation with which she may have been content to live quietly for the rest of her life.

♪

Of the fate of William Long Kingsman, a little more is known. Having saved the reputation of the Maunsell family by marrying their errant daughter, his in-laws received him into their bosom as one of their own, a member of the Irish establishment. Kingsman (with, we must assume, Dorothea and their children) lived in Ireland, where he enjoyed the patronage of the Maunsells and their well-connected kin. He purchased a seat as a representative in the Irish parliament for Granard (Longford) following the death of the incumbent, John Kilpatrick. This was possible since Kilpatrick had been the ward of Kingsman's brother-in-law, Thomas Maunsell, the eldest son of Thomas Maunsell, the persecuting barrister. For all his inheritance and connections, however, Kingsman did not prosper in the long term. His life ended in August 1793 in the Fleet prison, where he had been incarcerated for debt.[3]

As for Thomas Maunsell senior, there is no evidence that his daughter's personal conduct and career on the stage ever affected his public profile as an influential lawyer and politician. He became a King's Counsel in the Court of Exchequer in 1769, shortly after the scandal involving his daughter and Tenducci, and in the same year was elected MP for Kilmallock in the Irish parliament, a seat which he held until 1776. His prosperity increased in 1775 when he was made Counsel to the Revenue by Lord Harcourt, an office worth £800 a year. He died in 1783, his legacy secured through the survival of his namesake son and heir.[4]

Whether by accident or design, later generations of Maunsells effectively changed the historical record, erasing an embarrassing episode in their family's history. When it was published in the early part of the twentieth century, the official history of the Maunsell family made no mention of Dorothea's first marriage, and backdated her wedding to Kingsman to 1762, when she would have been about 12 years old.[5] Similar fictions and half-truths are still repeated in the annals of Irish history whenever the Maunsells are mentioned. One recent authoritative study of prominent Irish families records that Dorothea was a widow when she married Kingsman, her first husband being called 'Tenucci'.[6]

♪

It has been possible to trace some further details about the identity and fate of William and Dorothea's children.[7] Their first child, named Dorothea after her mother and grandmother, is of especial interest. Married women from this period often left few historical records, since their legal identity was formally merged with that of their husbands, and there are often few traces of them in the archives as a result. But the same was not true of spinsters, and Dorothea Frances Kingsman, daughter of Dorothea, formerly Maunsell 'falsely called' Tenducci, and William Long Kingsman, never married. Her will records that she lived out her days as a resident of Upper Seymour Street in Marylebone, most likely in modest gentility, in property inherited from her great-uncle Robert Long, although she later moved to Hertfordshire.[8] It is not possible to confirm exactly how old Dorothea Frances was when she died in October 1800, but it seems highly likely that she was born before 1771, and that she was the same child who was once acknowledged by Tenducci as his own. Dorothea Frances's will indicates that she left her estate worth £1,600—a considerable fortune—to her biological father, who evidently needed the money.[9]

Item 13 of the libel issued against Tenducci on 24 May 1775, in a still-legible part of the document that was excised from the official record, suggested that 'immediately after the solemnization of their Marriage at Rome...[William Kingsman and Dorothea] did live and cohabit together as lawfull Husband and Wife and have consummated their said Marriage by Carnal Copulation and procreation of two Children both of whom are now living'.[10] Church courts (unlike common law at this time) reserved the right retrospectively to legitimize children whose parents were not married but wed later on. The timing of the births was misrepresented, since Dorothea already had a child before her first marriage to Kingsman. But it was indeed the case that Emily, another daughter, was born after Dorothea and William Kingsman had married in Rome. Little is known about her, except that in the event of her father's death she was left the residual legacy of Dorothea's property, minus £500, which went to Dorothea's other sibling, her 'Brother Kingsman'.[11] This was Henry, born in 1775, who was the only son of Dorothea and William Long Kingsman. Henry went to Winchester School aged 9 in 1784, which means he must have been born around the time that the trial to annul his mother's first marriage was taking place in 1775. Sadly, his fate was not a happy one. Like his father before him, he was confined to the Fleet, the debtor's prison, in 1802. Upon release, he went to Jamaica, where he met an untimely death that same year.[12] In the face of outrageous fortune, the legacy of the Kingsmans' legitimated marriage was by no means guaranteed.

♪

The formal annulment of the Tenduccis' marriage in February 1776 received some attention in the English press, but was quickly followed by more news: that the singer planned to return to London for the first time in over five years.[13] Speculation ensued regarding whether he would be engaged by one of the opera houses, or whether he had come solely to 'assert his claim to his wife'.[14] His return to England was precipitated not by his intention to win back Dorothea, however, but by the opportunity to make a clean slate of his financial problems. Tenducci's debts in England were said to have amounted to the extraordinary sum of £10,000.[15] The law was gradually recognizing that imprisoning debtors was an unsatisfactory means of securing repayment for creditors, since the individual concerned had no means of working to pay them off. As part of the reform of laws relating to debt, the so-called 'Lords Act' stipulated that an imprisoned debtor could henceforth secure his release by swearing an oath guaranteeing that his assets would be handed over to his creditors, to be divided proportionately among those to whom he owed money.[16] Accordingly, Tenducci surrendered himself to the Keeper of the Fleet prison. His name was published in the *London Gazette*, the government-sponsored newspaper, declaring he was insolvent and unable to pay his creditors. He thereby succeeded in clearing his outstanding debts in England, but at some personal cost, since he was soon reported to have fallen 'dangerously ill', presumably from the notoriously insanitary prison conditions.[17]

Once he had been released from prison and recovered his health, Tenducci remained in England and made a new start in his career. Though his days of performing in large productions of *opera seria* were over, he resumed his former round of benefit concerts and solo appearances, performing popular works such as Handel's oratorios.[18] He was engaged by Sheridan to perform at Drury Lane in the 1776–7 season, and succeeded in renewing his popular following among English audiences by singing musical interludes in the *Maid of Oaks*. This merry pastoral play (first staged in 1774) attracted attention as it had been written by one of the most famous commanders of British troops in the American War of Independence, General John Burgoyne, whose surrender at Saratoga in 1777 eventually proved to be a decisive moment in the loss of the American colonies.[19] The English press, who had given Tenducci a rough reception in previous years, approved of his contribution to this patriotic production. He was now described as a 'capital singer', whose voice had 'improved beyond imagination' during his sojourn in Italy. The *London Chronicle* published a rave review of Tenducci's performance in the *Maid of Oaks*: 'All our encomiums could not but fall short of his high deserts. The powers of his voice are not less astonishing than his execution, and his method of singing is such as amazes the ears of the Connoisseurs, while it enchants the generality of the auditors.' Tenducci was now 'the most delightful singer of Italy', who also had 'the peculiar advantage of singing in English' at a time of heightened nationalist fervour.[20] Productions of the ever-popular *Artaxerxes* were constantly judged against the memory of his defining 1762 performance.[21]

There was a growing mismatch, however, between Tenducci's now-excellent critical reputation as a singer of the first order, and the growing tide of public feeling against the grisly practice of castration. Tastes and fashions were quickly changing in the volatile political climate of the 1770s. The Enlightenment appeal to reason and dedication to nature reviled the production of castrati as singing 'men-machines'. This was overlaid with a new sense of patriotism in the English press, in an era when British imperial might was consolidated by the gains of the Seven Years War (1756–63), but also threatened by the rumblings of rebellion in the American colonies.[22] Whether Italian or French, it made no difference: fancy foreign imports began to be criticized as having a corrosive effect upon the body politic and the moral fibre of the nation. The *Morning Post* had to admit that 'Signor Tenducci's pipe is certainly very fine', but it opined that 'to rank him among the list of first rate English Oratorio singers who cannot articulate a syllable of our language, is the greatest absurdity'. English singers were superior since they had 'derived their musical education from the principles of nature, and reason'.[23] The press continued in similar vein when they reported Tenducci's sudden withdrawal from a performance of the *Maid of Oaks* during the production's otherwise successful run at Drury Lane in February 1777. Tenducci was criticized for incurring 'ruinous expence' owing to the fact that he was 'suddenly seized with a hoarseness, which injuring the *emasculate* delicacy of his voice, an apology was obliged to be made to the audience'. The criticism in this instance was based not just on Tenducci's supposed effeminacy but upon general xenophobia, since the paper went on to advise the proprietors of the Drury Lane Theatre that 'Should they have a similar occasion to apologize for their French dancers, it is highly probable that it would be received with equal indifference'. The piece concluded that the episode was 'proof [of] how little this very expensive train of foreigners are considered by an English audience, as an *essential* part of their entertainment'.[24]

Shortly afterwards, another critic, writing in the guise of 'Corelli' under the influence of the leading Enlightenment philosopher Jean-Jacques Rousseau, dismissed Tenducci's talent, since it was tainted by being contrary to nature:

> Rousseau affirms, that singing does not appear natural to man; for though the savages of America sing, because they talk, yet the true savage never sings; *ergo* castration was invented, and Tenducci is . . . a fresh wonder . . . Heavens preserve any man from such natural notes! He neither sings in tune, nor with any new cantabile.[25]

For some critics, castrati continued to represent the kind of absolutist political system and high Baroque fashion that was now highly out-dated in an era when radical ideas circulated among intellectual circles. These had found political expression in republican movements which were soon to have real and lasting impact in France and America. In the midst of these debates, Tenducci was something of a paradox. On one hand, he evidently enjoyed the patronage of *ancien régime* royalty and nobility wherever he could. On the other, he was no Farinelli, kept as a princeling's private pet, but a popular celebrity, who sang songs with patriotic associations in English, and took his music to mass audiences.

In 1778 he travelled to France, where, together with his friend J. C. Bach, he was received at Versailles, where he performed music from the Bach and Abel concerts. While in Paris, he became reac-quainted with Mozart, whom he had first met in London during the 1764–5 season. At that time the composer, and his sister, had first become renowned in English society as 'prodigies of Nature', being then only 8 and 13 years of age respectively.[26] Mozart composed a *scena* for Tenducci in Paris, a short musical piece for concert performances. This work is now presumed lost, but it was described by Charles Burney as 'a very elaborate and masterly composition', consisting of fourteen parts including two violins, horns, oboe, clarinets, pianoforte, and three voices, including two tenors in addition to Tenducci's soprano.[27] With an eye to the commercial benefits deriving from his association with French royal patronage, upon his return to London Tenducci published *Favourite Italian Songs* from his repertoire and dedicated them to Marie Antoinette, subscribing himself 'Count Ferdinando Tenducci'.

The English, while mostly eschewing the radical republicanism that was taking hold elsewhere in Europe and the American colonies, were famously sceptical of those who flaunted social pretension and titles.[28] Tenducci had been mocked in the press for styling himself 'Count' but defended his right to use the title of 'Count Palatine', explaining he had been given the title while in Italy by his patron, the Grand Duke of Tuscany. Some years earlier, he had taken the unusual step of issuing a public statement in the press, which read:

> GIUSTO FERDINANDO TENDUCCI observing in the London Evening Post... and in the General Advertiser of yesterday, a most ill natured paragraph calculated to render him ridiculous and presumptuous, he thinks it a duty he owes himself to observe, that whenever he may have used the title of Count, he was legally authorized so to do, having a patent from a sovereign Prince for holding and using such a title, as has been before granted to Farinelli, and some other professors of music.[29]

He blamed the envy of some members of his own profession for the imputation of this previous notice, and, ever-conscious of the need to cultivate public esteem, assured his English fans that he 'retains the most grateful remembrance of the many favours they have conferred on him'.[30] His pin-up portrait from 1770 was reprinted in the early 1780s to mark his revived popularity and ennoblement. Tenducci's new public image portrayed him, if not exactly younger, then certainly more plump and prosperous, with fewer wrinkles. Another addition was the medal upon his lapel, the badge of his new title: 'Justus Ferdinand Tenducci, Count Palatine and Knight of the Noble and Ancient Order of St. John'.[31]

♪

Tenducci's musical legacy was his flexibility and ability to adapt with the times. Within a single career, he not only made his mark upon Italian *opera seria*, but pioneered Arne's experiment with the genre of Italian-style opera in English, and a new, sincere, and expressive lyrical style introduced by Gluck; his influence therefore extended beyond the élite realm of Europe's great opera houses. A champion of Scottish songs, he reached wide audiences through his performances at the Pantheon and Ranelagh. His own compositions, though not enduringly popular, suited the pastoral tastes of the day. He continued to experiment with vocal styles and to mature as a performer, which earned him widespread acclaim. In the late 1770s, he pioneered the 'Rondeau', a new genre of singing 'in the round' popularized in London at Bach and Abel's concerts in which Tenducci was the lead male vocalist.[32] In his own country, he was remembered posthumously for having introduced the rondo to Italian audiences, which soon gained widespread popularity.[33] But his versatility also extended beyond his vocal talent. His ability to adapt to the changing tastes of the age highlights the success with which he overcame the prejudices in England against his cultural contribution as a foreigner and a castrato. As one contemporary commentator observed:

> Through every street of London we are charmed by the barrel organs with Tenducci's new Rondeau. This good Professor of Music has

charmed the town every season with an elegant publication; and he has been always very lucky in suiting the taste of the English people.[34]

But the longevity of Tenducci's career and popularity among British audiences was more than just luck: it was testimony to the quality of his maturing talent, and to his willingness constantly to adapt to changing tastes in an era which prized novelty and ingenuity. His ongoing participation in the Salisbury Music Festivals, and Handel commemoration concerts at Westminster Abbey in 1785, is confirmation of his success in securing a lasting position at the heart of fashionable musical culture in England well into the mid-1780s.[35] Further proof of this is provided in a rare surviving letter which Tenducci wrote during this period to Maria, Baroness Cosway (1760–1838) (Plate 15). Born and educated in Florence, Maria Cosway was a highly accomplished woman said to be conversant in five or six languages.[36] She was an artist in her own right, who painted portraits of, among others, Georgiana, Duchess of Devonshire, the leading Whig society hostess. She moved in fashionable artistic circles with figures such as Sir Joshua Reynolds, Cipriani, Bartolozzi, and Angelica Kaufmann. Her musical concerts drew in the *bon ton*, a circle of young aristocrats headed by the Prince of Wales.[37] Tenducci's letter is proof of their friendship, and his contribution to the success of these concerts. Writing in Italian, as one native speaker to another, he relayed news of the programme at Drury Lane, the proofs for his *Orpheus*, and various details concerning concert programmes, as well as his courteous formulaic regards to her husband, Richard Cosway.[38] He also continued his professional association well into the 1780s with leading female sopranos of the upcoming generation such as Mrs Billington.[39]

Tenducci's personal and professional network ought to have provided him with enough patronage to make a profitable living. His popularity continued to extend socially beyond the confines of the élite, and outwards from the metropolis. In fashionable Bath, he could draw

audiences of eight hundred people, and inspired the Master of Ceremonies at the Bath assembly to break with their tradition of never
requesting encores.[40] During the 1780s, Tenducci was associated, and
often appeared on programmes with Rauzzini, a young castrato who
dominated concert life in late-Georgian Bath.

But outside of London, the fashionable centres of provincial
musical culture, and the private concerts catering to the luxurious
tastes of the rich, castrati could still attract suspicion and even
hostility. In Bristol, Tenducci and Rauzzini were given a lukewarm
reception, in spite of the fact that they performed a programme of
music that had been a great success in Bath. One press report
mentioned that the Bristol audience 'neither relished, nor affected
to relish, the[ir] efforts . . . they appeared to be thoroughly sensible of
their excellence; but the moderation with which they dealt out their
applause they evinced that it was not the species of excellence they
wished most to encourage'.[41] Another report was more explicit
about what had happened: the 'rude *Bristolians*, uncorrupted by
the vicious taste of the times, looked upon [the castrati] . . . as objects
of ridicule rather than admiration, and laughed immediately at their
efforts to please'. On the second night, Tenducci claimed he was
indisposed, and refused to go on stage.[42] He was welcomed rather
differently upon his return to Dublin, where he gave an acclaimed
performance in the *Castle of Andalusia*.[43]

Another significant aspect of Tenducci's legacy was as a music
teacher, both as a private tutor to gifted male and female pupils, and
as a publisher of guides aimed at young people interested in developing
their vocal techniques and refining their musical taste. In addition to
general guides, such as his *Instruction of Mr. Tenducci to his Scholars*
(*c.*1785), he continued to provide private tuition to promising young
singers. One of his pupils, 'Miss Madden', premiered at a Hanover
Square concert in January 1786. Tenducci earned 'much honour from
the proficiency of his scholar', who was commended for her 'considerable degree of sensitivity and taste'.[44]

Though his voice was still highly praised, he may have sensed that his best performances were over, and that his future income would depend upon his talents as a tutor. Like the modern rock star who announces their retirement and gives one last, farewell tour, Tenducci placed the following advertisement in the *Public Advertiser* in March 1786:

> Mr. TENDUCCI, knowing by the example of others, as well as by his own Judgment, that a Time must arrive when every Professor ought to retire from the public Eye, and foreseeing that the Period at which he should make his Exit was hastening on, he has for some Time past devoted himself to the teaching of Singing, in which he flatters himself he has given perfect Satisfaction to the Nobility and Gentry, who have condescended to employ him ... Therefore at the End of the present Musical Season he intends to quit the Occupation of a public Singer.[45]

In the summer of 1786, he travelled to the West Country, where he was engaged by a 'Devonshire Lady of the first consequence' to spend his summer instructing her daughter in singing. He took part in the Royal Sovereign at Plymouth, a concert series of the kind that were then popular across provincial towns in imitation of the Handel jubilee celebrations in Salisbury, and was handsomely paid, reputedly the grand sum of £200, by the mother of his genteel pupil. 'Bravo, Signor Tenducci,' quipped the London press, 'you still deal in Notes!'[46]

♪

Just as his career was undergoing a successful revival, Tenducci again had his portrait painted, aged about 45 (Plate 16). Though some satirists commented upon his cadaverous appearance, this portrait emphasized his plump prosperity and rich attire, wearing a dark blue jacket with gold buttons and a red turned-down collar, a white silk waistcoat, and expensive lace at his collar and cuffs, representing a well-established and recognizable public figure. The artist, Thomas Beach, had painted Tenducci so that he could include him in his 'picture rooms' in Westgate Buildings, Bath. These rooms were festooned with well-known performers, the leading actors, vocalists, and musicians of the day. In order to celebrate the addition of his portrait, Tenducci gave a 'little private concert' in May that year while his effigy in oil gazed down upon the audience. Horace Walpole, who attended the concert, recorded the atmosphere enjoyed by the audience of fifty ladies and gentlemen: 'A fine light and shade being thrown upon the paintings, everyone found himself surrounded, as if by magic, by a number of his acquaintances breathing in canvass...in such natural shapes did the pictures look upon, and seem to listen to us, that it was difficult not to persuade ourselves they were not auditors also.'[47]

The fact that Tenducci's presence in the public eye provoked another round of satires indicates the success of his revived career in the late 1770s and early 1780s. In addition to a production of a new play, *The Son-In-Law*, in which he was parodied by the actor Bannister, a poem in the *New Bath Guide* summarized him thus:

> I need not say much about Mr. *Tenducci*,
> Repetitions, I know very well, will not suit ye.
> He's such an old stager—the *thing* is worn out,
> His *airs*, many years, have been hawking about!
> Yet I do not perceive that his voice seems to break,
> And the Ladies still talk of his charming long shake![48]

Tenducci continued to be associated with rumours of affairs with women, and it may be that he never gave up hope of finding a female companion with whom he could share his life. As late as January 1788, though by now he was said to be suffering from incurable gout, the talk of the town was that he had 'actually entered into the *serious* Opera of Matrimony with a foreign lady of youth, beauty, and fortune, whose *passion*, fortunately for the *Count*, is entirely centred in music'. There is no evidence that this rumour was based upon reality, but the fact that Tenducci continued to attract gossip of this kind suggests that his marriage to Dorothea Maunsell was not the only contribution to his reputation as a ladies' man.[49] An advertisement quickly followed announcing that one of his more famous pupils, the Scottish soprano Mrs Stewart, had not quitted her studies with the singer, as reported, and that the young lady alluded to was 'a pupil placed under the tuition of Tenducci by the Queen of France . . . possessed of voice and taste that will ere long make a distinguished figure in the vocal world, to the no small credit of her celebrated tutor'.[50]

But it seems that for all his distinguished patrons and promising pupils, Tenducci still could not live within his means. In mid-February 1788, the papers announced that 'Ferdinando Tenducci . . . music-seller' had declared himself bankrupt.[51] His lifelong inability to stay in credit had been exacerbated by a speculative venture that went wrong. In the early autumn of 1787, it was reported that Tenducci was going to establish a 'Musical Nunnery' at Bromley, 'assisted by proper masters, for the complete education of twelve young ladies, in the theory and practical knowledge of Vocal and Instrumental Music'. Here, the young ladies would reside 'constantly in this Convent of Apollo, sequestered from the world and society', in preparation for a career in opera or upon the stage.[52] The fact that other sources confirm that Tenducci was at that time a resident of 'Bromley, near Bow' lend credibility to the report that he had planned to set up a music school, but there is no evidence that this scheme ever materialized.[53]

The final indignity of Tenducci's last bankruptcy was that his possessions were sold by auction. The press reports indicate that, among his goods and personal effects, Tenducci had owned a remarkable range of valuable luxury items, including works of art: pictures, prints, bronzes, gold watches and snuff boxes, diamonds, antique rings, plates, household furniture, musical instruments of 'various kinds', books, bookcases, 'fine prints by Bartolozzi', and 'little statues of men and cattle in Italian bronze'.[54] In an age when owning a single set of bed linen was the norm, and only relatively wealthy households possessed more than basic furniture, Tenducci's home contained expensive 'piano-fortes, violins, violincellos, and musical publications... enough to set up a shop with'.[55] Of course, his musical instruments, books, and sheet music were not only valuable but essential to Tenducci's livelihood as a composer and tutor. Of especial value among his personal belongings sold at auction in April 1788 was a fine topaz jewel, sold for seven guineas, which at 'an inch in diameter and of most uncommon brilliancy' was said to be 'the finest in the kingdom'. The press noted that 'what perhaps would increase its value in the estimation of many people, [is that] this topaz once belonged to QUEEN ANNE'.[56] Tenducci's ownership of expensive decorative objects, including a jewel fit for a queen, is suggestive of the standard of living to which the servant's son from Monte San Savino became accustomed at the height of his boom-and-bust fortunes. But, whatever precious and tasteful items he had earned at the top of his profession he was again forced to relinquish as he quit England's shores and fled penniless once again to Italy, this time for good.

♪

In July 1789, just as news was spreading across Europe of the momentous revolutionary uprisings in France, 'Count Tenducci' was reported to be residing in comfort in the home of a Genoese nobleman.[57] Earlier that same month, Tenducci had made a guest appearance at the musical celebrations in Rapallo, in commemoration of the Feast Day of Our Lady of Monte Allegro, where he received particular mention among a grand orchestra as a distinguished *virtuoso* and professor of music.[58] As the summer waned, he travelled further along the Ligurian coast near Genoa, to the seaside town of Camoglia, where he contributed to the Feast Day of their patron Saint Prospero, to general applause. Now approaching his mid-fifties, and certainly in more modest venues than the great opera houses of Florence and Rome,

Tenducci still had the power to move audiences with the beauty of his singing voice, and its natural, expressive quality.[59]

Giusto Ferdinando Tenducci lived out his last days in the vicinity of Genoa, where he had found hospitality and appreciative audiences. He died from a sudden 'apoplectic fit' on 25 January 1790, at the age of about 54. His remains were interred in the parochial church of San Salvatore, just two days later on 27 January, confirming that by the end of his life he had made a full reconciliation with the Church of Rome.[60] It is pleasing to reflect that his funeral befitted a life dedicated to music. A special Requiem Mass for Tenducci's soul was said on the day his remains were interred, accompanied by the celebrated tenor, Guiseppe Carri, and a select orchestra of the finest musicians.[61] Just a decade later, Napoleon's invading army rolled into Genoa and razed the church of San Salvatore to the ground, of which there is now not a trace to be seen.

# Coda

Historical facts about men and women born in obscurity are not easy to come by. Even those exceptional people who by quirk of fate or sheer determination make it into the history books leave a body of historical evidence that is like a fine old musical instrument long infested with woodworm: some material traces of the original do survive, but these have become pockmarked with holes, till all that is left is a fragile shell and hollow space. This book has endeavoured to squeeze a tune from ephemeral materials using the different varieties of time-tempered fragments that are left to us: not just the written words, but the objects, art, and music that are the legacy of previous generations. By engaging with reconstructed sounds, visiting sites of interest, and touching material traces, as well as reading and looking hard in archives, both historian and reader may in future be able to gain a deeper insight into the long-forgotten cadences, the pulses, and social rhythms of previous generations.[1]

I came across the story of Tenducci and his marriage to Dorothea Maunsell by chance while researching another book on the history of the family with a friend and colleague, the historian Elizabeth Foyster. Knowing that seventeenth- and eighteenth-century society placed great importance upon men marrying and fathering legitimate children, she and I were interested in finding out about the experiences of men who were husbands, but not fathers. We wondered how childless men were regarded by others in their local community in the past: were they stigmatized or, did they, like Samuel Pepys, the famous diarist who was himself childless, find other ways of parenting and procuring heirs, such as nephews or godchildren?[2] Here the detective story began. My friend mentioned the survival of documents from lawsuits relating to marriages that were annulled on the grounds of male impotence, and a curious case she had come across involving a castrato singer who had married. The search took me to the London Metropolitan Archives and the records of the London Consistory Court, the church court which dealt with marital disputes in the early modern period. This led to a hunt in the archives, and a thick bundle tied with string. Alphabetized and produced as exhibits in court, these were the original documents presented in the case of 'Kingsman, formerly Maunsell, falsely called Tenducci' during May 1775, together with some of the original depositions or witness statements recorded by court scribes. These papers yielded up the details of how Dorothea Kingsman, née Maunsell, had petitioned the court for an official annulment of her marriage to Giusto Ferdinando Tenducci so that her freedom to marry another man, William Long Kingsman, would be recognized in law. More exciting still, attached to these intriguing 230-year-old documents were the original depositions from the court hearing in Florence. The originals were written in Italian and Latin, embellished with the seals and signatures of the British consul, Sir Horace Mann, and the Florentine notaries and witnesses who provided evidence for the London court. The edited details of the hearing were printed in 1779 and 1780 as part of several volumes of scandalous cases, the *Trials for Adultery: or, the History of Divorces. Being Select Trials at Doctors Commons, for Adultery, Fornication, Cruelty, Impotence, etc., from the Year 1760, to the Present Time.* This printed version indicates that not all of the original statements were preserved in the archives: likewise the archives contained much that was omitted from the printed version of the court proceedings. I realized that these documents were uniquely valuable, not least because they provide the only detailed surviving eyewitness account of how one small boy came to be handed over by his own family for castration.

We are not strangers in our own time to the immediate and close relationship between luxury and suffering. Force-feeding birds to make *fois gras* of their livers, bleeding veal-calves to procure perfectly white meat, rearing ermine in cages to be skinned for their fur: such examples of cruelty to animals in the making of luxury commodities cause outrage today, and rightly so. In Western societies the human suffering caused by our constant demand for novelty is usually pushed further afield, outside of the favoured trading zones of Europe and America to the sweatshops of the developing world. Recovering Tenducci's history has provided one step towards reclaiming the history of thousands of boys who suffered a similar fate. This previously hidden story of child mutilation and trafficking that took place between the sixteenth and nineteenth centuries in Italy, like the history of the trade in African slaves, is part of the wider cultural inheritance of modern Europeans. It is another important dimension in the history of the rise of modern consumer society, where the moral limits of human commodification were starting to be questioned just as the ideas of the Enlightenment movement were gaining ground.

I was spurred on to write this book having been jolted out of a cosy familiarity with the Georgians by the Tenducci court case, encouraged to think anew about the period as a time when Europeans deemed it acceptable to mutilate young boys in the pursuit of art, or at least colluded in the process by buying tickets to hear them sing. In particular, I was curious to know why the British public went crazy for what was the ultimate in Catholic Baroque fashion at a moment in their history when, governed by austerely Protestant Hanoverians, they were supposed to be turning their faces against Continental tyranny and absolutism. The answer to this particular question lay in the overriding influence and receptiveness of the British to all things Italian, including castrati. This was the era of the Grand Tour, when fashion leaders took time in their youth to visit the Continent, returning with cargoes of antiquities—lawfully purchased or merely looted—and a desire to replicate what they saw in their own country estates. By attending Italian operas, or engaging the services of an Italian music tutor or dancing instructor, members of polite society cultivated a form of leisure which expressed their idea that Italy, the seat of classical learning, architecture, and art, was the home of true taste. The Catholicism of their Italian continental neighbours could be accommodated in relation to the much more ancient history of the Roman Empire, in an era of nascent British imperial expansion. It was no coincidence that Handel, under the patronage of the militaristic Hanoverian monarchs, chose *Giulio Cesare* (Julius Caesar) as the theme for one of his most successful experiments in Italian operatic style. Though these cultural influences were always appropriated and adopted to suit specific political ends, and were never uncontroversial, the evidence of Italian cultural influence throughout the British Isles presented here has challenged the supposedly xenophobic and insular character of British national identity in the eighteenth century.[3]

Tenducci's story has also shown how attitudes towards men and manhood changed over time, and how society has chosen to define, and redefine, the institution of marriage when presented with variables in humanity that do not conform to strict social norms. The castrato lived in a period of European history where, not for the first time, but certainly to an unprecedented extent, increasing literacy and mass communication via the newspaper press and other forms of popular printed media gave public expression to new ideas about individualism, social mobility, and cultural aspiration.[4] A new emphasis was placed upon the market values of urbanizing European societies that promoted and valued new types of artistic virtuosity—in literature, music, and the visual arts. Brute strength came to matter less to the middling sorts and aristocracy than social polish and cultural refinement as a means of progressing in the world, and within this context (which provided the market demand for the castrato's original and terrible production) a new kind of masculinity, based upon cultural fashioning rather than biological determination, found a niche that was both recognized and celebrated. Tenducci married, and was the first under

English law to test whether a castrato could live as an 'ordinary' husband. His chosen identity was as a husband and father, even if his biological destiny suggested the impossibility of this choice.

'In a Settecento [eighteenth-century] history of gender and sexuality, the castrato might well be cast at center stage', observes Martha Feldman, one of the leading musicologists to have studied the phenomenon of the castrato in history.[5] Others have argued that the castrato was both at the centre and on the margins of society.[6] This was less paradoxical than it might seem. Tenducci was not a man permanently on the margins of eighteenth-century society, unlike the 'mollies' or rakes of his day. Mollies were exclusively homosexual and formed a subculture of their own in certain London taverns.[7] The rake or libertine was a legacy of the Restoration period, a notorious hell-raiser and drunken womanizer, usually rich and from an aristocratic background, who revelled in his extreme conduct, boasting of his prowess with the sword, his atheism in a society where profession of Christian faith was practically obligatory, and his sexual excesses through which he flouted the boundaries of virtue, honour, and social convention.[8] Such men, like the notorious Earl of Rochester, lost their capacity to father healthy sons, and hastened themselves to an early, horrific death from tertiary syphilis.[9] The castrato, the molly, and the libertine became stereotypes against which 'normal' manhood was defined.[10] Seldom sophisticated, frequently brutal in their visual and verbal assaults, popular satires and cartoons portrayed castrati as monstrous, worthy only of laughter or pity. But Tenducci's story has shown how the reality was more complex, with some castrati inspiring adulation, desire, love, and admiration as performers and as people. Even satires against castrati were themselves capitalizing upon the popularity of these singers in order to make a quick profit: one of their functions was to generate further interest and consumer demand for the products associated with Italian opera stars. The castrato's place was not at the margins, but at centre-stage in fashionable eighteenth-century European culture. The castrato was sometimes figured as a social outcast, an example of masculinity 'gone wrong'. But countering this idea has been the evidence presented in this book for the mass appeal of castrati as performers, their central role in the economic and cultural life of cities across Europe, and their enduring appeal throughout most of the eighteenth century. Together, these formed the bedrock of a mainstream popularity upon which a tiny minority of castrati like Tenducci found fame, making (and losing) personal fortunes in the process.

Tenducci did not want to be a dissident, but to have a wife like any 'normal' man. He married in spite of his status as a castrato, knowing he could not physically consummate the union according to the definition of the act that the law required. Perhaps he felt he would get away with it because of his fame, confident that public opinion would back his cause. Like generations of European aristocracy, and centuries of popes and cardinals belonging to the Roman Catholic Church, whose wealth and power licensed them to bend the rules of conventional morality, Tenducci's actions suggest that he believed that his fame allowed him to marry, and to have a wife of his choosing, in spite of the prohibitions in his native country. In this sense, he anticipated the modern culture of celebrity, by which anything is possible, provided it is both popular and profitable.

The story of the castrato and his wife has brought into question the nature and limits of love, sex, and marriage in the Tenduccis' own day, and ours as well. For this extraordinary episode—the elopement and marriage of a young girl with a castrato—was analogous to how marriage between two women was regarded in many Western cultures until very recently. Regardless of whatever sexual activity may have taken place between the parties, it was never regarded as a 'proper' consummation in law, and as a result was deemed to be (to use the terminology of the London Consistory Court) an 'Effigy of a marriage', what in our own times would be deemed a 'pretend' marriage. These unions, where they occurred, were effectively erased from the historical record through annulment. Such marriages did happen, albeit rarely, before modern times.[11]

Historians writing about the history of sexuality during the past few decades have often emphasized the marginal and dissident character of same-sex relationships, as deeply subversive events, often without making a distinction between all-male and all-female unions. Yet there were significant differences. Same-sex marriages between men, unlike those between women, took place not in churches but in secret 'molly-house' ceremonies, and were dangerous since they were associated with a particular sex act, sodomy, which was punishable by death. Unlike marriages between men, those between women were seldom punished in England, but simply erased through eventual annulment, much like the marriage of Giusto Ferdinando Tenducci and Dorothea Maunsell. This emphasis upon subcultures and dissidence played an important part in writing a new history that informed political struggles over the sexual identity politics of the late twentieth and twenty-first centuries.[12] But focusing upon marginality and dissidence has led to something of a historical dead-end. The evidence is there to allow fresh insights into pre-modern attitudes towards sexuality (the history of the castrato being just one example), but it is sometimes so all-pervasive, and so mainstream, that it has been overlooked.[13] Castrati are referred to all over the newspapers and correspondence of Georgian Britain, but they are simultaneously everywhere and nowhere. Their histories were largely forgotten with the advent of the Romantic movement and a new fashion in music for deep tenor voices with a 'darker and more powerful' masculine sound.[14] The revised sensibilities of European audiences came to reject the cruel practices and outmoded tastes of previous generations. The last Italian castrato, Alessandro Moreschi, who died in 1922, was a historical anomaly, lost in time like a survivor from the Battle of Waterloo. The only recording of his broken voice in old age gives no indication of the talent and charismatic power with which castrati like Tenducci and

Rauzzini continued to win over even sceptical audiences during the 1770s, at a time when the fashion for castrati was in decline.[15]

The impact of female marriages, like the marriage of Dorothea Maunsell and Giusto Ferdinando Tenducci, did not immediately alter the institution of heterosexual marriage, traditionally defined as a union between a man and a woman, for the procreation of children. It did demonstrate very publicly however the capacity of a new eighteenth-century doctrine of romantic love to open up a variety of possible relationships, and the ability of society to accommodate such relationships, often treating them as marriages, ahead of the Church, the State, and the legal establishment in reforming marriage laws. Tenducci was not ostracized for his marriage, nor did his career suffer as a result of his elopement with Dorothea. Though he was aware of the prospect of punishment had he married in his native country, in England he was able to cohabit, sharing bed and board with Dorothea: he referred to her as his wife, and she referred to him as her husband. What is more, they were received socially in London, Edinburgh, and provincial British towns, by people who recognized them as a married couple.

Dorothea found the 'loophole' of a relationship with a castrato not 'counting' in law provided her with a temporary degree of autonomy which many women never enjoyed. Though she was subjected to disinheritance and disgrace in her family, and the same degree of public vilification that any young woman suffered who did not at least pay lip service publicly to paternal authority, she found a space through her marriage to Tenducci to avoid the patriarchal dictates of her father's choice of husband. She was eventually able to negotiate a second marriage to a man of her choosing, one who was able to give her children. Dorothea's story illustrates the extraordinary lengths to which some women had to go in order to find a degree of control over their lives, within the confines and expectations of a patriarchal household. She lived in an increasingly literate society, where newspapers were within reach of servant girls, and new ideas were opened up which modelled alternatives to the dictates of male authority. A very few, like Dorothea, were bold enough to translate rebellion from the printed page into real life.

In many respects, the love story that has been explored in these chapters is remarkably conservative. Dorothea Maunsell and Giusto Ferdinando Tenducci wanted to conform to the ideal of romantic love and heterosexual marriage that had been popularized in their day through a variety of dominant cultural influences, most notably the novel. Husband and wife both accounted for their actions in the press, in Dorothea's detailed published account of their elopement, and in conversations with friends recorded in court, by appealing to what was fast becoming the single most desirable reason for getting wed: they loved one another. Though most ordinary people may have tempered their romantic inclinations with more practical considerations such as financial security and prospects, including the prospect of children, Tenducci and (through her marriage to him) Dorothea were cultural leaders who took the social trends of their day one step further. The notoriety of their elopement produced a shocking foretaste of what was to come in a changing modern world where the dictates of patriarchal marriage would ultimately be sacrificed at the altar of romantic love. Ultimately it was the nature of marriage, and not the innate range of human emotions and desires, regardless of disability, creed, or gender, which had to change.

How did Tenducci regard his fate, and come to terms both with great celebrity, and with his disability, deliberately inflicted at the behest of his own family? The archival records that were unearthed in the process of researching the story of Giusto and Dorothea, the castrato and his wife, have revealed some of the closest fragments we have to oral history, accounts of conversations with Tenducci written down by those who met him and by those who provided witness statements in court. Such moments are very rare in the history of castrati, since there are almost no personal diaries or letters in which they recorded their innermost feelings.[16] These have offered a glimpse of how Tenducci came to terms with the fate he had suffered as a boy, and how he dealt with the fact of his castration. In the statement of the poet Nicolo Tassi from the Teatro di Cocomero in Florence, Tassi recalled a conversation he had witnessed between Tenducci and a fellow-castrato named Tapi, when the three of them were seated at a table, perhaps enjoying some relaxed conviviality in a sunny courtyard. The memory of this conversation led Tassi to reflect upon how Tenducci had confided his feelings about the surgery that had made such an irrevocable impact upon his life:

> When ever he was calld upon and so requird ... I have heard ... Ferdinando Tenducci say he submitted to undergo the Operation with great Courage to be cured and get rid of a relaxation which he sufferd of both parts rather choosing to be Castrated than to pass his Life with such an Irksome Imperfection which often filled his Scrotum with gross Humours.[17]

Though he could not accrue honour to himself on the public stage of the battlefield as other men did, Tenducci's own claim to courage in facing personal suffering was one means for him to assert his masculinity through valour, confronting head-on the popular stereotype of the cowardly eunuch. The story which Tenducci told about his castration may have been the same one that he had been told as a boy by his parents in order to make sense of it. If so, then he chose to repeat the story as his own. By giving this explanation as to why he had been operated upon, he emphasized his own control of his situation ('choosing to be Castrated') rather than his powerlessness as a child-victim. In later life, as an artist, a connoisseur, and musical *virtuoso*, he preferred to see his mutilation as an almost aesthetic choice against a troublesome and unhealthy 'Imperfection' of his body. Like many victims of

219

trauma, Tenducci found solace in constructing a story which displaced the actual horror of what he had suffered. The conversation recalled by Tassi is a hint that, wherever he went, Tenducci must have been asked time and again to relate the story of how he came to be castrated. He strove to find dignity in his misfortune, and to make sense of his life through his friendships, through his art, and through his relationship with his wife. In a world not yet obsessed with his pioneering style of celebrity and audacious self-fashioning, many regarded him as less than a man, and some even doubted his full humanity. Yet Tenducci and Dorothea's marriage anticipated the struggle to reconcile biological destiny and individual choice, legally inscribed norms and personal freedom, that was destined to shape the lives of so many men and women in the course of the modern era.

# Notes

BL                    British Library, London

*General History*     Charles Burney, *A General History of Music, From*
*of Music*            *the Earliest Ages to the Present Period*, 4 vols.
                      (London, 1789), edited with critical and historical
                      notes by Frank Mercer (London, 1935).

*DNB*                 Lawrence Goldman (ed.), *New Oxford Dictionary of*
                      *National Biography*, first published September 2004
                      (ed. H. C. G. Matthew and Brian Harrison), Online
                      edition: http://www.oxforddnb.com (September
                      2010 version).

LMA                   London Metropolitan Archives

NLS                   National Library of Scotland, Edinburgh

NLI                   National Library of Ireland, Dublin

TNA                   National Archives, Kew

*Trials for Adultery* Anon., *Trials for Adultery: or, the History of Divorces.*
                      *Being Select Trials at Doctors Commons, for Adultery,*
                      *Fornication, Cruelty, Impotence, etc., from the Year*
                      *1760, to the Present Time... Taken in Short-Hand by*
                      *A Civilian*, 7 vols. (London, 1780), Volume VII.

*True and Genuine*    Dorothea Tenducci, *The True and Genuine Narra-*
*Narrative*           *tive of Mr. and Mrs. Tenducci. In a Letter to a Friend*
                      *at Bath. Giving a Full Account, From their Marriage*
                      *to the Present Time* (London, 1768).

## Prelude

1. The concert re-imagined here is based upon an account of an actual concert given by Farinelli: see *London Evening Post*, no. 1119 (18 Jan. 1735).
2. *London Evening Post*, nos. 1077 and 1078 (12 and 15 Oct. 1734).
3. Anon., *Do You Know What You are About? Or, a Protestant Alarm to Great Britain* (London, 1733), 16.
4. Quotations are from Paolo Rolli and the Dowager Duchess of Leeds, in Thomas McGeary, 'Farinelli's progress to Albion: the recruitment and reception of opera's "blazing star"', *British Journal for Eighteenth-Century Studies*, 28.3 (2005), 347, 349.
5. Antonio Mazzeo, *I Tre 'Senesini' Musici ed Altri Cantanti Evirati Senesi* (Siena: Cantagalli, 1979) quotes a letter by Metastasio dated 17 February 1755 which records that Tenducci was generally called Senesino: this has occasionally resulted in him being confused with two other castrato singers, Francesco Bernardi (b. 1686) and Andrea Martini (b. 1761). Tenducci's name is missing, however, from the baptismal records that survive in the Sienese archives: Archivio di Stato, Siena, *Battezzati Maschi*, 1152–3 (1728–41). Ansano Rossi, who knew Tenducci, recalled under oath that the singer was born at 'Colle di Valdenza near Sienna' (possibly Colle di Val d'Elsa, 12 km north-west of Siena), although no further substantiating evidence for this claim has been found. LMA/DL/C/639/Consistory Court of London, deposition book (Nov. 1772–Apr. 1777), fo. 310[r].
6. A useful summary of the differences between microhistory and biography is in Jill Lepore, 'Historians who love too much: reflections on microhistory and biography', *Journal of American History* (2001), 129–44.

## Chapter One.
## The Pig Man Arrives in Monte San Savino

1. C. J. Wickham, *The Mountains and the City: The Tuscan Appenines in the Early Middle Ages* (Oxford: Clarendon Press, 1988), pp. xxviii, 37–9, and *passim.*
2. My thanks to Renato Giulietti for this information (pers. com.).
3. Cinzia Cardinale (ed.), *Archivo Prennitario del Comune di Monte San Savino,* Vol. II (Arezzo: Progetto Archivi, 2004), 86–7.
4. LMA/DL/C/558/21, Deposition of Tomasso Massi (23 Oct. 1775), fo. 3, reveals Tenducci's father 'was then Servant of the Commissary of the . . . Village'.
5. For the emergence of banking houses among the most powerful families in medieval Europe, see Peter Spufford, *Power and Profit: The Merchant in Medieval Europe* (London: Thames and Hudson, 2002).
6. Cardinale (ed.), *Archivo Prennitario del Comune di Monte San Savino,* Vol. II, 'Commissari Fiorentini di Monte San Savino', 331–2.
7. Beatrice Gottlieb, *The Family in the Western World* (Oxford: Oxford University Press, 1993).
8. Ibid. 13.
9. Ibid. 17–23, 35–7.
10. Pieve che di S. Agata, MSS APREM, inv. 2108–9. I am most grateful to Dr Angelo Gravano for sharing his intensive research on the baptismal records from this region, and to Dr Renato Giulietti (*Archivista Storico Comunale,* Monte San Savino), for his communication on this subject.
11. Helen Berry and Elizabeth Foyster, 'Childless men in early modern England', in eadem (eds.), *The Family in Early Modern England* (Cambridge: Cambridge University Press, 2007), 164–5.

12. LMA/DL/C/558/21, Deposition of Antonio Massi (28 Oct. 1775), fo. 3.

13. Berry and Foyster, 'Childless men', 163–5; see also *The Histories of Gargantua and Pantagruel*, ed. and trans. J. M. Cohen (Harmondsworth: Penguin, 1955).

14. Alison Rowlands, 'The conditions of life for the masses', in Euan Cameron (ed.), *The Family in Early Modern Europe* (Oxford: Oxford University Press, 2001), 35.

15. Many historians now question Philippe Ariès's assertion that childhood was 'invented' in the eighteenth century, but it is certain that in the majority of pre-modern European households, child labour was an important part of the household economy. See Ariès, *Centuries of Childhood: A Social History of Family Life*, ed. and trans. Robert Baldick (New York: Random House, 1962), and for a more recent overview, Hugh Cunningham, *Children and Childhood in Western Society Since 1500* (Harlow: Longman, 1995), ch. 4.

16. Baldassare Castiglione, *The Book of the Courtier* (1528), trans. Leonard Epstein Opdycke (New York, 1929), 26.

17. Karen Harvey, 'The history of masculinity, *circa* 1650–1800', *Journal of British Studies*, 44.2 (2005), 296–311. See also in the same issue, Karen Harvey and Alexandra Shepard, 'What have historians done with masculinity? Reflections on five centuries of British history, c. 1500–1950', 274–80.

18. Anthony Ashley Cooper, *Characteristics of Men, Manners, Opinions, Times, etc.* (1711), ed. John M. Robertson (London, 1900), Vol. II, p. 256.

19. Quoted in Jeremy Gregory, '*Homo religious*: masculinity and religion in the long eighteenth century', in T. Hitchcock and M. Cohen (eds.), *English Masculinities, 1660–1800* (London and New York, 1999), 99.

20. See Peter Laslett, K. Oosterveen, and R. Smith (eds.), *Bastardy and its Comparative History: Studies in the History of Illegitimacy and*

*Marital Nonconformism in Britain, France, Germany, Sweden, North America, Jamaica and Japan* (London: Edward Arnold, 1980).

21. For a discussion of the idea of 'hegemonic' codes of masculinity, taken from sociological theory, see Alexandra Shepard, *Meanings of Manhood in Early Modern England* (Oxford: Oxford University Press, 2003), *passim*.

22. LMA/DL/C/558/21, Deposition of Nicolo Tassi (23 Oct. 1775), fo. 8.

23. The Chiesa di Sant'Agostino, Monte San Savino was the burial place of Sansovino, and was improved during the eighteenth century. See Renato Giulietti, *Monte San Savino* (Monte San Savino: Associazione Pro Loco di Monte San Savino, 2004), 154–5.

24. Balatri, unpublished account, quoted in Angus Heriot, *The Castrati in Opera* (London: Secker and Warburg, 1956), 211.

25. Mary E. Fraudsen, '*Eunuchi conjugium*: the marriage of a castrato in early modern Germany', *Early Music History 24: Studies in Medieval and Early Modern Music*, ed. Iain Fenlon (Cambridge: Cambridge University Press, 2005), 64–5.

26. C. Donahue Jr., 'The canon law on the formation of marriage and social practice in the later Middle Ages', *Journal of Family History*, 8 (1983), 144–58.

27. Berry and Foyster, 'Childless men', 163–9.

28. For an overview, see Valeria Finucci, *The Manly Masquerade: Masculinity, Paternity and Castration in the Italian Renaissance* (Durham, NC and London: Duke University Press, 2003), ch. 6 and *passim*.

29. Acts 8: 26–40.

30. Quoted in Isobel Grundy, *Lady Mary Wortley Montagu* (Oxford: Oxford University Press, 1999), 145, 148.

31. The variety of operations undertaken to perform an effective castration was described in gruesome detail for Georgian readers in Anon. [Charles Ancillon], *Eunuchism Display'd. Describing all*

*the Different Sorts of Eunuchs; the Esteem They Have Met With in the World, and How They Came to be Made So* (London, 1718). For a detailed discussion of *Eunuchism Display'd*, see Chapter 7.

32. Heriot, *Castrati in Opera*, 10.
33. Giuseppe Gerbino, 'The quest for the soprano voice: castrati in Renaissance Italy', *Studi Musicali*, 33.2 (2004), 307, 309.
34. Ibid. 307, 309–10.
35. Gabriele Falloppio, *La Chirurgia* (Venice, 1687), Vol. III, p. 193, quoted and translated in ibid., 350.
36. Edward Behrend-Martínez, *Unfit for Marriage: Impotent Spouses on Trial in the Basque Region of Spain, 1650–1750* (Reno and Las Vegas: University of Nevada Press, 2007), 129–30.
37. Gerbino, 'Quest for the soprano voice', 324.
38. Ibid.
39. J. R. Hale, *Florence and the Medici: The Pattern of Control* (Plymouth: Thames and Hudson, 1977), 187–92.
40. The requirement that priests be both physically intact and masculine, yet effectively 'castrated' through prescriptive celibacy, led to a rich tradition of popular anti-clerical satire in Europe: see Daron Burrow, *The Stereotype of the Priest in the Old French Fabliaux: Anticlerical Satire and Lay Identity* (Bern: Peter Lang, 2005), 185 and *passim*.
41. These themes are explored in Jacqueline Murray, 'Sexual mutilation and castration anxiety: a medieval perspective', in Mathew Kuefler (ed.), *The Boswell Thesis: Essays on Christianity, Social Tolerance and Homosexuality* (Chicago and London: University of Chicago Press, 2006).
42. Matt. 18: 8.
43. This association was highlighted in the title of a recent recording by Cecilia Bartoli of arias written for castrati: *Sacrificium* (conductor Giovanni Antonini, Decca recording, 2009).
44. John Rosselli, 'The castrati as a professional group and a social phenomenon, 1550–1850', *Acta Musicologica*, 60 (1988), 154.

45. Quoted in J. S. Jenkins, 'The voice of the castrato', *The Lancet*, 351 (1998), 1878.

46. P. A. Scholes (ed.), *Dr Burney's Musical Tours in Europe*, Vol. I (Oxford: Oxford University Press, 1959), 247.

47. *General History of Music*, 530, n. (a).

48. Heriot, *Castrati in Opera*, 42–7.

49. Ibid. 53.

50. '...*son maschio, Toscano, e...si trova* | *galli nelle mie parti che anno uova,* | *dalle quali i soprano son al mondo;* | *Che li galli si nomano Norcini*' ('I am male, Tuscan, | and . . . there are | cockerels in my part of the world that lay eggs, | from which sopranos are born. | That these cockerels are called *Norcini* . . . '), Balatri, '*Frutti del Mondo, esperimentati da Filippo Balatri nativo dell'Alfea in Toscana*', unpublished extract quoted in Heriot, *Castrati in Opera*, 209–10.

51. LMA/DL/C/558/21 (23 Oct. 1775), fo. 5, Tomasso Massi deposed that he had been fetched by the lawyer Ansano Rossi from 'Figlini'. Gaetano Mugni, his father's servant, was described as a 'book seller' but could not sign his name. His testimony was written down and signed by Dr Antonio Frascani. See LMA/DL/C/558/21 (23 Oct. 1775), fo. 22.

52. Margaret Pelling, 'Appearance and reality: barber-surgeons, the body and disease', in A. L. Beier and Roger Finlay (eds.), *London: The Making of the Metropolis, 1500–1700* (London: Longman, 1986).

53. LMA/DL/C/558/21, Deposition of Tomasso Massi (23 Oct. 1775), fo. 1. Massi's testimony is reprinted in full in the Appendix.

54. Ibid., fo. 4.

55. Ibid.

56. Ibid., fo. 5.

57. Ibid., fo. 4.

58. Ibid., fo. 2.

59. LMA/DL/C/558/21, Deposition of Gaetano Mugni (23 Oct. 1775), fo. 20.
60. LMA/DL/C/558/21, Deposition of Tomasso Massi, fo. 2. The circumstances in which these details came to light are explored in Chapter 8.

## Chapter Two. Schooling Angels in Naples

1. Antonio Mazzeo, *I Tre 'Senesini' Musici ed Altri Cantanti Evirati Senesi* (Siena: Cantagalli, 1979), 27.
2. Martha Feldman, 'Strange births and surprising kin: the castrato's tale', in Paula Findlen, Wendy Wassyng Roworth, and Catherine M. Sama (eds.), *Italy's Eighteenth Century: Gender and Culture in the Age of the Grand Tour* (Stanford: Stanford University Press, 2009), 183–4.
3. Anthony R. DelDonna, 'Opera in Naples', in Anthony R. DelDonna and Pierpaolo Polzonetti (eds.), *The Cambridge Companion to Eighteenth-Century Opera* (Cambridge: Cambridge University Press, 2009), 215.
4. Ibid., *passim.*
5. Patrick Barbier, *The World of the Castrati: The History of an Operatic Phenomenon* (1989), trans. Margaret Crosland (London: Souvenir Press, 1996), 41.
6. Michael Snodin and Nigel Llewellyn, *Baroque: Style in the Age of Magnificence, 1620–1800* (London: V&A Publishing, 2009).
7. Joanna Norman, 'Performance and performativity: Baroque art and design for the theatre', in Snodin and Llewellyn, *Baroque*, 144–6.
8. Ibid.
9. DelDonna, 'Opera in Naples', 225–6.
10. The church of Santa Maria della Pietà dei Turchini survives on the Via Medina in Naples, across the street from the Teatro di San Carlo. The building next door to the church, which once housed

the musical conservatory of the same name where Tenducci received his musical education, is now occupied by the Palazzo Turchini hotel.

11. Martha Feldman, *Opera and Sovereignty: Transforming Myths in Eighteenth Century Italy* (Chicago and London: University of Chicago Press, 2007), 1–5, for a particular discussion of the spatial layout of the Teatro di San Carlo. See also Michael F. Robinson, *Naples and Neapolitan Opera* (Oxford: Clarendon Press, 1972), 7–9.

12. Feldman, *Opera and Sovereignty*, 8.

13. Francesco Cotticelli and Paolgiovanni Maione, 'Metastasio: the dramaturgy of eighteenth-century heroic opera', in DelDonna and Polzonetti, *Eighteenth-Century Opera*, 74.

14. Feldman, *Opera and Sovereignty*, 8.

15. Lucie Marién, *The Art of Singing: A Manual of Bel Canto* (London, 1974), 1–5.

16. Pierpaolo Polzonetti, 'Opera as process', in DelDonna and Polzonetti, *Eighteenth-Century Opera*, 6.

17. Feldman, *Opera and Sovereignty*, 9.

18. David Schulenberg, *Music of the Baroque* (New York and Oxford: Oxford University Press, 2001), 161.

19. See Nicholas Clapton, 'Carlo Broschi Farinelli: aspects of his technique and performance', in a special edition of the *British Journal for Eighteenth-Century Studies* devoted to Farinelli: 28.3 (2005), 323–38.

20. The observations are from the conductor René Jacobs, whose insights derive from performances of music written for castrati, in 'There are no castratos left: what now?', *Arias for Farinelli* (Berlin: Akademie für Alte Musik, 2002), 28.

21. Jacob Simon (ed.), *Handel: A Celebration of His Life and Times, 1685–1759* (London: National Portrait Gallery, 1985), 145.

22. Michael Kelly, *Reminiscences of Michael Kelly of the King's Theatre and Theatre Royal Drury Lane*, 2nd edn., 2 vols. (London: Henry Colburn, 1826), Vol. I, pp. 40–4.

23. Tenducci's harpsichord was built in London in 1766, and is the only example by this harpsichord-maker to have survived to the present day. For an expert interpretation of the instrument's significance within the history of music, and a recording of the harpsichord in use, see David Leigh, *Tenducci's Harpsichord*, Harpsichords: Historic, Rare and Unique, Vol. 2 (Acanthus International Records: 94012).

24. This useful schema for eighteenth-century stage deportment was formulated by Dene Barnett: see Melania Bucciarelli, *Italian Opera and European Theatre, 1680–1720: Plots, Performers, Dramaturgies* (Amsterdam and Cremona: Brepolis, 2000), 11–12.

25. Ibid. 15.

26. Angus Heriot, *The Castrati in Opera* (London: Secker and Warburg, 1956), 48.

27. Giusto Ferdinando Tenducci, 'Address to the Public', in *Orpheus and Eurydice, a Musical Drama...The Poetry by the Celebrated Councellor Calsabigi* (London, 1785), 3.

28. Christopher Hogwood, *Handel* (Bath: Thames and Hudson, 1984), 144.

29. Stanley Sadie (ed.), *The New Grove Dictionary of Music*, Vol. 3 (London: Macmillan, 1980), 595.

30. Heriot, *Castrati in Opera*, 48.

31. Tenducci, 'Address to the Public', 3.

32. Feldman, 'Castrato's tale', 183–4.

33. Heriot, *Castrati in Opera*, 41–2.

34. Olive Baldwin and Thelma Wilson, 'Giusto Ferdinando Tenducci', *DNB*, date the end of his musical training to 1750, but according to Mazzeo, *I Tre 'Senesini'* (p. 28), he entered the conservatory at 1748: two years would not have been enough time to train a castrato. It is not inconceivable that he entered the conservatory earlier, in 1744 (Baldwin and Wilson), but in this case he would already have been at the conservatory for four years before his castration.

35. Heriot, *Castrati in Opera*, 45.
36. Robinson, *Naples and Neapolitan Opera*, 21.
37. DelDonna, 'Opera in Naples', 216.
38. Mazzeo, *I Tre 'Senesini'*, 28.
39. Ibid.
40. Curtis Price, Judith Milhous, and Robert D. Hume, *The Impresario's Ten Commandments: Continental Recruitment for Italian Opera in London, 1763–64*, Royal Musical Association Monographs, No. 6 (London: Royal Musical Association, 1992), 6–8. The fortunes of the King's Theatre were uncertain at this time and there were frequent changes of management.
41. Ibid. 10.
42. Ibid.
43. Price *et al.*, *Impresario's Ten Commandments*, 27.G. W. Stone (ed.), *The London Stage, 1660–1800: A Calendar of Plays, Entertainments and Afterpieces. Part IV: 1747–1776* (Carbondale, Ill.: Southern Illinois University Press, 1962), 681–2.
44. Simon McVeigh, 'Introduction', in Susan Wollenberg and Simon McVeigh (eds.), *Concert Life in Eighteenth-Century Britain* (Aldershot: Ashgate, 2004), 8–9; see also eidem, 'The benefit concert in nineteenth-century London: from "tax on the nobility" to "monstrous nuisance"', in Bennett Zon (ed.), *Nineteenth-Century British Music Studies*, 1 (Aldershot: Ashgate, 1999).
45. Tenducci, 'Address to the Public', 1.
46. The form of Tenducci's contract is derived from Mazziotti's contract for 1763–4, which survives due to the court case prosecuted between Leone and Giardini following a disastrous season. The wording of such contracts, as Price *et al.* have noted, was 'highly formulaic'. See their Appendix B.

## Chapter Three. The Castrato in London

1. Frederick C. Petty, 'Italian Opera in London, 1760–1800', *Studies in Musicology*, 16 (1972), 4.

2. Lowell Lindgren, 'The staging of Handel's operas in London', in Stanley Sadie and Anthony Hicks (eds.), *Handel Tercentenary Collection*, Royal Musical Association (Basingstoke and London: Macmillan, 1987), 93–117.

3. G. W. Stone (ed.), *The London Stage, 1660–1800: A Calendar of Plays, Entertainments and Afterpieces. Part IV: 1747–1776* (Carbondale, Ill.: Southern Illinois University Press, 1962), 707–10.

4. John Brewer, *The Pleasures of the Imagination: English Culture in the Eighteenth Century* (London: HarperCollins, 1997), p. xxvii. For the diminution of the English court as a cultural centre, see ibid., ch. 1.

5. Ibid.

6. For a useful exploration of the range of cultural activities on offer in Georgian London, see Jeremy Black, *A Subject for Taste: Culture in Eighteenth-Century England* (London and New York: Hambledon, 2005).

7. Edward A. Langhans, 'The theatres', in Robert D. Hume (ed.), *The London Theatre World, 1660–1800* (Carbondale, Ill.: Southern Illinois University Press, 1980), 56.

8. Brewer, *Pleasures of the Imagination*, 27.

9. Heriot, *Castrati in Opera*, 58–61.

10. The Royal Society was repeatedly low on funds, and the Royal Academy of Arts was not founded until the 1760s, in spite of repeated attempts at establishing a national society for the arts. I am grateful to Jason Kelly for highlighting this anomaly with the Royal College of Music.

11. Brewer, *Pleasures of the Imagination*, 364.

12. The commemoration of the 350th anniversary of Handel's death in 2009 was one mark of his enduring influence on English music: for an earlier collection published to celebrate his tercentenary in 1987, see Stanley Sadie and Anthony Hicks (eds.), *Handel Tercentenary Collection*, Royal Musical Association (Basingstoke and London: Macmillan, 1987).

13. John Rosselli, 'The castrati as a professional group and a social phenomenon, 1550–1850', *Acta Musicologica*, 60 (1988), 143.

14. Samuel Pepys, *Diary* (16 Feb. 1667).

15. John Evelyn recorded in his diary that 'Mr. Pepys' invited Siface to his house to perform to 'a select number of persons'. *Diary and Correspondence of John Evelyn* (19 Apr. 1687), ed. William Bray (London: Routledge, 1827), 460.

16. Ibid. (30 Jan. 1678), 457.

17. Mark Goldie (ed.), *The Entring Book of Roger Morrice, 1677–1691. Vol. I: Roger Morrice and the Puritan Whigs* (Woodbridge: Boydell and Brewer, 2007), 421.

18. Elizabeth Krimmer, '"Eviva il Coltello?" The castrato singer in eighteenth-century German literature and culture', *PMLA*, 120.5 (2005), 1543–59.

19. Anon., *Do You Know What You are About? Or, a Protestant Alarm to Great Britain: Proving Our Late Theatric Squabble, a Type of the Present Contest for the Crown of Poland; and that the Division between Handel and Senesino, has more in it than we imagine. Also, That the Latter is No Eunuch, but a Jesuit in Disguise; with Other Particulars of the Greatest Importance* (London, 1733), 1–18.

20. Ibid.

21. For an introduction, see Jeremy Black, *The British Abroad: The Grand Tour in the Eighteenth Century* (London: Sandpiper, 1999); for the extensive historiographical literature on the Grand Tour, see Jason M. Kelly, *The Society of Dilettanti: Archaeology and Identity in the British Enlightenment* (New Haven and London:

Paul Mellon Centre for Studies in British Art, Yale University Press, 2009).

22. Clare Haynes, *Pictures and Popery: Art and Religion in England, 1660–1760* (Aldershot: Ashgate, 2006), 13.

23. Colin Haydon, *Anti-Catholicism in Eighteenth-Century England, c. 1714–1780* (Manchester: Manchester University Press, 1998), 102. The quotation is from Gibbon.

24. E. W. Brayley, *Historical and Descriptive Accounts of the Theatres of London* (London, 1826), 28.

25. For an introduction to Hogarth's life and work, including the *Rake's Progress* series, there is no better single volume than Jenny Uglow, *Hogarth: A Life and a World*, 2nd edn. (London: Faber and Faber, 2002).

26. Patrick Barbier, *The World of the Castrati: The History of an Operatic Phenomenon* (1989), trans. Margaret Crosland (London: Souvenier Press, 1996), 182; Jacob Simon (ed.), *Handel: A Celebration of His Life and Times, 1685–1759* (London: National Portrait Gallery, 1985), 14–16.

27. Lien Bich Luu, *Immigrants and the Industries of London, 1500–1700* (Aldershot: Ashgate, 2005) highlights the treatment of immigrants in early modern London, although the focus is chiefly upon migration to England from the Low Countries. Much research remains to be done on Italian communities in England before 1800.

28. *Public Advertiser*, no. 7870 (12 Feb. 1760).

29. Kelly, *Society of Dilettanti*, ch. 5 and *passim*.

30. Massimo Becattini, *Filippo Mazzei, Mercante Italiano a Londra, 1756–1772* (Prato: Pentalinea, 1997), 59, and n. II, p. 63.

31. James Boswell, entry for 1 July 1785, reproduced in Irwin S. Lustig and Frederick A. Pottle (eds.), *Boswell: The Applause of the Jury, 1782–1785* (London and New York: McGraw-Hill, 1980), 316; and 23 June 1786, in idem, *Boswell: The English Experiment* (London and New York: McGraw-Hill, 1986), 74. I am grateful to Jim Caudle for these references.

32. *Public Advertiser*, no. 7530 (16 Dec. 1758).

33. Langhans, 'The theatres', 68, 71.

34. Ibid. 65.

35. For a statistical comparison of the dimensions of eighteenth-century London theatres, see ibid. 62–5.

36. Gioacchino Cocchi, b. *c*.1720, d. *c*.1788. Cocchi remained at the King's Theatre until 1762; in the mid-1760s, he returned permanently to Italy. See Stanley Sadie (ed.), *The New Grove Dictionary of Music*, Vol. 4 (London: Macmillan, 1980), 509.

37. Stone, *The London Stage*, 707.

38. *General History of Music*, 858.

39. *Public Advertiser*, no. 7642 (3 May 1759).

40. Michael F. Robinson, *Naples and Neapolitan Opera* (Oxford: Clarendon Press, 1972), 102.

41. Barbier, *World of the Castrati*, 69.

42. *London Chronicle, or Universal Evening Post*, no. 398 (14 July 1759).

43. Hagley Hall MSS, Lyttelton family papers, Worcester Record Office: George Lyttelton to William Lyttelton, fo. 41 (20 July 1759). This collection was unavailable, pending recataloguing at the time of publication. I am most grateful to Mr Michael Cousins of Hagley Hall in assisting me with a transcript.

44. The rarity of such cases is highlighted in Lawrence Stone, *The Road to Divorce: England 1530–1987* (Oxford: Oxford University Press, 1990), 301–46. In the late eighteenth century, the number of divorce bills rose, from 20 to 41 per decade (p. 325).

45. Ibid. 242.

46. Hagley Hall MSS, Lyttelton family papers, Worcester Record Office: George Lyttelton to William Lyttelton (20 July, 1759), fo. 41$^v$.

47. 'I think poor Lady Lyttelton's affair is in a manner settled.' Letter from Henry Conway to Horace Walpole (17 June 1759), in W. S. Lewis (ed.), *The Yale Edition of Horace Walpole's*

*Correspondence*, Vol. 38 (London and New Haven: Yale University Press, 1974), 14, n. 9.

48. Huntington Library, San Marino, California, Elizabeth Montagu Letters, MO1281, George Lyttelton to Elizabeth Montagu (10 Aug. 1759), fo. 2$^v$. My thanks to Gayle Richardson for assistance with this reference.

49. BL Add. MS 22130, Elizabeth Lyttelton to Mrs Payne (22 Mar. 1785), fo. 19.

50. Ibid. (8 July 1789), fo. 24$^v$.

51. See also Christine Gerrard, 'Lyttelton, George, first Baron Lyttelton (1709–1773)', *DNB*.

52. Michael Kelly, *Reminiscences of Michael Kelly of the King's Theatre and Theatre Royal Drury Lane*, 2nd edn., 2 vols. (London: Henry Colburn, 1826), Vol. I, p. 60.

53. *Public Advertiser*, no. 7870 (12 Feb. 1760).

54. *Public Ledger, or The Daily Register of Commerce and Intelligence*, no. 204 (5 Sept. 1760).

55. Daniel Defoe, *Essay Upon Projects* (London, 1697), 192–227.

56. *Public Advertiser*, no. 8173 (13 Jan. 1761).

57. *General History of Music*, 868.

58. See for example *Public Advertiser*, no. 7537 (3 Jan. 1759); no. 7914 (27 Mar. 1760); no. 8505 (5 Feb. 1762).

59. The account of Ranelagh is taken from N. Wroth, *London Pleasure Gardens of the Eighteenth Century* (London, 1896), 199–205.

60. Ibid.

61. See *Six New English Songs Composed by Ferdinando Tenducci and to be Sung by him at Ranelagh* (c.1763), Harding MUS. E474, Bodleian Library, Oxford.

62. See *London Magazine, or Gentleman's Monthly Intelligence*, no. 31 (Aug. 1762), 44; *Public Advertiser*, no. 8910 (26 May 1763).

63. *Public Advertiser*, no. 9198 (23 Apr. 1764). The expensive garments on sale at this shop were paid for in 'Ready Money' alone: an innovation in an era when many sales were made on a credit

basis, particularly when dealing with the gentry. See H. Berry, 'Polite consumption: shopping in eighteenth-century England', *Transactions of the Royal Historical Society*, 6th ser., Vol. 12 (2002), 375–94.

64. *The British Muse, Containing Original Poems, Songs &c.*, Vol. 33, no. 230 (Nov. 1763), 261.

65. Tobias Smollett, *The Expedition of Humphry Clinker* (1771), ed. Lewis M. Knapp (Oxford: Oxford University Press, 1966), 92.

66. *Gazetteer and London Daily Advertiser*, no. 11298 (30 May 1765).

67. *Public Advertiser*, no. 9245 (15 June 1764).

68. Keith Wrightson, 'Mutualities and obligations: changing social relationships in early modern England', *Proceedings of the British Academy*, 139 (Oxford: Oxford University Press, 2006), 186–7.

69. See *Public Advertiser*, no. 8875 (13 April 1763); no. 9140 (18 Feb. 1764).

70. A 'stone' was a colloquial term for a testicle. Such witticisms persisted for many years. See for example *Morning Post*, no. 8308 (17 Sept. 1783).

71. *Dramatic Magazine* (Oct. 1829), 244. The aria was 'Let not rage thy bosom firing'.

72. Brian Robins, *Catch and Glee Culture in Eighteenth-Century England* (Woodbridge: Boydell and Brewer, 2006) is the finest study to date of this aspect of provincial musical life.

73. Preface, Tenducci, *Six New English Songs* [n.p.].

74. John Kay, *A Series of Original Portraits and Character Etchings*, 2 vols. (Edinburgh: Birlinn Limited, 2007).

75. Todd Gilman, 'Arne, Handel, the beautiful and the sublime', *Eighteenth-Century Studies*, 42.4 (2009), 530.

76. For an account of the riot, see the *Gentleman's Magazine*, Vol. 33 (1763), 97; see also Frederic George Stephens, *Catalogue of Prints and Drawings in the British Museum: Personal and Political Satires*. Vol. IV: 1761–1770 (London, 1883), 228.

77. Ibid. 40, 228.

NOTES TO PP. 68–69

## Chapter Four. Fancying Tenducci

1. The emergence of a 'two-sex' theory of the body from a pre-modern 'one-sex' model with roots in classical antiquity was charted by Thomas Laqueur in his *Making Sex: Body and Gender from the Greeks to Freud* (Cambridge, Mass. and London: Harvard University Press, 1990). Though physiological understanding of the body evolved and changed over time, the superiority of male anatomy remained a remarkably durable hypothesis.

2. J. Cuthbert Hadden, *George Thompson, the Friend of Burns* (London, 1898), 20.

3. Ibid. 21.

4. Linda Kelly, *Susanna, the Captain and the Castrato: Scenes from the Burney Salon, 1779–80* (London: Starhaven, 2004), 34. See also Anita McConnell, 'Beckford, William Thomas (1760–1844)', *DNB*; William Beckford, *Vathek* (1786), ed. Roger Lonsdale (Oxford: Oxford University Press, 1998), 108–9 for the fictional transformation of Splendens into the Palace of Eblis, complete with unearthly music echoing around its 'vaulted and lofty rows of columns and arcades'.

5. A useful summary of the historical context in relation to same-sex relations is H. G. Cocks and Matt Houlbrook, 'Introduction', in idem (eds.), *The Modern History of Sexuality* (London: Palgrave Macmillan, 2006).

6. This tripartite system of orientation, identification, and behaviour is widely accepted in modern psychology, and is especially helpful in systematically analysing a historical person's sexuality, though the issue of whether it is correct to consider a category such as 'sexual orientation' in a pre-modern context is much debated. See Lisa M. Diamond, *Sexual Fluidity* (Cambridge, Mass.: Harvard University Press, 2008), 12–14 and *passim*.

7. *Trials for Adultery*, 20–1.

8. Elizabeth Foyster, *Manhood in Early Modern England: Honour, Sex and Marriage* (London: Longman, 1999), 42–3.

9. Ibid. 45.

10. Keith Thomas, *The Ends of Life: Roads to Fulfilment in Early Modern England* (Oxford: Oxford University Press, 2009), 160–86 on the importance of honour in establishing social reputation, 'an essential precondition of every one's fulfilment, for on it hinged personal identity and self-esteem'. Though equally important for both sexes, a woman's honour was based upon her chastity, a man's upon his creditworthiness.

11. Philip Carter, 'James Boswell's manliness', in T. Hitchcock and M. Cohen (eds.), *English Masculinities, 1660–1800* (London: Longman, 1999), 111.

12. Anthony Fletcher, *Gender, Sex and Subordination, 1500–1800* (New Haven and London: Yale University Press, 1995), 92; G. J. Barker-Benfield, *The Culture of Sensibility: Sex and Society in Eighteenth-Century Britain* (Chicago and London: Chicago University Press, 1992), 50.

13. David Hume, *Essays and Treatises on Several Subjects* (London, 1758), 'Of the Standard of Taste', 138. Hume's ideas echoed those of Joseph Addison and Richard Steele in *The Spectator*, and found poetic expression in the poetry of Mark Akenside.

14. Giusto Ferdinando Tenducci, *Amintas: An English Opera. As Performed at the Theatre-Royal, in Smock-Alley. The music Selected by Mr. Tenducci, from the Following Eminent and Favourite Composers, viz. Rauzzini, Glordani, Anfossi, Bach, Sacchini, Rameah, Alessandri, David Rizzo, Doctor Arnold, Rush, &c.* ... (Dublin, 1783), preface (n.p.). The *pasticcio*, of which this is an example, is discussed in Chapter 5.

15. *True and Genuine Narrative*, 59. See the ensuing chapters of this book for a full exploration of the circumstances of this comment.

16. Jacob Simon (ed.), *Handel: A Celebration of His Life and Times* (London: National Portrait Gallery, 1985), 82, shows a rotund Nicolini in a cartoon, one of 45 caricatures of opera singers from the early eighteenth century in a collection owned by Count Francesco Algarotti.

17. For a detailed summary of the physical effects of castration upon the human male, see Roger Freitas, 'The eroticism of emasculation: confronting the Baroque body of the castrato', *Journal of Musicology*, 20.2 (2003), 214, 226.

18. Elizabeth Harris to James Harris Jr. (29 Jan. 1771), in Donald Burrows and Rosemary Dunhill (eds.), *Music and Theatre in Handel's World: The Family Papers of James Harris, 1732–1780* (Oxford: Oxford University Press, 2002), 619.

19. A second portrait emerged at the sale of the private collection of Yves St Laurent and Pierre Berge at Christies in February 2009, where early owners were thought to include a Mr Broderip, Custodian of the Haymarket Theatre, and the English tenor John Braham. My thanks to Tim Hitchcock for alerting me to this sale.

20. A remarkable study of this subject is Colin Jones, 'Pulling teeth in eighteenth-century Paris', *Past & Present*, 166.1 (2000), 100–45.

21. See Martha Feldman, 'Strange births and surprising kin: the castrato's tale', in Paula Findlen, Wendy Wassyng Roworth, and Catherine M. Sama (eds.), *Italy's Eighteenth Century: Gender and Culture in the Age of the Grand Tour* (Stanford: Stanford University Press, 2009), 176–85, for a detailed and fascinating analysis of the complex intersections between animal similes applied to castrati and their linkage with images of displaced fertility—including cartoons of them as castrated roosters, born of hens laying castrato-producing eggs.

22. Tobias Smollett, *The Expedition of Humphry Clinker* (1771), ed. Lewis M. Knapp (Oxford: Oxford University Press, 1966), 92.

23. Fletcher, *Gender, Sex and Subordination*, 34–6.

NOTES TO PP. 74–77

24. Debates surrounding the shifting models of human anatomy and conception are explored in Roy Porter and Mikulas Teich, *Sexual Knowledge, Sexual Science: The History of Attitudes to Sexuality* (Cambridge: Cambridge University Press, 1994).

25. See Philip Carter, *Men and the Emergence of Polite Society, 1660–1800* (Harlow: Longman, 2001).

26. This highly convincing analysis is presented by Roger Frietas, 'Sex without sex: an erotic image of the castrato singer', in Findlen *et al.*, *Italy's Eighteenth Century*, 209. Frietas argues here and elsewhere that the essentially boyish characteristics of castrati appealed to a Renaissance aesthetic that still shaped responses to ideals of beauty among male and female audiences in this period.

27. Thomas, *The Ends of Life*, 44–77.

28. Lawrence Sterne, *The Life and Opinions of Tristram Shandy, Gentleman* (1759–67), ed. Graham Petrie (Harmondsworth: Penguin, 1967, repr. 1985), Vol. I, p. 91; Vol. V, chs. 17–27, pp. 369–77.

29. See Fletcher, *Gender, Sex and Subordination*.

30. The question of the relationship between the audience and the castrato on stage, and the gendered aspects of this dynamic, are explored more fully in Chapter 3.

31. Curtis Price, Judith Milhous, and Robert D. Hume, *The Impresario's Ten Commandments: Continental Recruitment for Italian Opera in London, 1763–64*, Royal Musical Association Monographs, No. 6 (London: Royal Musical Association, 1992), 10.

32. *The Winter's Amusement, Consisting of Favourite Songs and Cantatas . . . The Whole Composed by Thomas Arne* (n.d., 1762?). A rare copy of this collection of songs is in the Beinecke Library, Yale University.

33. *Queen Mary's Lamentation, As Sung by Mr. Tenducci at the Pantheon, London* (Dublin, n.d., 1773?).

34. The *Morning Chronicle* judged Mrs Mattocks to be a finer actor, although Tenducci was 'so capital a singer' (no. 1505, 21 Mar. 1774). Isabella Mattocks (née Hallam, 1746–1826) was related to

NOTES TO PP. 77-80

the Covent Garden impresario John Rich and had a long and
varied career, first as an actress, then as a singer. See Olive Baldwin
and Thelma Wilson, 'Mattocks, Isabella (1746–1826)', *DNB*.

35. *Public Advertiser*, no. 15453 (6 Dec. 1783).
36. I am grateful to Professor Susan Staves for a preview of her
    chapter, 'The learned female soprano', in Elizabeth Eger (ed.),
    *Bluestockings Displayed: Portraiture, Performance and Patronage,
    1730–1830* (Cambridge: Cambridge University Press, forthcom-
    ing, 2011).
37. *Gazzetta Toscana*, no. 6 (Feb. 1772), reported Tenducci's triumph,
    '*rappresenta il personnaggio di Motezuma [sic], Imperatore del
    Messico*' at the Teatro di Roma. See also Chapters 8 and 9 for
    Tenducci's later career.
38. Patrick Barbier, *The World of the Castrati: The History of an
    Operatic Phenomenon* (1989), trans. Margaret Crosland (London:
    Souvenier Press, 1996), 184.
39. See Eger, *Bluestockings Displayed*.
40. BL Egerton MS 3690, fo. 18, Letter to Fanny Burney from Sus-
    anna Burney (6 Nov. 1782).
41. Ibid.
42. Continental travel by women tended to be undertaken for different
    reasons, such as honeymooning or 'rest cures' in foreign spa towns,
    although the daughter or wife of a diplomat and art connoisseur,
    such as Emma, Lady Hamilton or Lady Lambton spent much time
    in Italy. Some, like the Northumberland gentlewoman Harriet
    Carr, became artists in their own right under the influence of Italian
    culture, although this was exceptional. For an excellent recent
    study, see Anne French, *Art Treasures in the North: Northern
    Families on the Grand Tour* (Norwich: Unicorn Press, 2009).
43. Barbier, *World of the Castrati*, 183.
44. Giacomo Casanova, Chevalier de Seingalt, *History of My Life*,
    trans. Willard R. Trask, Vol. 10 (Baltimore and London, 1997),
    12; Todd S. Gilman, 'The Italian (castrato) in London', in Richard

Dellaora and Daniel Fischlin (eds.), *The Work of Opera: Genre, Nationhood and Sexual Difference* (New York: Columbia University Press, 1997), 57.

45. John Dryden, *Poems of John Dryden*, ed. J. Kinsley (Oxford: Oxford University Press, 1958), Vol. 2, p. 708. The quotation could also be a *double entendre,* the 'kiss' standing for sexual intercourse. I am grateful to an anonymous reader for highlighting the complexity of this reference.

46. Keith Thomas, 'The double standard', *Journal of the History of Ideas*, 20 (1959), 195–216; see also Bernard Capp, 'The double standard revisited: plebeian women and male sexual reputation in early modern England', *Past & Present*, 162 (1999), 70–100.

47. Kelly, *Susanna, the Captain and the Castrato*, 78.

48. Jonathan Swift, *Gulliver's Travels* (1726), ed. Paul Turner (Oxford: Oxford University Press, 1986), 106–7. My thanks to Nigel Thornton for this parallel. While Roger Freitas's analogy for the castrato is a boy, locked into perpetual adolescent splendour, the doll is another metaphor for the castrato which usefully encapsulates how they were treated by eighteenth-century consumers, both male and female.

49. Elizabeth Eger and Lucy Peltz (eds.), *Brilliant Women: Eighteenth-Century Bluestockings* (London: National Portrait Gallery, 2008).

50. Quoted in Susan B. Lanser, 'Bluestocking Sapphism and the economies of desire', *Huntington Library Quarterly*, 65.1–2 (2002), 267, 271.

51. See Chapter 5 for an exploration of the influence of the novel upon the emotional lives of young girls in this period.

52. Kelly, *Susanna, the Captain and the Castrato*, 103–10 and *passim.*

53. Ibid. 71, 77, 102.

54. The growing interest in this subject among literary scholars and eighteenth-century historians was anticipated in an early study by Lilian Faderman, *Surpassing the Love of Men: Romantic Love and*

NOTES TO PP. 82–84

*Friendship between Women from the Renaissance to the Present* (New York: Morrow, 1981).

55. Gerhard Croll and Irene Brandenburg, 'Guadagni, Gaetano', in Grove Music Online. Oxford Music Online, http://www.oxford musiconline.com/subscriber/article/grove/music/11885 (accessed 22 Nov. 2010). The life-size marionettes in Guadagni's domestic performances re-enacted his most famous role as the hero Orpheus.

56. Annie Raine Ellis (ed.), *The Early Diary of Frances Burney, 1768–1778* (London: George Bell, 1907), Vol. II, pp. 122–3.

57. Ian Woodfield, *Opera and Drama in Eighteenth-Century London: The King's Theatre, Garrick, and the Business of Performance* (Cambridge: Cambridge University Press, 2001), 171–2. The satire was complicated by rivalry between Brooke and David Garrick, the leading actor of his generation, whose company was established at Drury Lane.

58. 'J. Democritus', and 'W. Diogenes' [Anon.], *The Remarkable Trial of the Queen of Quavers and Her Associates for Sorcery, Witchcraft and Enchantment at the Assizes held in the Moon, for the County of Gelding before the Rt. Hon. Sir Francis Lash, Lord Chief Baron of the Lunar Exchequer* (London, 1777/8?), 7.

59. Ibid. 9.

60. Woodfield, *Opera and Drama*, 172; the quintessential tourist narrative in this period by a German gentlewoman visiting London sights is Marie Sophie von La Roche, *Sophie in London, 1786*, trans. C. Williams (London: Cape, 1933).

61. Anon., *An Epistle to John James H[ei]dd[e]g[e]r Esq on the Report of Signor F[a]r[i]n[e]lli's being with Child* (1736), 4. Johann Jakob Heidegger (1666–1749) was a Swiss-born impresario who took a lead as a man of taste and business acumen who helped introduce Italian opera to large audiences in London. He was assistant manager at Drury Lane, collaborated with Handel, and was active in the Royal Academy of Music. Stanley Sadie (ed.), *The New Grove Dictionary of Music*, Vol. 8 (London: Macmillan, 1980), 433.

62. Ibid. See also Karen Harvey, *Reading Sex in the Eighteenth Century: Bodies and Gender in English Erotic Culture* (Cambridge: Cambridge University Press, 2005).

63. Anon., *The Secrets of a Woman's Heart. An Epistle from a Friend to Signor F[arine]lli. Occasion'd by the Epistle of Mrs. C[onstantia] P[hilli]ps, to the Angelick Signior F[arine]lli* (1735), 15.

64. Anon., *Do You Know What You are About? Or, a Protestant Alarm to Great Britain* (London, 1733), 16.

65. Ibid.

66. The second is Tenducci's letter to Mrs Conway, BL Add. MS 33965: see Chapter 9.

67. '...*che Tenducci non sa esprimere in Inglese.*' Burney family papers, Beinecke Library, Yale University, OSB MSS 3/Box 15/folder 1146, Letter to Charles Burney from Tenducci [n.d.].

68. *True and Genuine Narrative*, 50.

69. Ibid. 18.

70. Ibid. 21.

71. Bachelors only boasted about sex with women if they did not intend to marry them, while a married man's honour rested upon his wife's sexual reputation *not* being discussed in his community. See Foyster, *Manhood in Early Modern England*, 55–67.

72. Mary E. Fraudsen, '*Eunuchi conjugium:* the marriage of a castrato in early modern Germany', *Early Music History 24: Studies in Medieval and Early Modern Music*, ed. Iain Fenlon (Cambridge: Cambridge University Press, 2005), 67. Sorlisi's alter ego was a soldier, 'Titius', through whom he was able to articulate his experiences.

73. Burney family papers, Beinecke Library, Yale University, OSB MSS 3/Box 15/folder 1146. The seal survives intact on the letter from Tenducci to Charles Burney [n.d.].

## Chapter Five. A Dublin Scuffle

1. The character sketch here is drawn not only from the *True and Genuine Narrative*, which may not have been authored by Dorothea herself, but from the unconventional actions of Dorothea herself, her social background and birth-order, and the impression of those who met her in person later in life: see for example Louisa Harris's description of Dorothea's 'genteel' manner and singing 'exceedingly well', in Donald Burrows and Rosemary Dunhill (eds.), *Music and Theatre in Handel's World: The Family Papers of James Harris, 1732–1780* (Oxford: Oxford University Press, 2002), 602.

2. Thomas Arne, *Amintas, or The Royal Shepherd. An English Opera. As Perform'd at the Theatre-Royal in Covent-Garden* (London, 1764).

3. *Public Ledger*, no. 1762 (28 Aug. 1765).

4. Elizabeth Harris, writing from Whitehall to James Harris Jr. in Oxford (20 Oct. 1764), recorded in her letter that 'he [Tenducci] does not care to leave us'. The Harris family were involved in organizing the highly successful annual music festival, and were already well acquainted with Tenducci. In Burrows and Dunhill, *Music and Theatre in Handel's World*, 430.

5. John Watson, *Gentleman's and Citizen's Almanack* (Dublin, 1769), end pages list the 'Remarkable Events' cited here.

6. T. C. Barnard, 'Grand metropolis or "the anus of the world"? The cultural life of eighteenth-century Dublin', in Peter Clark and Raymond Gillespie (eds.), *Two Capitals: London and Dublin, 1500–1840, Proceedings of the British Academy*, 107 (Oxford: Oxford University Press, 2001); Vandra Costello, 'Recreation in Georgian Dublin', in Gillian O'Brien and Finola O'Kane (eds.), *Georgian Dublin* (Dublin: Four Courts, 2008).

7. See Máire Kennedy, 'Book mad: the sale of books by auction in eighteenth-century Dublin', *Dublin Historical Record*, 54.1 (2001),

48–71. See also Robin Myers, Michael Harris, and Giles Mandel-brote (eds.), *Under the Hammer: Book Auctions since the Seventeenth Century* (London: Oak Knoll and the British Library, 2001).

8. Colum Kenny, *King's Inns and the Kingdom of Ireland: The Irish 'Inn of Court', 1541–1800* (Dublin: Irish Academic Press, 1992), 173.

9. See W. H. Grattan Flood, 'Eighteenth-century Italians in Dublin', *Music and Letters*, 3.3 (1922), 274–8; see also T. J. Walsh, *Opera in Dublin, 1705–1797: The Social Scene* (Dublin: Allen Figgis, 1973).

10. Kenny, *King's Inns and the Kingdom of Ireland*, 174; Watson, *Gentleman's and Citizen's Almanack*, 53.

11. R. F. Foster, *Modern Ireland, 1600–1972* (Harmondsworth: Penguin, 1989), 185.

12. Tenducci's inspiration was Thomas Hull's adaptation and translation of Antonio Maria Lucchini's *libretto* for the opera *Farnace*, first performed in Bologna in 1731. Hull's adaptation was called *The Revenge of Athridates*, and had been performed at Drury Lane in London in 1765. It seems there was some working agreement between Hull and Tenducci for the latter to take the production to Dublin and (later) Edinburgh: see Thomas Hull, *Pharnaces: or, the revenge of Athridates. An English opera. As it was to have been performed at the Theatre-Royal, Edinburgh. The music selected . . . by Mr. Tenducci* (Edinburgh, 1769).

13. G. F. Tenducci, *The Revenge of Athridates. An English Opera. As Perform'd at the Theatre in Smock-Alley. The Music Selected from the Most capital Composers, and Adapted by Mr. Tenducci* (Dublin, 1765).

14. Robert B. Shoemaker, 'The decline of public insult in London: 1660–1800', *Past & Present*, 169 (2000), 97–131.

15. *Trials for Adultery*, 6.

16. Ibid. 8.

17. Edith Mary Johnston-Liik, *History of the Irish Parliament, 1692–1800. Vol. 5: Commons, Constituencies and Statutes* (Belfast: Ulster Historical Foundation, 2002), 119. Maunsell was born c.1705 and

died before 5 May 1778 (ibid.). Watson, *Gentleman's and Citizen's Almanack*, 53, lists Thomas Maunsell Esq. as King's Council in the Court of Exchequer, with chambers near Exchequer Court.

18. Johnston-Liik, *History of the Irish Parliament*, 217–18.

19. H. A. C. Sturgess, *Register of Admissions to the Honourable Society of the Middle Temple from the Fifteenth Century to the Year 1944* (London: Butterworth Press, 1949), Vol. I, p. 318.

20. Edward Keane, P. Beryly Phair, and Thomas U. Sadler (eds.), *The King's Inns Admission Papers, 1607–1867*, Irish Manuscripts Commission, Dublin (1982), pp. viii, 332; Kenny, *King's Inns and the Kingdom of Ireland*.

21. Ibid. 162.

22. Robert George Maunsell, *History of Maunsell, or Mansell* (Cork, 1903), 46–53.

23. Ibid. 49–50; Johnston-Liik, *History of the Irish Parliament*, 219.

24. *True and Genuine Narrative*, 1.

25. Many historians and literary scholars are now at pains to emphasize the difficulties over interpreting the 'truth' in so-called 'ego documents', not least when their authorship is in question, but even when an identified author purports to be giving a dispassionate account of events. For an authoritative exploration of these issues, see Natalie Zemon Davis, *Fiction in the Archives: Pardon Tales and their Tellers in Sixteenth-Century France* (Cambridge: Polity Press, 1987).

26. M. O. Grenby, 'The origins of children's literature', in M. O. Grenby and Andrea Immel (eds.), *The Cambridge Companion to Children's Literature* (Cambridge: Cambridge University Press, 2009), 3–18.

27. See for example *Public Advertiser*, no. 9942 (12 Sept. 1766); *St James's Chronicle, or the British Evening Post*, no. 879 (18 Oct. 1766); *Dublin Chronicle*, no. 1374 (1–3 Sept. 1766).

28. G. J. Barker-Benfield, *The Culture of Sensibility: Sex and Society in Eighteenth-Century Britain* (Chicago: University of Chicago Press, 1996), 164.

29. Richard Allestree, *The Ladies Calling* (London, 1673), quoted in Anthony Fletcher, *Gender, Sex and Subordination in England, 1500–1800* (New Haven and London: Yale University Press, 1995), 386.
30. Barker-Benfield, *Culture of Sensibility*, 162.
31. See Brean Hammond, *Professional Imaginative Writing in England, 1680–1740: 'Hackney for bread'* (Oxford: Oxford University Press, 1997).
32. Barker-Benfield, *Culture of Sensibility*, 169.
33. *Gazetteer and London Daily Advertiser*, no. 72119 (6 Jan. 1768).
34. The comparison of Dorothea's elopement with Lawrence Stone's theory of the rise of companionate marriage presented in his classic and controversial work *The Family, Sex and Marriage in England, 1500–1800* (Harmondsworth: Penguin, 1977) is tempting, although Stone's work has been largely dismissed by historians for (among other things) taking liberties with the evidence.
35. Fletcher, *Gender, Sex and Subordination*, 393–5.
36. *True and Genuine Narrative*, 66.
37. Ibid. 4.
38. Ibid.
39. These tensions had a long precedent, and are explored by Katharine Hodgkin in relation to one Elizabethan composer's diary: see 'Thomas Whythorne and the problem of mastery', *History Workshop Journal*, 29.1 (1990), 20–41.
40. Ibid.
41. *Wilson's Dublin Directory*, 21, lists Thomas Maunsell, barrister, as resident in 'York-street' in 1764 and 1765.
42. The Earl of Kildare was created Marquis in 1761 and Duke of Leinster in 1766. Originally Kildare House, Leinster House is now the home of the Irish parliament. Christine Casey, *The Buildings of Ireland: Dublin* (New Haven and London: Yale University Press, 2005), 498.
43. Charles Baroe recalled the detail of the coach trips to Molesworth Street. See *Trials for Adultery*, 11.

44. Mary Astell, *A Serious Proposal to the Ladies, for the Advancement of their True and Greatest Interest* (London, 1694), 11.
45. *True and Genuine Narrative*, 5.
46. *Trials for Adultery*, 23.
47. *True and Genuine Narrative*, 5.
48. *Trials for Adultery*, 11.
49. Ibid.
50. *True and Genuine Narrative*, 4. On Hester Thrale see Norma Clarke, *Dr. Johnson's Women* (London: Hambledon, 2000), ch. 4.
51. *True and Genuine Narrative*, 24, 'Letter from North Goal' (2 Sept. 1766). The lack of survival of the *Cork Evening Post* for 1766 (verified in *NEWSPLAN–Report of the Newsplan Project in Ireland*, ed. James O'Toole, rev. edn. Sara Smyth, London and Dublin, 1998) makes it impossible to verify the original form in which this letter was printed.
52. *Trials for Adultery*, 24.
53. *True and Genuine Narrative*, 6.
54. Keith Wrightson, *English Society, 1580–1680* (London: Hutchinson, 1982, repr. Routledge, 1990), 72.
55. Ingrid Tague, 'Aristocratic women and ideas of family in the early eighteenth century', in H. Berry and E. Foyster (eds.), *The Family in Early Modern England* (Cambridge: Cambridge University Press, 2007), 184–208.
56. *True and Genuine Narrative*, 5.
57. Ibid. 6.

## Chapter Six. The Elopement

1. *True and Genuine Narrative*, 6.
2. Ibid.
3. LMA/DL/C/558/20/fos. 7–8, 'Sayings and depositions' presented to the Lord Bishop of Cork and Ross in the case of 'Kingsman,

falsely called Tenducci v. Tenducci'. Deposition of Mary Holland (taken 30 Oct. 1775, brought in to the London Consistory Court, 28 Feb. 1776).

4. Ibid.
5. Ibid.
6. *Trials for Adultery*, 29.
7. Rebecca Probert, *Marriage Law and Practice in the Long Eighteenth Century: A Reassessment* (Cambridge: Cambridge University Press, 2009), 138–9.
8. Ibid.
9. Edith Mary Johnston-Liik, *History of the Irish Parliament, 1692–1800. Vol. 5: Commons, Constituencies and Statutes* (Belfast: Ulster Historical Foundation, 2002), 117–19.
10. T. C. Barnard, *The Abduction of a Limerick Heiress: Social and Political Relations in Mid-Eighteenth Century Ireland*, Maynooth Studies in Local History, no. 20 (1998), 11–12.
11. R. G. Maunsell, *History of Maunsell, or Mansell* (Cork, 1903), 39–53.
12. *True and Genuine Narrative*, 11.
13. Ibid. 8–10.
14. Ibid. 11.
15. *Trials for Adultery*, 27.
16. Ibid. 28.
17. Ibid.
18. *True and Genuine Narrative*, 12.
19. Ibid.
20. *Trials for Adultery*, 30.
21. *True and Genuine Narrative*, 14.
22. Ibid.
23. Ibid. 16.
24. *Trials for Adultery*, 30.
25. For use of *habeas corpus* to regain possession of runaway wives, see Lawrence Stone, *Road to Divorce: England 1530–1987*

(Oxford and New York: Oxford University Press, 1992), 165–6. Maunsell's attempted use of *habeas corpus* here as a father claiming right of possession over custody of his daughter reflects his lack of recognition of the legitimacy of her marriage.

26. *True and Genuine Narrative*, 17–18. On clandestine marriage see R. B. Outhwaite, *Clandestine Marriage in England, 1500–1850* (London: Hambledon, 1995).

27. Dorothea must have been familiar with Shakespeare's play: she mentions the advertisement of a production of *The Merchant of Venice* for Tenducci's benefit in Cork. See *True and Genuine Narrative*, 28.

28. *True and Genuine Narrative*, 17.

29. Ibid. 26.

30. Ibid. 20.

31. The dilemmas of patriarchy in the face of female intransigence, among many other aspects of gender relations at this time, are explored in Amanda Vickery, *The Gentleman's Daughter: Women's Lives in Georgian England* (New Haven and London: Yale University Press, 1998), 49 and *passim*.

32. *True and Genuine Narrative*, 19–21.

33. *Dublin Mercury*, no. 51 (2–6 Sept. 1766).

34. *Dublin Courant*, no. 1374 (1–3 Sept. 1766).

35. *Dublin Mercury*, no. 51 (2–6 Sept. 1766).

36. *Public Advertiser* (London), nos. 9442, 9944 (12–13 Sept. 1766); *St James's Chronicle, or the British Evening Post*, no. 879 (18 Oct. 1766). 'Friends' meant anyone who had a stake in her interests, blood-relatives as well as friends in the modern sense: see N. Tadmor, 'The concept of the household-family in eighteenth-century England', *Past & Present*, 151 (1996), 111–40.

37. *True and Genuine Narrative*, 48.

38. *Dublin Courant*, no. 1377 (8–18 Sept. 1766).

39. Hannah Barker, *Newspaper, Politics and Public Opinion in Late-Eighteenth Century England* (Oxford: Clarendon Press, 1998); see

also Victoria Gardner, 'Newspaper proprietors and the business of newspaper publishing in provincial England, 1760–1820', unpublished D.Phil. thesis (University of Oxford, 2008); and Vic Gatrell, *City of Laughter: Sex and Satire in Eighteenth-Century London* (London: Atlantic, 2006) for the connections between politics, sex, satire, and reputation in popular prints of the period.

40. I am much indebted to the work of Professor Barnard in the contextual detail about Dorothea's 'abduction' that follows, and the social milieu of the Maunsells.

41. Barnard, *Abduction of a Limerick Heiress*, 9.

42. Ibid.

43. Ibid. 12.

44. Ibid. 21.

45. *True and Genuine Narrative*, 32; *Trials for Adultery*, 34.

46. *True and Genuine Narrative*, 32–3.

47. Elizabeth Foyster, *Marital Violence: An English Family History, 1660–1857* (Cambridge: Cambridge University Press, 2005), 28.

48. Stone, *Road to Divorce*, 167–8.

49. *True and Genuine Narrative*, 35.

50. Ibid. 36. It is possible to make a satirical interpretation of Dorothea's list of her so-called 'deprivations' in the clothing department. For example, the colour of the worsted stockings was italicized for emphasis (unfashionable '*black*') and she lists seven shifts as a deprivation, where most working people made do with one. Dorothea could have been satirizing the fact that her parents' efforts to make her suffer were in retrospect trivial hardships. Or this could be taken as evidence that the author was not really Dorothea, but someone satirizing the fashion obsessions of a young girl. Ultimately, it is for the individual reader to decide, as would have been the case in the eighteenth century. See John Styles, *The Dress of the People: Everyday Fashion in Eighteenth-Century England* (New Haven and London: Yale University Press, 2007).

51. *True and Genuine Narrative*, 41.

52. Other types of print culture in this period played upon a similar fascination with 'low life'. See for example Helen Berry, 'Rethinking politeness in eighteenth-century England: Moll King's coffee house and the significance of "flash talk"', *Transactions of the Royal Historical Society*, 6th ser., 11 (2001), 65–81.

53. *True and Genuine Narrative*, 43.

54. Ibid. 43, 47. For an excellent analysis of Cleland's work and the genre from which it emerged, see Karen Harvey, *Reading Sex in the Eighteenth Century: Bodies and Gender in English Erotic Culture* (Cambridge: Cambridge University Press, 2005), 24 and *passim*.

55. *True and Genuine Narrative*, 60.

56. As readers of *Pamela* and *Clarissa* would have been only too aware, since the plots in both novels hinge on the consequences of attempted, and actual, rape. See Gregory Durston, 'Rape in the eighteenth-century metropolis', *British Journal for Eighteenth-Century Studies*, part 1, 28.2 (2005), 167–79; part 2, 29.1 (2006), 15–31.

57. The *Old Bailey Proceedings Online* (www.oldbaileyonline.org, 3 July 2010), contains over two thousand rape cases: see for example Richard Green, prosecuted on 10 May 1769, for the rape of his neighbour's servant, 19-year old Elizabeth Jervis (t17690510-15). See also Miranda Chaytor, 'Husband(ry): narratives of rape in the eighteenth century', *Gender and History*, 7.3 (1995), 378–407.

58. *True and Genuine Narrative*, 44.

59. Ibid. 48.

60. Ibid. 52.

61. Ibid. 57.

62. The details of this were repeated in a letter purportedly by Tenducci to Dorothea's father, ibid. 58–60. Whether the letter was

genuine is uncertain, but the main representation of the humiliation that Dorothea had suffered is contained within these pages.

63. Ibid. 58.
64. Ibid. 68.
65. *London Evening Post*, no. 6842 (11 July 1767).
66. LMA/DL/C/557/102/1/Exhibit A, fo. 1, copy of an extract from the registry of the Consistory Court of the Diocese of Waterford and Lismore (1775). Confirmed in the deposition of Thomas Maunsell, *Trials for Adultery*, 30.
67. *True and Genuine Narrative*, 68. The postscript is dated 'Clogheen, Sept. 21, 1767'.
68. LMA/DL/C/557/102/1/Exhibit A, fo. 1.
69. Ibid.; see also *True and Genuine Narrative*, 29.

## Chapter Seven. Married Life

1. These principles had a long lineage: see Diana O'Hara, *Courtship and Constraint: Rethinking the Making of Marriage in Tudor and Stuart England* (Manchester: Manchester University Press, 2000).
2. LMA/DL/C/557/102/2 (1775), fo. 1.
3. Keith Thomas, 'The double standard', *Journal of the History of Ideas*, 20 (1959), 198–9.
4. Ibid.
5. *St James's Chronicle, or the British Evening Post*, no. 879 (18 Oct. 1766).
6. *Dublin Mercury*, no. 53 (9–13 Sept. 1766).
7. *Public Advertiser*, no. 9942 (12 Sept. 1766).
8. *True and Genuine Narrative*, 20.
9. See Laura Gowing, *Common Bodies: Women, Touch and Power in Seventeenth-Century England* (New Haven and London: Yale University Press, 2003), *passim*.
10. *Trials for Adultery*, 27.

11. The classic work on this subject is Martin Ingram, *Church Courts, Sex and Marriage in England, 1570–1640* (Cambridge: Cambridge University Press, 1987).

12. Rebecca Probert, *Marriage Law and Practice in the Long Eighteenth Century: A Reassessment* (Cambridge: Cambridge University Press, 2009), 34.

13. See Roy Porter and Lesley Hall, *The Facts of Life: The Creation of Sexual Knowledge in Britain, 1650–1950* (New Haven and London: Yale University Press, 1995). Letters sent to early periodical newspapers from this period ask about the fundamentals of sex and reproduction, suggesting a widespread curiosity and lack of information on the subject, unsurprising in an era when medical science had not resolved the function of sperm and egg. See Helen Berry, *Gender, Society and Print Culture in Late-Stuart England* (Aldershot: Ashgate, 2003), ch. 5.

14. *Monthly Review*, no. 38 (Jan. 1768), 63.

15. Ibid.

16. Anthony Fletcher, *Gender, Sex and Subordination: 1500–1800* (New Haven and London: Yale University Press, 1995), 76–7.

17. See ibid. 291–2 on the implications of anatomist Thomas Willis's research on the brain and nervous system.

18. See Janet Todd, *Mary Wollstonecraft: A Revolutionary Life* (London: Weidenfeld and Nicolson, 2000), 180.

19. Ibid. See particularly pp. 169–87 for a summary of these debates. Wollstonecraft's own relationship with William Godwin, whom she married, was a famously companionate one.

20. *Critical Review, or, Annals of Literature*, no. 26 (Oct. 1768), 317.

21. Juvenal, *The Satires*, 6.366–79, trans. Niall Rudd (Oxford: Clarendon Press, 1991).

22. Ibid.

23. William Wycherley, *The Country Wife* (1675), ed. John Dixon Hunt (London, A. & C. Black, 1972), Act I, scene 1, pp. 8–9 and *passim*.

24. *True and Genuine Narrative*, 65–6.

NOTES TO PP. 137–141

25. *St James's Chronicle, or the British Evening Post*, no. 879 (18 Oct. 1766).

26. Mary E. Fraudsen, '*Eunuchi conjugium*: the marriage of a castrato in early modern Germany', *Early Music History*, 24 (2005), 64.

27. See Paul Baines and Pat Rogers, *Edmund Curll, Bookseller* (Oxford: Clarendon Press, 2007), 114, 117.

28. Anon. [Charles Ancillon], *Eunuchism Display'd. Describing all the Different Sorts of Eunuchs; the Esteem They Have Met With in the World, and How They Came to be Made So* (London, 1718), p. ix.

29. Ibid., p. xi.

30. For a discussion of eighteenth-century controversies surrounding the *Priapeia*, see Jason M. Kelly, *The Society of Dilettanti: Archaeology and Identity in the British Enlightenment* (New Haven and London: Paul Mellon Centre for Studies in British Art, Yale University Press, 2009), 243–58. The Dilettanti book of the same name, translated as the *Worship of Priapus*, caused a sensation that reverberated in élite circles during the late-eighteenth century.

31. Baines and Rogers, *Edmund Curll*, 114–15.

32. *Eunuchism Display'd*, p. xviii.

33. See Karen Harvey, 'The history of masculinity, *circa* 1650–1800', *Journal of British Studies*, 44.2 (2005), 296–311.

34. Lawrence Stone, *The Road to Divorce: England 1530–1987* (Oxford: Oxford University Press, 1990), *passim*.

35. *Eunuchism Display'd*, p. xiv.

36. Ibid., p. xv.

37. Ibid. 214–18.

38. The Reformation had made some allowances for marriages that would not lead to children: the Book of Common Prayer had a form of wording for a marriage ceremony in circumstances where the bride was beyond childbearing age. There is also evidence that having *too many* children was frowned upon in northern Europe, unless a couple could support them. For a discussion of these issues, see Helen Berry and Elizabeth Foyster, 'Childless men in early

modern England' in eadem (eds.), *The Family in Early Modern England* (Cambridge: Cambridge University Press, 2007), *passim.*

39. *Eunuchism Display'd*, pp. xiv and 232–5.
40. Berry and Foyster, 'Childless men', 163–79.
41. James A. Brundage, *Law, Sex and Christian Society in Medieval Europe* (Chicago and London: University of Chicago Press, 1987), 37.
42. Ibid., 144–55, 163–4.
43. For an exploration of gender, rhetoric, and shifting political circumstances, particularly revolution, see Michèle Cohen, 'Manliness, effeminacy and the French: gender and the construction of national character in eighteenth-century England', in Tim Hitchcock and Michèle Cohen (eds.), *English Masculinities, 1660–1800* (London: Longman, 1999).
44. See R. I. Moore, *The Formation of a Persecuting Society: Power and Deviance in Western Europe, 950–1250* (Oxford: Blackwell, 1987). Professor Moore charts the definition and persecution of minorities as a necessary part of the process of state formation and the exercise of power by ruling élites. See also the influential work of John Boswell on the history of Christianity and homosexuality, explored in Mathew Kuefler (ed.), *The Boswell Thesis: Essays on Christianity, Social Tolerance and Homosexuality* (Chicago and London: University of Chicago Press, 2006).
45. R. H. Helmholz, *Roman Canon Law in Reformation England* (Cambridge: Cambridge University Press, 1990), 69–77.
46. Ibid. 74.
47. See Jacqueline Murray, 'On the origins and role of wise women in causes for annulment on the grounds of male impotence', *Journal of Medieval History*, 16.3 (1990), 235–49; a comparative study is Pierre Darmon, *Damning the Innocent: A History of the Persecution of the Impotent in Pre-Revolutionary France* (New York: Viking Press, 1986).

48. Roger Freitas, 'The eroticism of emasculation: confronting the Baroque body of the castrato', *Journal of Musicology*, 20.2 (2003), 223–33.

49. See Patricia Crawford and Sara Mendelson, 'Sexual identities in early modern England: the marriage of two women in 1680', *Gender and History*, 7.3 (1995), 362–77.

50. Edward Behrend-Martínez, *Unfit for Marriage: Impotent Spouses on Trial in the Basque Region of Spain, 1650–1750* (Reno and Las Vegas: University of Nevada Press, 2007), 126.

51. Karen Harvey, *Reading Sex in the Eighteenth Century* (Cambridge: Cambridge University Press, 2004), 134, 139–45.

52. *General History of Music*, 528.

53. R. B. Outhwaite, *The Rise and Fall of the English Ecclesiastical Courts, 1500–1860* (Cambridge: Cambridge University Press, 2006), 50–1 and *passim*.

54. For an example of the distinctive honour code of the social élite see Donna Andrew, 'The code of honour and its critics: the opposition to duelling in England, 1700–1850', *Social History*, 5 (1980), 409–34.

55. *Trials for Adultery*, 22.

56. Ibid. 13.

57. *St James's Chronicle*, no. 1029 (3 Oct. 1767). Signora Cremonini had arrived in Edinburgh, most probably from Naples, in the early 1760s and commanded large fees upward of £150. Like Tenducci, she had persistent problems with defaulting on debts and unfulfilled contracts. See Jennifer Macleod, 'The Edinburgh Musical Society: its membership and repertoire, 1728–1797', unpublished Ph.D. thesis (University of Edinburgh, 2001), 164–5.

58. Valentine Green, *The History and Antiquities of the City and Suburbs of Worcester*, Vol. 2 (London, 1796), 76, n. 1.

59. This is inferred from an entry in the *Public Advertiser*, no. 10938 (21 Nov. 1769), in which 'Mr. Tenducci, being returned to London, and it being his Intention to pay every Person to whom he is

in debted as soon as he is able', desired 'all Persons would send in an Account of their Demands' to his rather swanky new address: 'No. 35, in New Bond-street'.

60. See James Mackay, *Burns: A Biography* (Darvel: Alloway Publishing, 2004), 66–8.

61. Ibid. 72.

62. *Edinburgh Advertiser*, no. 462 (31 May–3 June 1768), 357; no. 463 (3–7 June 1768), 363; no. 465 (10–14 June 1768), 381; no. 470 (28 June–1 July 1768), 5.

63. Claire Nelson, 'Tea-table miscellanies: the development of Scotland's song culture, 1720–1800', *Early Music*, 28.4 (2000), 597.

64. *Public Advertiser*, no. 10468 (21 May 1768).

65. For an excellent history of the Society, see Macleod, 'Edinburgh Musical Society'.

66. 'A list of the members of the musical society at Edinburgh, 1767', National Library of Scotland, APS.1.80.40 [n.p.].

67. Macleod, 'Edinburgh Musical Society', 169.

68. A recent study is Daniel Szechi, *1715: The Great Jacobite Rebellion* (New Haven and London: Yale University Press, 2006); see also Christopher A. Whatley, *Scottish Society 1707–1830: Beyond Jacobitism, Towards Industrialization* (Manchester: Manchester University Press, 2000).

69. Nelson, 'Tea-table miscellanies', 597–603.

70. J. Cuthbert Hadden, *George Thomson, the Friend of Burns* (London, 1898), 20–1.

71. Macleod, 'Edinburgh Musical Society', 169.

72. Ibid. 53.

73. John Kay, *A Series of Original Portraits and Character Etchings, Vol. II*, introd. Alan Bell (Edinburgh: Birlinn Ltd, 2007), 92–3.

74. Ibid. 93.

75. Olive Baldwin and Thelma Wilson, 'Tenducci, Giusto Ferdinando (*c.*1735–1790)', *DNB*.

76. *Gazetteer and London Daily Advertiser*, no. 12724 (12 Dec. 1769).

77. *Lloyd's Evening Post and British Chronicle*, no. 1942 (13 Dec. 1769).
78. *St James's Chronicle*, no. 1374 (14 Dec. 1769). The affidavit has not been traced.
79. See R. H. Helmholz, 'Bastardy litigation in Medieval England', *American Journal of Legal History*, 13.4 (1969), 360–83, esp. 370.
80. Farinelli's brother Ricardo, as has already been noted, was the biological father of the children belonging to Farinelli's mistress, who were his designated heirs. See Martha Feldman, 'Strange births and surprising kin: the castrato's tale', in Paula Findlen, Wendy Wassyng Roworth, and Catherine M. Sama (eds.), *Italy's Eighteenth Century: Gender and Culture in the Age of the Grand Tour* (Stanford: Stanford University Press, 2009), 188–90.
81. *Trials for Adultery*, 13–14.
82. *Gazetteer and London Daily Advertiser*, no. 12842 (28 Apr. 1770).
83. Ibid., no. 12845 (2 May 1770).
84. Ibid., no. 12855 (14 May 1770). J. C. Bach was the same age as Tenducci (also born in 1735) and was the youngest of Johann Sebastian Bach's eighteen children (most of whom died in infancy). He was court musician to Queen Charlotte between 1763 and 1782. Carl Friedrich Abel had been a pupil of J. S. Bach and was practised in the 'mellifluous Italian' style of playing the viola da gamba. See Heinz Gärtner, *Johann Christian Bach: Mozart's Friend and Mentor*, trans. Reinhard G. Pauly (Portland: Amadeus Press, 1994), 39–40 and *passim*.
85. *Lloyd's Evening Post and British Chronicle*, no. 1982 (16 Mar. 1770).
86. *London Evening Post*, no. 6677 (28 Aug. 1770); *Public Advertiser*, no. 11122 (30 Aug. 1770).
87. *General Evening Post*, no. 5756 (30 Aug. 1770).
88. Elizabeth Harris to James Harris Jr. (22 Sept. 1770), in Donald Burrows and Rosemary Dunhill (eds.), *Music and Theatre in Handel's World: The Family Papers of James Harris, 1732–1780* (Oxford: Oxford University Press, 2002), 601.

89. Rosemary Dunhill, 'Harris, James (1709–1780)', *DNB*.
90. Burrows and Dunhill, *Music and Theatre*, 393.
91. Louisa Harris to James Harris Jr. (26–27 Sept. 1770), ibid. 602.
92. Ibid.
93. Elizabeth Harris to James Harris Jr. (30 Sept. 1770), ibid. 602–3.
94. Elizabeth Harris to James Harris Jr. (6 Oct. 1770), ibid. 603–4.
95. Elizabeth Harris to James Harris Jr. (24 Oct. 1770), ibid. 605.
96. The harrowing domestic incarceration of Anne Dormer at Rousham is one extreme example of the power that a paranoid husband could exert over his wife if he merely suspected she was unfaithful. See Amanda Vickery, *Behind Closed Doors: At Home in Georgian England* (New Haven and London: Yale University Press, 2009), 194–6.
97. Lady Catherine de Bourgh was of course one of the most memorable fictional characters of Jane Austen in *Pride and Prejudice* (1813).
98. Huntington Library, San Marino, California/John Marsh Diaries/ HM54457, Vol. 3 (Mar. 1770), fos. 9–11.
99. Ibid. See also Helen Berry, 'Sense and singularity: the social experiences of John Marsh and Thomas Stutterd in late-Georgian England', in Jonathan Barry and H. R. French (eds.), *Social Identity, Class and Status, England c.1500–1800* (London: Palgrave, 2005).
100. *Trials for Adultery*, 19.
101. Ibid. 21–2.
102. Giacomo Casanova, *History of My Life*, trans. Willard R. Trask (Baltimore: Johns Hopkins Press, 1970), Vol. 10, p. 12. The commentary on Tenducci in this (sole) translation is riddled with errors: Trask dates this meeting to 1764, which would have been impossible since Tenducci had not met Dorothea at that time.
103. On intersex people known formerly as 'hermaphrodites', and the 'one-sex' body, see *Herculine Barbin: Being the Recently Discovered Memoirs of a Nineteenth-Century French Hermaphrodite*, introd. Michel Foucault, trans. Richard McDougall (New York:

Pantheon Books, 1980); Thomas Laqueur, *Making Sex: Body and Gender from the Greeks to Freud* (Cambridge, Mass. and London: Harvard University Press, 1990).

104. *Public Advertiser*, no. 11231 (3 Nov. 1770).

105. Ibid., no. 11257 (8 Dec. 1770).

106. Burrows and Dunhill, *Music and Theatre*, 625, note.

107. *Gazetteer and London Daily Advertiser*, no. 13082 (2 Feb. 1771). This was an early attempt at adapting Voltaire's *Semiramis* for the operatic stage: a more famous later adaptation was by Rossini.

108. Quoted in Burrows and Dunhill, *Music and Theatre*, 625, note.

109. Macleod, 'Edinburgh Musical Society', 170.

110. Ibid.

111. Giusto Ferdinando Tenducci, 'Preface', to *Orpheus and Eurydice: a Musical Drama* (London, 1785), 3.

## Chapter Eight. The Trial

1. *General History of Music*, 497.

2. W. S. Lewis *et al.* (eds.), *Horace Walpole's Correspondence with Sir Horace Mann* (New Haven and London: Yale University Press, 1967), Vol. 7, p. 353 (29 Nov. 1771). Walpole, writing to Lord Hertford, had described Tenducci (surely mistakenly) as only a 'moderate tenor' when he heard him in a performance of the *pasticcio Ezio* at the Haymarket Theatre in 1764. See ibid., Vol. 38 (25 Nov. 1764), 466–7.

3. *Trials for Adultery*, 16–17.

4. Ibid. Baroe recalled that he had visited the Tenduccis at a country house outside Florence.

5. This production was later taken to London: see 'Preface' to *Orpheus and Eurydice, a Musical Drama . . . as Performed at the King's Theatre in the Haymarket* (London, 1785), in which Tenducci recalled that 'I have resolved humbly to present to [the public] . . . that same

Orpheus, which was so much applauded at Florence, by persons of the first rank, and of the purest and most refined taste in music', p. 4. Retrospectively, critics have condemned the 'watering-down' of Gluck's original opera in *pasticcio* style. Tenducci has received particular blame for this, although Georgian audiences expected nothing less. The interjection of pieces by Handel, for example, would seem especially peculiar to the modern opera-goer, but surely not to many contemporaries, who would have considered them to have been an especial treat. See Patricia Howard, *C. W. von Gluck, Orpheo* (Cambridge: Cambridge University Press, 1981), 62–5.

6. G. F. Tenducci, 'Preface', *Orpheus and Eurydice*, 3.
7. Martha Feldman, 'Denaturing the castrato', *Opera Quarterly*, 24.3–4 (2009), 186–90. Professor Feldman describes the 'line in the sand' (p. 189) that emerged after the castrato Guadagni's 1762 performance of Gluck's *Orpheo*, between an expressive and lyrical (new) style of opera, pioneered by Gluck, and the older 'flamboyant' line favoured by castrati such as Rauzzini. Tenducci's style belonged to the Guadagni/Gluck side of this divide.
8. The legend of Orpheus and Eurydice had been perennially popular as an operatic theme since the earliest production by Monteverdi. Writing in collaboration with Gluck, the librettist Calzabigi's innovation was to highlight the human tragedy of the story: '[Orpheus] is, above all, a husband'. See Howard, *Orpheo*, 39.
9. *Trials for Adultery*, 15–16.
10. *General Evening Post*, no. 5943 (14 Nov. 1771).
11. *Trials for Adultery*, 16.
12. See start of Chapter 7 for a discussion of Dorothea's age. She was about 19 years old when she left Tenducci in November 1771.
13. *Gazzetta Toscana*, no. 43 (24 Oct. 1772), 174.
14. William Long Kingsman was admitted on 2 November 1762, *Records of Lincoln's Inn* (Lincoln's Inn, London, 1896), Vol. 1.2, *Admissions, 1420–1799*, 453.

15. Edith Mary Johnston-Liik, *History of the Irish Parliament, 1692–1800: Commons, Constituencies and Statutes* (Belfast: Ulster Historical Foundation, 2002), Vol. 5, p. 35.

16. LMA/DL/C/177, Allegations, Libels and Sentences Book (24 May 1775), Kingsman formerly Maunsell, falsely called Tenducci, fo. 355ᵛ.

17. Ibid.; TNA/PCC/Prob. 11/969 Will of Robert Long (proved 11 July 1771), fos. 253–58. See also John Roque's survey of London, completed and indexed in 1747. Reproduced as *The A to Z of Georgian London*, with introductory notes by Ralph Hyde (London: Harry Margary in association with Guildhall Library, 1981), plate 1.

18. See D. Weir, 'Rather never than late: celibacy and age at marriage in England. Cohort fertility, 1541–1871', *Journal of Family History*, 9 (1984), 340–54.

19. See Will Coster, *Baptism and Spiritual Kinship in Early Modern England* (Aldershot: Ashgate, 2002), 222–45; *Records of Lincoln's Inn*, 453.

20. LMA/DL/C/177, Allegations, Libels and Sentences Book (24 May 1775), Kingsman formerly Maunsell, falsely called Tenducci, fo. 355ᵛ, item 13.

21. TNA/PCC/Prob. 11/969, Will of Robert Long (proved 11 July 1771), fo. 258. Long's will was complicated by three codicils and the naming of other executors and beneficiaries. William Long Kingsman may also have exaggerated his actual income from his uncle's legacy.

22. Ibid., fos. 253–5. See also Patricia Crawford, *Blood, Bodies and Families in Early Modern England* (Harlow: Longman, 2004).

23. The voting qualification was hugely complex in this period and varied according to place of residence, but the most common requirement for a male householder was that he should have an income of forty shillings or more from freehold property.

24. The definition of gentility was famously undergoing a transformation in the eighteenth century, with upwardly mobile tailors and shopkeepers styling themselves 'gentlemen'. Land ownership was still a critical marker of status, however. See Felicity Heal and Clive Holmes, *The Gentry in England and Wales, 1500–1700* (Basingstoke: Macmillan, 1994).

25. The concert given by *'Sig[nor] Kingsman Cavaliere Inglese'* featured the oboist Antonio Domenichini and violinist Francisco Piantanida, and was conducted by Antonio Mosel. *Gazzetta Toscana*, no. 43 (24 Oct. 1772), 174.

26. The character of this musical expatriate community is sketched in Elizabeth Gibson, 'Earl Cowper in Florence and his correspondence with the Italian opera in London', *Music and Letters*, 68.3 (1987), 235–52.

27. The legitimation of children born before their parents married was possible in canon law, but not common law. The very particular set of circumstances presented here had to be resolved in Doctors' Commons (see the remainder of this chapter). Rebecca Probert, *Marriage Law and Practice in the Long Eighteenth Century: A Reassessment* (Cambridge: Cambridge University Press, 2009), 44–5.

28. *Trials for Adultery*, 32–3.

29. As documented in LMA/DL/C/557/102/2, Exhibit B (17 Sept. 1775), fo. 1, 'Extracted from the Registry of the Office of Faculties belonging to his Grace the Lord Archbishop of Canterbury'.

30. Ibid.

31. John H. Chapman (ed.), *The Register Book of Marriages Belonging to the Parish of St. George Hanover Square in the County of Middlesex. Vol. I: 1725–1787* (London, 1886), 233.

32. *General History of Music*, 704.

33. Ibid. See also LMA/DL/C/557/102/2, Exhibit B (17 Sept. 1775), fo. 1.

34. R. B. Outhwaite, *The Rise and Fall of the English Ecclesiastical Courts, 1500–1860* (Cambridge: Cambridge University Press, 2006), 55.

35. LMA/DL/C/557/102/2, Exhibit B (17 Sept. 1775), fo. 1.

36. David M. Turner, 'Popular marriage and the law: tales of bigamy at the eighteenth-century Old Bailey', *London Journal*, 30.1 (2005), 6–21.

37. Outhwaite, *Rise and Fall*, 48–9.

38. Heather Smith, 'Women and marriage in the eighteenth century: evidence from the London church courts, 1730–1780', unpublished Ph.D. thesis (University of Bristol, 2000), Appendix 3, p. 218. Eighty-two separation cases were heard in the London Consistory Court between 1770 and 1779; see ibid. 219.

39. Further research on this subject is being conducted by Daphna Oren-Magidor at Brown University. Barbara Chubak gathered together thirty-two cases to analyse the symptoms presented in the cases from a modern medical perspective. See her 'Impotence and suing for sex in eighteenth-century England', *Urology*, 71.3 (2008), 480–4.

40. LMA/DL/C/177, Allegations, Libels and Sentences Book (24 May 1775), Kingsman formerly Maunsell, falsely called Tenducci, fos. 351$^r$–357$^v$. The London Consistory Court, together with the Court of Arches, were commonly known as 'Doctors' Commons', the location of hearings in the city of London. Lawrence Stone, *The Road to Divorce: England 1530–1987* (Oxford: Oxford University Press, 1990), 44.

41. LMA/DL/C/557/102/4, Exhibits A to D.

42. LMA/DL/C/177, Allegations, Libels and Sentences Book (24 May 1775), Kingsman formerly Maunsell, falsely called Tenducci, fo. 351$^r$.

43. Ibid.

44. The increasing social élitism of cases prosecuted in the London Consistory Court was noted in Smith, 'Women and marriage', 177. On legal costs, see pp. 125, 214.

45. Anne French, *Art Treasures in the North: Northern Families on the Grand Tour* (Norwich: Unicorn Press, 2009), 5–9.

46. Ibid. See also Jeremy Black, *The British Abroad: The Grand Tour in the Eighteenth Century* (Stroud: Sutton, 2003; 1st edn. 1992).
47. *Archivio Della Parrocchia di S. Donato*, Genoa: *Archivio della Parrocchia del SS. Salvatore* (1766–1800), 165, n. 13.
48. The exact date of his arrival is unknown: the estimate is made upon the lapse of time between the Kingsman marriage in London in September 1773 and the procurement by Wilbraham of the first witness statements in Florence in October 1775.
49. The allegation that Mann had 'borrowed the effeminacy of Italy' was made by William, 2nd Earl Fitzwilliam, who visited him in Florence. In Hugh Belsey, 'Mann, Sir Horace', *DNB*.
50. LMA/DL/C/639, Deposition book (Nov. 1772–Apr. 1777), Deposition of Ansano Rossi (12 Dec. 1775), fo. 310$^r$.
51. LMA/DL/C/558/21, Interrogation of Tomasso Massi. Massi deposed that Ansano Rossi 'came for me at Figlini and brought me to the City of Florence' (23 Oct. 1775), fos. 5–6.
52. Francesco Magnelli, *Pianta della Citta' di Firenze Rilevata Esattamente Nell'Anno 1783*, engraved by Cosimo Zocchi. Displayed in the permanent collection, Museo di Firenze Com'era, Florence.
53. Gaetano Auzzoni, *Pianta Topografica di Firenze* (1850). Permanent collection, Museo di Firenze Com'era, Florence. See also Paolo Lucchesini, *I Teatri di Firenze* (Rome: Newton Compton, 1991), 27–32, 40–4, 83–102.
54. See for example *Accademia degli Infuocati, 'Contratti e scritte dal 1771 al 1857'*: Mainero's name appears in the margin, where arrangements for procuring stage scenery and wardrobe are mentioned (*'per comodo del Palco Scenio, et del Vestiario . . .'*). Florence: *Archivio Storico/Comune di Firenze*/TN00083/IT ASCFI/TN/4/1/4, n.p., contract dated 24 Apr. 1774.
55. LMA/DL/C/558/21, Deposition of Nicolo Tassi (23 Oct. 1775), fos. 14–16.
56. Ibid., fos. 10–12. Tassi wrote the *libretto* to *La Contadina in Corte*, with music by Sacchini, performed at the King's Theatre on

14 March 1771; and *l'Amore Soldato*, also set to music by Sacchini, first performed at the King's Theatre on 5 May 1778. In Morris S. Levy and John Milton Ward (eds.), *The King's Theatre Collection: Ballet and Italian Opera in London, 1706–1883* (Cambridge, Mass.: Houghton Library of Harvard College Library, 2003), 101, 104.

57. This actual title, which was typical of the genre, was published in London in 1797.

58. Readers of Michel Foucault will recognize the relevance of Tenducci's predicament to Foucault's theory, reiterated in many of his most famous works such as *Madness and Civilization* (1962), *The Archaeology of Knowledge* (1972), and three volumes of *The History of Sexuality* (1976–84), that the creation of new discourses of scientific knowledge was constitutive of a power nexus in which individuals became effectively trapped, categorized, and pathologized, as society moved towards modernity. In Tenducci's case, the attempt by medico-juridical 'experts' to define the 'truth' of his body was elicited by the law's intervention in the Tenducci marriage. Countering this Foucauldian interpretation is the argument presented throughout this book for Tenducci's location at the centre of social and cultural life in eighteenth-century Europe (see *passim* and 'Coda').

59. Pietro Leopoldo d'Asburgo Lorena, *Relazioni Sul Governo della Toscana, II. Stato Fiorentino e Pisano*, ed. Leo S. Olschki (Florence, 1970), 270–1.

60. The courts overseen by the proconsul were described by the Grand Duke as '*tre camere buone e luminose*', ibid.

61. See for example LMA/DL/C/558/21, the foot of the testimony of Tomasso Massi (23 Oct. 1775), fo. 6, 'Confirmd in all its parts by the Intervention of the Oath by me duly administered to him and by him taken by touching the Scripture and declaring to have Sign'd the same with his own hand in quorum &c.'

62. See for example LMA/DL/C/558/21, Setti's endorsement of the testimony of Nicolo Tassi (23 Oct. 1775), fo. 12.

63. Ibid., fo. 7.
64. The town of Figline Valdarno, approximately 10 km south-east of Florence.
65. Ibid., fos. 3–4.
66. Ibid., fo. 1.
67. Ibid., fos. 1–2.
68. LMA/DL/C/558/21, Deposition of Nicolo Tassi (23 Oct. 1775), fo. 8.
69. Ibid., fo. 9.
70. See Chapter 1.
71. LMA/DL/C/558/21, Deposition of Antonio Frascani (24 Oct. 1775), fos. 25–6.
72. Ibid. 'Cuseiano' was probably Cusignano, a village 15 km south-west of Florence.
73. Ibid.
74. LMA/DL/C/558/21, Deposition of Tomasso Massi (23 Oct. 1775), fo. 3.
75. The persistent reference to Tenducci as being 'around' 11 years old suggests that the year was actually 1746, though the exact date is impossible to verify either way. If the operation was indeed performed upon Tenducci at the age of about 13 in 1748, this would have been very late indeed.
76. This was presumably under the pretext of medical necessity, since in this case the procedure, and financial transaction, were both documented in the form of a contract between the Church and Senesino's father. Elizabeth Avanzati, 'The unpublished Senesino', in *Handel and the Castrati* (London: Handel House Museum Exhibition Catalogue, 2006), 9, n. 5.
77. LMA/DL/C/558/21, Deposition of Tomasso Massi (23 Oct. 1775), fo. 4.
78. Avanzati, 'Unpublished Senesino', 9, n. 6.
79. Quoted in Martha Feldman, 'Denaturing the castrato', *Opera Quarterly*, 24.3 (2009), 178.

80. Ibid. 179.

81. Ibid. 181.

82. Lawrence Stone, *The Family, Sex and Marriage in England, 1500–1800* (Harmondsworth: Penguin, 1977). For a summary of subsequent critics of Stone, see Berry and Foyster, 'Introduction', in eadem (eds.), *The Family in Early Modern England* (Cambridge: Cambridge University Press, 2007).

83. The application of psychoanalysis to the study of pre-modern history has had varying degrees of success: one distinguished example is Lyndal Roper's application of the theories of Melanie Klein to the study of German witchcraft trials in *Oedipus and the Devil: Witchcraft, Sexuality and Religion in Early Modern Europe* (London: Routledge, 1994). It seemed necessary to mention the Oedipus complex in relation to a father having his son castrated, since it is one of the most immediate associations that is likely to be made in our own post-Freudian era. I have not pursued this line of analysis further, however, since we do not have access to further evidence such as records of Tenducci's dreams or fantasies, or those of his immediate family.

84. Cinzia Cardinale (ed.), *Archivo Prennitario del Comune di Monte San Savino*, Vol. II (Arezzo: Progetto Archivi, 2004), 331–2, '*Commissari Fiorentini di Monte San Savino*'.

85. The idea of sympathetic bonding, thought to have been necessary for conception, went back to Aristotle and was still widely believed in early modern Europe. See Anthony Fletcher, *Gender, Sex and Subordination in England, 1500–1800* (New Haven and London: Yale University Press, 1995), 51–3.

86. The conduct of official business in public houses was not unusual: they were the customary venues, for example, for coroners' inquests in this period.

87. The original deposition of Mary Holland, together with her signature, survives among the consistorial court depositions in LMA/DL/C/558/20 (30 Oct. 1775), fos. 6–8. The original depositions of

271

Samuel Griffith, Joanna Green, and Simon Preston were not preserved, but are reproduced in *Trials for Adultery*, 39–47.

88. *Trials for Adultery*, 8–9. The depositions of Charles Baroe, together with the other depositions of Lorenzo Lombardi, Thomas and Dorothea Maunsell (the parents of Dorothea Tenducci), and Francis Michael Passerini, taken in November 1775, were not preserved in the original, hence reliance upon the published version of their statements (pp. 18–37). Judging by comparison of the original deposition of Mary Holland with the version published in *Trials for Adultery*, the transcription was accurate, although some 'tidying up' had been done from the original court record, mostly via the insertion of punctuation and removal of legal terms, such as the repetition of deponent', to produce a narrative that was easier to read. Though we need to be aware that the oral testimonies were in effect mediated twice—once through the clerk of the court, and once by a journalist, the essential details are the same, as far as it is possible to judge. See 'A note on Sources'.

89. Quoted in Angus Heriot, *The Castrati in Opera* (London: Secker and Warburg, 1956), 47.

90. Heriot comments: 'One suspects that...this was a tale *pour les tourists*, swallowed wholesale by the gullible German', ibid.

91. *Trials for Adultery*, 18–19. See Chapter 4 for a fuller discussion of the outward signs of male virility, and their cultural meaning in this period.

92. The testimonies of Passerini, and more significantly Thomas Maunsell and his wife, are interwoven in Chapters 5, 6, and 7.

93. LMA/DL/C/639, Deposition of Peter Crawford (12 Dec. 1775), fos. 306$^v$–309$^r$ and Ansano Rossi, fos. 310$^r$–311$^v$.

94. See Daniel Heatz, 'Galuppi, Tenducci, and Montezuma: a commentary on the history and musical style of opera seria after 1750', in John A. Rice (ed.), *Essays on Opera, 1750–1800* (Aldershot: Ashgate, 2010).

95. *Gazzetta Toscana*, no. 6 (Feb. 1772).

96. Lambeth Palace Library, London, Court of Arches, Case 8932 (1677), Elizabeth Syler v. Edmund Syler; Case 1185 (1662), Mary Collings v. Samuel Collings. I am very grateful to Elizabeth Foyster for alerting me to these cases.

97. *The Cases of Impotency and Virginity fully Discuss'd* (London, 1732, 2nd edn. 1734).

98. LMA/DL/C/558/21 (23 Oct. 1775), fo. 14. The public notary attested that he had done this 'at the request of Mr Rossi', in order to comply with the requirements of the London court.

99. LMA/DL/C/177, Allegations, Libels and Sentences Book, 1777 (28 Feb. 1776), Kingsman formerly Maunsell, falsely called Tenducci, fo. 358$^r$.

100. *Trials for Adultery*.

101. LMA/DL/C/177 (28 Feb. 1776), fos. 358$^r$–359$^r$.

102. Ibid.

103. *Public Ledger, or the Daily Register of Commerce and Intelligence*, no. 4301 (6 Oct. 1773).

104. LMA/DL/C/639, Deposition book, Nov. 1772–Apr. 1777 (12 Dec. 1775), fo. 310$^r$.

## Chapter Nine. Legacy

1. See for example LMA/DL/C/177, Allegations, Libels and Sentences Book, Jan. 1772–June 1777 (24 May 1775), fos. 351$^v$, 352$^r$, 355$^r$.

2. *Trials for Adultery*, 1–50.

3. Edith Mary Johnston-Liik, *History of the Irish Parliament, 1692–1800: Commons, Constituencies and Statutes* (Belfast: Ulster Historical Foundation, 2002), Vol. 5, pp. 35, 218–19.

4. Ibid. 219–20. See also John Watson, *Gentleman's and Citizen's Almanack* (Dublin, 1769), 53.

5. Robert George Maunsell, *History of Mansell, or Maunsell* (Cork, 1903).

6. Johnston-Liik, *History of the Irish Parliament*, 35.
7. Other offspring were possible, even likely, given the high rate of infant mortality at this time and unrecorded miscarriages: the under-recording of these additional pregnancies is endemic and a source of constant difficulty to historical demographers. Suffice it to say that the Kingsmans had three children whose existence was recorded.
8. TNA/PCC/Prob 11/1348, Will of Dorothea Frances Kingsman, administered 4 Oct. 1800.
9. Ibid. This document is not without its curiosities. Dorothea Frances unambiguously left her property to 'my ffather W L Kingsman', but the will was drafted in 1800, which was supposedly after he had died in the Fleet prison. It may be that news of his shameful demise was kept hidden, or travelled slowly. Another discrepancy is the note of administration which refers to 'Richard Long Kingsman' as the testator's father and 'Universal Legatee'. I have assumed this is an error and that this referred to another close male relative, not that this is the will of an entirely different Dorothea, which seems highly unlikely.
10. LMA/DL/C/177, Allegations, Libels and Sentences Book, Jan. 1772–June 1777 (24 May 1775), fo. 355$^v$.
11. Ibid.
12. Johnston-Liik, *History of the Irish Parliament*, 35.
13. *St James's Chronicle*, no. 2346 (27 Feb. 1776); *Morning Chronicle*, no. 2189 (27 May 1776).
14. *London Packet or New Lloyds Evening Post*, no. 1111 (29 Nov. 1776).
15. Johan Wilhelm von Archenholz, *A Picture of England: Containing the Laws, Customs and Manners of England* (Dublin, 1790), 174.
16. Jay Cohen, 'The history of imprisonment for debt and its relation to the development of discharge in bankruptcy', *Journal of Legal History*, 3.2 (1982), 153–71, esp. 158–9.

17. *London Gazette,* no. 11723 (30 Nov. 1776); *St James's Chronicle, or the British Evening Post,* no. 2456 (30 Nov. 1776); *General Evening Post,* no. 6700 (10 Dec. 1776).

18. See for example *Gazetteer and London Daily Advertiser,* no. 14964 (8 Feb. 1777).

19. *Morning Post,* no. 1301 (21 Dec. 1776); *General Evening Post,* no. 6726 (8 Feb. 1777).

20. *London Chronicle, or Universal Evening Post,* no. 3149 (8 Feb. 1777).

21. *Morning Chronicle,* no. 1505 (21 Mar. 1774); *General Evening Post* (17 Oct. 1775); *London Evening Post,* no. 8552 (9 Jan. 1777).

22. On related themes, see Kathleen Wilson, *The Island Race: Englishness, Empire and Gender in the Eighteenth Century* (London and New York: Routledge, 2003); Michèle Cohen, 'Manliness, effeminacy and the French: gender and the construction of national character in eighteenth-century England', in Tim Hitchcock and Michèle Cohen, *English Masculinities, 1660–1800* (London: Longman, 1999).

23. *Morning Post,* no. 1353 (20 Feb. 1777).

24. *Gazetteer and London Daily Advertiser,* no. 14985 (5 Mar. 1777).

25. Ibid. For the transmission of Rousseau's ideas in English, Jean-Jacques Rousseau, *Appendix to Grassineau's Musical Dictionary, Selected from the 'Dictionnaire de Musique' of J. J. Rousseau* (London, 1769), which quotes the origins of Rousseau's idea that 'Singing does not appear to be natural to man, for tho' the savages of America sing, because they talk, the true savage never sings', p. 41.

26. The Harrises of Salisbury spent £1 on tickets for a Tenducci concert on 30 April 1765, and 10s. 6d. on the same day for a concert by Mozart: see 'London account book of Elizabeth Harris, 2 April–16 May, 1765', reproduced in Donald Burrows and Rosemary Dunhill (eds.), *Music and Theatre in Handel's World: The Family Papers of James Harris, 1732–1780* (Oxford: Oxford University Press, 2002), 442.

27. I leave debate concerning the provenance of surviving musical scores attributable to this *scena* to the musicologists. For a discussion of Mozart's K. 315b, see C. B. Oldman, 'Mozart's *scena* for Tenducci', *Music and Letters*, 42.1 (1961), 44–52. For the quotation from Burney, see ibid. 49.

28. See Paul Langford, *Englishness Identified: Manners and Character, 1650–1850* (Oxford: Oxford University Press, 2000), esp. ch. 2.

29. *Morning Post*, no. 1608 (16 Dec. 1777).

30. Ibid.

31. See Foundling Hospital Museum, London: Gerald Coke Handel Foundation Collection, HC4066, no. 5646, 'Justus Ferdinand Tenducci' [*sic*, n.d.].

32. See for example *London Evening Post*, no. 8754 (25 Apr. 1778). Tenducci even sold sheet music for the new rondo which he had performed at the following year's Bach and Abel's concert from his lodgings, 'No. 13, Poland-street . . . near Oxford Street'. Ibid., no. 8920 (10 June 1779).

33. Tenducci's obituary stated he was '*il primo a introdurre nelle sceniche rappresentanze l'uso di cantare i Rondò*'. *Avvisi di Genova*, no. 5 (30 Jan. 1790).

34. *General Evening Post*, no. 710 (3 July 1779).

35. As reported by John Marsh, the musical impresario, who was not uncritical of Tenducci's abilities, but who noted that his Salisbury concerts in the early 1780s were still attracting good audiences of about 300 people. See Brian Robins, *The John Marsh Journals*, Sociology of Music, no. 9 (New York: Stuyvesant, 1998), 251, 253, 273.

36. Stephen Lloyd, 'Cosway, Maria Louisa Catherine Cecilia, Baroness Cosway in the nobility of the Austrian empire (1760–1838)', *DNB*.

37. Ibid.

38. Letter from Giusto Ferdinando Tenducci to Mrs Cosway, BL Add. MS 33965 [n.d., early 1780s?], fos. 396$^r$–397$^r$.

39. Olive Baldwin and Thelma Wilson, 'Tenducci, Giusto Ferdinando', *DNB*.

40. *Public Advertiser*, no. 15805 (20 Jan. 1785).
41. *Morning Herald and Daily Advertiser*, no. 444 (2 Apr. 1782).
42. Ibid., no. 445 (3 Apr. 1782).
43. *Public Advertiser*, no. 15453 (6 Dec. 1783).
44. *Morning Post*, no. 4046 (21 Jan. 1786).
45. Ibid., no. 16165 (15 Mar. 1786).
46. *Public Advertiser*, no. 16332 (25 Sept. 1786). It seems highly likely that Tenducci's hosts and benefactors were the Parker family of Saltram House, given the proximity to Plymouth, and the refashioning of Saltram as a centre of artistic patronage at this time by the family matriarch, Thereza Parker.
47. Quoted in Susan Sloman, *Pickpocketing the Rich: Portrait Painting in Bath, 1720–1800*, exhibition catalogue (Bath: Holburne Museum of Art, 2002), 16.
48. Reprinted in *Morning Herald and Daily Advertiser*, no. 79 (31 Jan. 1781).
49. *Public Advertiser*, no. 16739 (11 Jan. 1788).
50. Ibid., no. 16742 (15 Jan. 1788).
51. *General Evening Post*, no. 8463 (16 Feb. 1788).
52. Ibid., no. 8394 (8 Sept. 1787).
53. *Morning Post*, no. 4687 (26 Mar. 1788).
54. *Morning Chronicle*, no. 5905 (12 Apr. 1788).
55. Ibid., no. 5906 (14 Apr. 1788). For the contrasting standards of living in eighteenth-century England between rich and poor, see Amanda Vickery, *Behind Closed Doors: At Home in Georgian England* (New Haven and London: Yale University Press, 2009), esp. chs. 2 and 5.
56. *Morning Post*, no. 4706 (17 Apr. 1788).
57. *Bath Chronicle*, no. 1451 (30 July 1789).
58. '...*con scelta numerosa orchestra, in cui si distinse il Virtuoso Accademico Sig. Giusto Ferdinando Tenducci.*' *Avvisi di Genova*, no. 28 (11 July 1789).
59. Ibid., no. 36 (5 Sept. 1789).

60. 'Die 27 dicti [ianuarii, 1790], Ferdinandus Tenducci quo[ndam] ... Florentinus 54 annis circiter a syncope coreptus obiit die 25 [ia-nuarii] et hodie in hac nostra [ecclesia] sepultus est.' Genoa, Arch-ivio Della Parrocchia di S. Donato: Archivio della Parrocchia del SS. Salvatore: Defunti (1766–1800), 165, n.13. I am most grateful to Maria Rosa Moretti for confirmation of these details, which for the first time enable Tenducci's exact date of birth, cause of death, and place of burial to be confirmed.

61. Avvisi di Genova, no. 5 (30 Jan. 1790).

## Coda

1. An interesting overview of this increasingly popular approach to the study of history is Mark M. Smith, *Sensing the Past: Seeing, Hearing, Smelling, Tasting and Touching in History* (Berkeley: University of California Press, 2004).

2. See Helen Berry and Elizabeth Foyster, 'Childless men in early modern England', in eadem (eds), *The Family in Early Modern England* (Cambridge: Cambridge University Press, 2007).

3. The enduring influence of Linda Colley's *Britons: Forging the Nation, 1707–1837* (New Haven and London: Yale University Press, 1992) was marked by the publication of the second edition of this book in 2005.

4. Though controversial, the theory of the rise of modern individual-ism is usefully articulated in Michael Mascuch, *The Origins of the Individualist Self* (Cambridge: Polity Press, 1997); see also Jona-than I. Israel, *Radical Enlightenment: Philosophy and the Making of Modernity* (Oxford: Oxford University Press, 2001).

5. Martha Feldman, 'Strange births and surprising kin: the castrato's tale', in Paula Findlen, Wendy Wassyng Roworth, and Catherine M. Sama (eds.), *Italy's Eighteenth Century: Gender and Culture in the Age of the Grand Tour* (Stanford: Stanford University Press, 2009), 175.

6. For the autobiographical poem by the castrato Balatri, see Angus Heriot, *The Castrati in Opera* (London: Secker and Warburg, 1956), 209–11 and *passim*. There is also the story of Sorlisi voiced as the soldier 'Titius' in Mary E. Fraudsen, *'Eunuchi conjugium:* the marriage of a castrato in early modern Germany', *Early Music History 24: Studies in Medieval and Early Modern Music*, ed. Iain Fenlon (Cambridge: Cambridge University Press, 2005), 67.

7. See Randolph Trumbach, *Sex and the Gender Revolution. Vol. I: Heterosexuality and the Third Gender in Enlightenment London* (Chicago: Chicago University Press, 1998); Rictor Norton, *Mother Clap's Molly House: The Gay Subculture in England, 1700–1830*, 2nd edn. (Stroud: Chalford Place, 2006).

8. Peter Clark, *British Clubs and Societies: The Origins of an Associational World* (Oxford: Clarendon Press, 2000).

9. Jason Kelly, 'Riots, revelries, and rumor: libertinism and masculine association in Enlightenment London', *Journal of British Studies*, 45.4 (2006), 759–95.

10. In this, castrati were examples of what Judith Butler has called 'abject bodies', in *Bodies that Matter: On the Discursive Limits of Sex* (New York and London: Routledge, 1993), p. xi.

11. See for example Patricia Crawford and Sara Mendelson, 'Sexual identities in early modern England: the marriage of two women in 1680', *Gender and History*, 7.3 (1995), 362–77. There were also the famous 'Boston' marriages in New England, and widely accepted female partnerships in Victorian society: see Sharon Marcus, *Between Women: Friendship, Desire and Marriage in Victorian England* (Princeton: Princeton University Press, 2007).

12. The approach of Rictor Norton for example has been to try to 'recover' gay men's history from the surviving archives, difficulties notwithstanding in terms of applying modern identity categories to the pre-modern period: see for example 'Recovering gay history from the Old Bailey', *London Journal*, 30.1 (2005), 39–54.

13. My approach has been influenced by the pioneering work of Sharon Marcus on the importance of female friendships and love in the negotiation of heterosexual marriage in Victorian England. Through a variety of evidence, for mother–daughter relationships, the plots of novels and mainstream fashion illustrations, doll stories and material culture, Marcus shows how female relationships, including eroticized ones, were not marginal or dissident, but an essential part of brokering male–female bonds (*Between Women, passim*). See also Marjorie Garber, *Bisexuality and the Eroticism of Everyday Life* (New York and London: Routledge, 2000), which richly explores the potential that exists to move beyond binary categories (such as homo- and heterosexual), and to re-evaluate mainstream cultural messages about gender and sexuality.

14. Nicholas Clapton, *Moreschi: The Last Castrato* (London: Haus Publishing, 2004), 23–5.

15. Ibid., *passim*. The recording of Moreschi's voice is in the British Library Sound Archive.

16. The exception is Bartolomeo Sorlisi, the castrato who was a resident of the German city of Dresden in the 1660s. Fraudsen, '*Eunuchi conjugium*', 67.

17. LMA/DL/C/558/21, Deposition of Nicolo Tassi (23 Oct. 1775), fo. 9.

# Grazie

Thanks to Newcastle University for financial support, a semester of research leave, and additional teaching relief in 2009/10 which enabled me to complete this book. At OUP, I am grateful to my Editor, Luciana O'Flaherty, for her excellent advice, and to Matthew Cotton and Deborah Protheroe for help with illustrations and permissions. In providing vital assistance with my research, I should like to thank the staff of the following institutions: The National Library of Ireland; The Beinecke Library, Yale University; The British Library, London; The National Library of Scotland; State Archives, Siena; and Bodleian Library, Oxford. For patiently sharing their time and scholarly expertise, my thanks go to Amanda Bevan of The National Archives; Bridget Howlett of the London Metropolitan Archives; Martin Wyatt at the Handel House Museum; Colin Coleman of the Foundling Museum; Mike Cousins at the Hagley Hall Archive; and my friend Gayle Richardson of the Huntington Library, San Marino, California. Angelo Gravano generously shared his research on the local archives of the Arezzo region, and Maria Rosa Moretti was most helpful in locating Genoese sources. My Newcastle colleague Claudia Baldoli steered me through the complexities of the Italian rail network, and gave me invaluable help translating archival documents, and some memorable present-day menus. Without her, this project would have been a lot less fun. In Monte San Savino, I met with tremendous generosity from Renato Giulietta, the local archivist, and Martino, who drove me back to Siena after the last bus had left.

I should also like to acknowledge and thank the many friends and colleagues who have given the research that went into this book their encouragement, inspiration, generous support, time, and hospitality: Keith Wrightson and Eva Wrightson, Todd Gilman, Nicholas Clapton, Kathryn James, Lisa Ford, Enrica Cappusotti, Joanne Bailey, Joan Allen, Fergus Campbell, Richard Wistreich, Jim Caudle, Lisa Cody, Joanna Huntington, Rowland Smith, Susan Walker, Steven Wallace, Catherine Harbor, Cathy McClive, Margaret McCollum, Alecia Moore, Sîan Broadhurst, Quinn Fidler, Heidi Shultz, Campbell Storey, Sophie McCann, Kristen Cooper, Steven Wallace, Freya Jarman-Ivens, Roger Dawson SJ, Rachel Hammersley, Kate Chegdzoy, David Saunders, Jeremy Boulton, R. I. Moore, Rowland Smith, Susan Staves, Martha Feldman, Caroline Nielsen, and Elizabeth Burke. Ria Snowdon provided essential help with research and compiled the index; Anjali Joseph was a diligent transcriber. Scott Ashley shared his vast knowledge of so many historical periods and subjects, from Molesworth Street to medieval parallels. He made me think harder, and was kind enough to share his idea for a title. At Newcastle University, I received many stimulating questions from the Early Modernists Group, postgraduate students on the MA in British History, and undergraduates taking HIS3078. Further thought was provoked by postgraduate students and colleagues attending the 'History of the Senses' seminar at the Institute for Historical Research, and the Universities of Sheffield and Yale, where I gave papers from work in progress in 2008/9.

I am especially grateful to Jason Kelly, Anthony Fletcher, Elizabeth Foyster, and Karen Harvey for reading draft chapters and finding the time in their busy schedules to provide detailed comments. Nigel Thornton gamely took part in a walking tour of Tenducci's London. Kate Thick listened and sorted out the 'Tenducci knot', and my ever-supportive parents John Berry and Julia Berry developed a new interest in everything Baroque. More than most, Sarah Duffy understands the limits of language and thus the difficulty in formulating my final expression of gratitude. Her courage and loyalty extended to the moped-infested streets of Naples, which was more than could be expected of any merry accomplice.

Morpeth
December 2010

# A Note on Sources

Where possible, the details of the marriage annulment case between Giusto Ferdinando Tenducci and Dorothea Kingsman, née Maunsell, have been taken directly from the original London Consistory Court records relating to the case of 'Kingsman, falsely called Tenducci v. Tenducci' preserved in the London Metropolitan Archives (see 'Manuscript Sources', below). These include the original papers brought into court as Exhibits when the case opened in May 1775; the 'Sayings and depositions' made by witnesses; the Deposition book (1772–7) covering the period that witness statements were taken down in London, Italy, and Ireland, and the 'Allegations, Libels and Sentence Book' (1772–7) which recorded both the grounds for the annulment and the judge's final verdict. It is still possible to consult the original depositions from Florence that were gathered for the annulment hearing. Written in Italian and Latin and embellished with official stamps, seals, and signatures, these were translated at the time into English before being presented before the presiding judge, Dr Bettesworth. It is these original translations that have, as far as possible, been quoted in this book. Fewer English and Irish depositions for this case have survived in their original form, and for these it was necessary to refer to a published account of the Tenducci annulment hearing, contained in *Trials for Adultery: or, the History of Divorces* (1780). For instance, the original depositions of witnesses Samuel Griffith, Joanna Green, and Simon Preston were not preserved in the consistory court archives, but were printed in *Trials for Adultery* (pp. 39–47). Neither were the depositions taken down in November 1775 from Charles

Baroe, Lorenzo Lombardi, Thomas and Dorothea Maunsell (Dorothea's parents), and the music professor Francis Michael Passerini
preserved, hence quotations from these witnesses were taken from
the published version of their statements (*Trials for Adultery*, pp. 18–
37). The reliability of the printed copy of the depositions merits some
attention. The survival of the original deposition of 59-year-old Mary
Holland (LMA/DL/C/558/20/fos. 6–8), authenticated by her shaky
signature, makes it possible to compare it with the version published
in *Trials for Adultery* (pp. 47–50). This reveals that some minor 'tidying
up' of punctuation was done to produce a printed narrative that was
easier to read than the original court record, but it is remarkable that
the two versions are substantively the same. A necessary caution is that
the oral testimonies produced by eyewitnesses to the Tenducci marriage annulment case in court were in effect mediated by at least two
different hands: the clerk of the court, and a journalist writing a version
transcribed from shorthand. However, the result of comparing the two
records of Mary Holland's deposition indicates that the content of the
published version of the trial is essentially accurate, as far as it is
possible to judge.

Perhaps surprisingly, and in spite of its tabloid-sounding title (which
was without doubt designed to sell copy), the *Trials for Adultery*
omitted to print the eyewitness statements taken down in Florence
which provided graphic detail about the circumstances of Tenducci's
castration. It was unlikely that this was to spare the sensibilities of
Georgian readers, who were used to a diet of sexual scandal in the
press, but rather because the Italian depositions were tabled ('brought
in') before the judge rather than being read out loud in court. The
general public at the time would therefore have been unaware of the
crucial account of Tomasso Massi, the son of the surgeon who castrated
Tenducci, who was witness to the operation. Since this unique document provided critical evidence, and is of wider historical significance,
its translation is reproduced in full in the Appendix that follows.

# Appendix:

## Deposition of Tomasso Massi

[Transcribed from LMA/DL/C/558/21/fos. 1–7, 'Kingsman formerly Maunsell falsely called Tenducci against Tenducci several Depositions marked No. 1 Translated from Latin & Italian brought in the 28th February 1776'].

**In the Name of God Amen**

Be it Known to all to whom these presents shall see that on the twenty third Day of the Month of October in the Year of Our Lord One Thousand Seven Hundred and Seventy five & the Eighth Indiction Pius Sextus being Reigning Pope His Serene Highness Petro Leopaldo Arch Duke of Austria Prince Royal of Hungaria and Bohemia &c. &c. being the Ninth and present Reigning Grand Duke of Tuscany at the request of Ansani Rosi Attorney Duly Authorised and appointed I the underwritten Notary was required to Interrogate Thomas the Son of Petro Antoni Massi of Nurcia upon the Contents of the Facts set forth in the within faithful Attestation by him made upon the said Twenty third Day of October of this present Year One Thousand Seven Hundred and Seventy five, the Tenor whereof is as follows Viz. I the underwritten Tommasso Massi Son of the late Petro Antonio Massi of Nurcia do upon my Solemn Oath attest to all whom it may concern to be valid in Court and thereout that in the Year One Thousand Seven Hundred and forty Eight or thereabout my said Father Pietro Antonio Massi did in the Village of Monte St. Savino in my presence Castrate Mr. Giusto Ferdinando Tenducci by making an Amputation of both his Testicles and the Spermatick Ducts to which Operation Gaetano di Antonio Figlini a Servant and Assistant to my said Fa[ther] was

286

present and held the said Tenducci fast and secure at the time of the said Operation that the said might be done Effectual[ly] and which being happily Executed I the aforesaid and underwritten by way of my said Father did upon the successive Days after the Operation as often as was necessary go to the House where the said Tenducci resided situated in the said Village Del Monti St. Savino to Apply his Plaisters and do whatever Else was wanting to the Incision of the Wound given to the said Tenducci at the time of Castrating him In Testimony thereof I have sign[e]d this present Attestation with my own Hand on this Twenty third Day of October One Thousand Seven Hundred and seventy five.

Tommasso Massi my own Handwriting

Whereupon I the underwritten Notary having read the foregoing Attestation to the said Tommassi Massi and the same being by him understood at the request of the said Mr Ansani Rossi did require of and interrogate the said Tomasso Massi in the following manner Viz:

**Whether** he did clearly recollect all what he had set forth and deposed in the foregoing Attestation and if he could truly Confirm the Contents thereof and whether he could particularly prove that the said Tenducci was Castrated.

**Answer:** I do recollect very well when my said Father in the Year One Thousand Seven Hundred and Forty Eight Castrated the said Mr Giusto Ferdinando Tenducci who resided in the Village of Monti St. Savino in the presence of Gaetano Mugni of Figlini Assistant and Servant of my said Father, and I do clearly recollect that the said Operation of Castrating was performed by Order of the said Tenducci's Father who was then Servant of the Commissary of the said Village and that such Operation was made at a House in the said Village where the said Tenducci resided.

**Interrogated** further at the request of the said Mr Rossi for what reason and in what manner was the said Witness present at the said Operation and what Age he was of when the same was done.

**Answer** My Father brought me up to the Profession of a Surgeon which I exercise at present and used to take me with him to all his Operations that I might practice and **I do** clearly recollect that my Father

Castrated the said Tenducci of both parts by making the usual Incisions in the Groin and of having Executed and cut out his Two Testicles and the Spermatick Ducts. I do recollect amongst other Circumstances that when my said Father was paid for that operation he complain[e]d of not being satisfied what he merited and that he was answer[e]d that he must have patience and consider that he made the Operation on the Son of a Poor servant which the said Tenducci was, **and** when the Operation was made I the Witness was of the Age of Seventeen Years or thereabouts.

**Interrogated** in what manner and for what reason did he the Witness go to Cure the said Tenducci after the aforesaid operation and by whose Orders and Directions did he go and make that Cure.

**Answer** as my said Father as I have above declared brought me up to the Profession of a Surgeon and which I now practice after he made his Operations in order that I might become proficient therein he used to send me to attend upon and Cure those persons he had Castrated and to heal up their wounds &c. &c. which I did to the said Tenducci who was cured by me of the wounds he had upon being Castrated by my having at the time and according to the rules of the profession changed his Plaisters and restored his Health in the manner it happened.

**Interrogated** whether anything had been given or promised him to make his Attestation.

**Answer** I made the said Attestation because I was requested so to do, but nothing was promised neither has any recompence been given me but I did it being the entire Truth.

**Interrogated** in General and as to his Person &c.

**Answer** that he was forty Years of Age and an Inhabitant of Figlini and that he profess[e]d the Business of a Surgeon.

**Interrogated** as to what he knew of his own Knowledge.

**Answer** because that he was present as above related to the Castrating of the said Tenducci.

**Interrogated** by whom he was requested to make the said Attestation.

**Answer** Mr Ansano Rossi requested me to make it. Came for me at Figlini and brought me to the City of Florence.

We the underwritten were together present as Witnesses to all the foregoing and to what the Witness declared and so deposed and saw the said Tomasso Massi sign the same of his Hand writing **and in Testimony** &c.

I **Guiseppe Setti** Clerk Curate of the Parrochial Church of St. Felice In Piazza my own Hand Writing.

I **Lorenzo Rossi** clerk my own hand Writing.

On the Twenty Third Day of October One Thousand Seven Hundred and Seventy Five.

The foregoing Attestation and Subsequent Deposition of the said Witness Tomasso Massi was in the presence of the aforesaid Priests Ratified and Confirmd in all its parts by the Intervention of the Oath by me duly administered to him and by him taken by touching the Scripture and declaring to have Sign'd the same with his own hand in **quorum** &c. . . .

I **Cosmus Gigliolini** Judge and Doctor of Laws Son of Antonius Francisci Councellor and Florentine Notary Public having been requested to Attest all the foregoing having signd the same with my own hand and in Confirmation thereof have sign and subscribd the same with my accustomed and usual Signature—Florence this Twenty third Day of October one Thousand Seven Hundred and Seventy Five.

We **Proconsul** and **Consul** of the College of Judges and Notaries of the City of Florence do Certify and Publicly attest that the above names **Cosmus Gigliolini** was and is such a Florentine Public Notary as he stiles himself faithful Loyal and Trustworthy to whose Writings and Signatures due faith and Credit is and always has been given in Court and thereout **In testimony thereof** We have caused these to be Impressd with our usual and Accustomed Seal Given at Florence this Twenty fourth Day of this Month of October One Thousand Seven Hundred and Seventy five.

Josephus Maria Mulatio Signorimus Proconsul.

Then follows the Attestation in English of Sir Horace Mann of the above Proconsul being such as He stiles himself . . .

# Select Bibliography

## Manuscript Sources

ARCHIVIO STORICO, COMUNE DI FIRENZE

TN00083/IT ASCFI/TN/4: Contracts and papers relating to the Teatro Niccolini (formerly Teatro di Cocomero), 1771–1857.

ARCHIVIO DI STATO, COMUNE DI SIENA

MS 1152–1153: Baptismal records, 1728–41.

BEINECKE LIBRARY, YALE UNIVERSITY

OSB MS 3/Box 15/1146: Burney family collection, Giusto Ferdinando Tenducci to Charles Burney, n.d.
OSB MS 146/Box 861 and 864: Hanover Royal Music Archive, Glees and songs from Vauxhall, 1770s.
Cupboard Ma31 Ar6 S81: 'The Winter's Amusement, Consisting of Favourite Songs and Cantatas Performed by Mr. Tenducci...', n.d.

BODLEIAN LIBRARY, OXFORD

Harding MUS. E474: Collection of English songs.

BRITISH LIBRARY, LONDON

Add. MS 22130: Correspondence of Elizabeth Lyttelton, 1784–9.
Add. MS 33965: Giusto Ferdinando Tenducci to Maria Cosway, n.d.
Egerton MS 3690–3708: Commonplace books and correspondence of Susanna Phillips, née Burney, 1780–97.

HUNTINGTON LIBRARY, SAN MARINO, CALIFORNIA

MO1281: Correspondence of Elizabeth Montagu.
HM54457: John Marsh Diaries.

LONDON METROPOLITAN ARCHIVE

Documents relating to the case of 'Kingsman, falsely called Tenducci v. Tenducci'.
LMA/DL/C/557/102/Exhibits, depositions and interrogations, 1775–6.
LMA/DL/C/558/20–21/Sayings and depositions, 1775–6.
LMA/DL/C/639/Deposition book, 1772–7.
LMA/DL/C/177/Allegations, Libels and Sentence Book, 1772–7.

THE NATIONAL ARCHIVES, KEW

TNA/PCC/Prob. 11/969 Will of Robert Long, 1771.
TNA/PCC/Prob 11/1348 Will of Dorothea Frances Kingsman, 1800.

WORCESTER RECORD OFFICE

Hagley Hall MS, Lyttelton family papers.

## Primary Printed Sources

NEWSPAPERS AND PERIODICALS

*Avvisi di Genova*
*Bath Chronicle*
*Dublin Courant*
*Dublin Mercury*
*Edinburgh Advertiser*
*Gazetteer and London Daily Advertiser*
*Gazzetta Toscana*
*General Evening Post*
*Gentleman's and Citizen's Almanack*
*Gentleman's Magazine*
*Lloyd's Evening Post and British Chronicle*
*London Chronicle, or Universal Evening Post*

*London Evening Post*
*London Gazette*
*London Magazine, or Gentleman's Monthly Intelligence*
*Monthly Review*
*Morning Chronicle*
*Morning Herald and Daily Advertiser*
*Morning Post*
*Public Advertiser*
*Public Ledger, or The Daily Register of Commerce and Intelligence*
*St James's Chronicle, or the British Evening Post*

PAMPHLETS/BOOKS

Anon. [Ancillon, Charles], *Eunuchism Display'd. Describing all the Different Sorts of Eunuchs; the Esteem They Have Met With in the World, and How They Came to be Made So* (London, 1718).

Anon., *Do You Know What You are About? Or, a Protestant Alarm to Great Britain* (London, 1733).

Anon, *The Happy Courtezan: Or, the Prude Demolish'd. An Epistle from the Celebrated Mrs. C[onstantia] P[hillips] to the Angelick Signor Far[i]n[el]li* (London, 1735).

Anon., *The Secrets of a Woman's Heart. An Epistle from a Friend to Signor F[arine]lli* (London, 1735).

Anon., *The Remarkable Trial of the Queen of Quavers and Her Associates for Sorcery, Witchcraft and Enchantment at the Assizes held in the Moon* (London, 1777/8?).

Anon., *Trials for Adultery: or, the History of Divorces. Being Select Trials at Doctors Commons, for Adultery, Fornication, Cruelty, Impotence, etc., from the Year 1760, to the Present Time... Taken in Short-Hand by A Civilian*, 7 vols. (London, 1780).

Archenholz, Johan Wilhelm von, *A Picture of England. Containing the Laws, Customs and Manners of England* (Dublin, 1790).

Arne, Thomas, *Artaxerxes. An English Opera. As it is Performed at the Theatre-Royal in Covent Garden* (London, 1762).

——*Amintas, or The Royal Shepherd. An English Opera. As Perform'd at the Theatre-Royal in Covent-Garden* (London, 1764).

Astell, Mary, *A Serious Proposal to the Ladies, for the Advancement of their True and Greatest Interest* (London, 1694).

Brayley, E. W., *Historical and Descriptive Accounts of the Theatres of London* (London, 1826).

Burney, Charles, *A General History of Music, from the Earliest Ages to the Present Period* (4 vols., London, 1789), ed. Frank Mercer (London, 1935).

Burney, Frances, *The Early Diary of Frances Burney, 1768–1778*, ed. Annie Raine Ellis (London, 1907).

Burrows, Donald, and Dunhill, Rosemary (eds.), *Music and Theatre in Handel's World: The Family Papers of James Harris, 1732–1780* (Oxford, 2002).

Casanova, Giacomo, *History of My Life*, trans. Willard R. Trask (Baltimore, 1970).

d'Asburgo Lorena, Pietro Leopoldo, *Realzioni Sul Governo della Toscana, II. Stato Fiorentino e Pisano*, ed. Leo S. Olschki (Florence, 1970).

Defoe, Daniel, *Essay Upon Projects* (London, 1697).

Kelly, Michael, *Reminiscences of Michael Kelly of the King's Theatre and Theatre Royal Drury Lane*, 2nd edn., 2 vols. (London, 1826).

Rousseau, Jean-Jacques, *Appendix to Grassineau's Musical Dictionary, Selected from the 'Dictionnaire de Musique' of J. J. Rousseau* (London, 1769).

Smollett, Tobias, *The Expedition of Humphry Clinker* (1771), ed. Lewis M. Knapp (Oxford, 1966).

Sterne, Lawrence, *The Life and Opinions of Tristram Shandy, Gentleman* (1759–67), ed. Graham Petrie (Harmondsworth, 1967, reprinted 1985).

Tenducci, Dorothea, *The True and Genuine Narrative of Mr. and Mrs. Tenducci. In a Letter to a Friend at Bath. Giving a Full Account, From their Marriage to the Present Time* (London, 1768).

Tenducci, Giusto Ferdinando, *Six New English Songs Composed by Ferdinando Tenducci and to be Sung by him at Ranelagh* (c.1763).

— *The Revenge of Athridates. An English Opera* (Dublin, 1765).

— *Amintas: An English Opera* (Dublin, 1783).

— *Orpheus and Eurydice, a Musical Drama* (London, 1785).

Walpole, Horace, *The Yale Edition of Horace Walpole's Correspondence*, ed. W. S. Lewis et al., 48 vols. (London and New Haven, 1937–83).

Watson, John, *Gentleman's and Citizen's Almanack* (Dublin, 1769).

Wycherley, William, *The Country Wife* (London, 1675), ed. John Dixon Hunt (London, 1972).

## Secondary Sources

### GENERAL

Barker, Hannah, *Newspaper, Politics and Public Opinion in Late-Eighteenth Century England* (Oxford, 1998).

Barry, Jonathan, and French, H. R. (eds.), *Social Identity, Class and Status, England c. 1500–1800* (London, 2005).

Black, Jeremy, *The British Abroad: The Grand Tour in the Eighteenth Century* (London: 1999).

——*A Subject for Taste: Culture in Eighteenth-Century England* (London and New York, 2005).

Blanning, T. C. W., *The Triumph of Music: The Rise of Composers, Musicians and their Art* (Cambridge, Mass., 2008).

Brewer, John, *The Pleasures of the Imagination: English Culture in the Eighteenth Century* (London, 1997).

Brooks, Chrisopher, *Law, Politics and Society in Early Modern England* (Cambridge, 2008).

Bucciarelli, Melania, *Italian Opera and European Theatre, 1680–1720: Plots, Performers, Dramaturgies* (Amsterdam and Cremona, 2000).

Clarke, Norma, *Dr. Johnson's Women* (London, 2000).

Cohen, Jay, 'The history of imprisonment for debt and its relation to the development of discharge in bankruptcy', *Journal of Legal History*, 3.2 (1982), 153–71.

Crawford, Patricia, *Blood, Bodies and Families in Early Modern England* (Harlow, 2004).

Foster, R. F., *Modern Ireland, 1600–1972* (Harmondsworth, 1989).

French, Anne, *Art Treasures in the North: Northern Families on the Grand Tour* (Norwich, 2009).

Gardner, Victoria, 'Newspaper proprietors and the business of newspaper publishing in provincial England, 1760–1820', unpublished D.Phil. thesis (University of Oxford, 2008).

Hale, J. R., *Florence and the Medici: The Pattern of Control* (Plymouth, 1977).

Haynes, Clare, *Pictures and Popery: Art and Religion in England, 1660–1760* (Aldershot, 2006).

Johnston-Liik, Edith Mary, *History of the Irish Parliament, 1692–1800. Vol. 5: Commons, Constituencies and Statutes* (Belfast, 2002).

Lepore, Jill, 'Historians who love too much: reflections on microhistory and biography', *Journal of American History* (2001), 129–44.

Kelly, Jason M., *The Society of Dilettanti: Archaeology and Identity in the British Enlightenment* (New Haven and London, 2009).

Kenny, Colum, *King's Inns and the Kingdom of Ireland: The Irish 'Inn of Court', 1541–1800* (Dublin, 1992).

Moore, R. I., *The Formation of a Persecuting Society: Power and Deviance in Western Europe, 950–1250* (Oxford, 1987).

O'Brien, Gillian, and O'Kane, Finola (eds.), *Georgian Dublin* (Dublin, 2008).

O'Hara, Diana, *Courtship and Constraint: Rethinking the Making of Marriage in Tudor and Stuart England* (Manchester, 2000).

Robins, Brian, *Catch and Glee Culture in Eighteenth-Century England* (Woodbridge, 2006).

Robinson, Michael F., *Naples and Neapolitan Opera* (Oxford, 1972).

Schulenberg, David, *Music of the Baroque* (New York and Oxford, 2001).

Simon, Jacob (ed.), *Handel: A Celebration of His Life and Times, 1685–1759* (London, 1985).

Smith, Mark M., *Sensing the Past: Seeing, Hearing, Smelling, Tasting and Touching in History* (Berkeley, 2004).

Snodin, Michael, and Llewellyn, Nigel, *Baroque: Style in the Age of Magnificence, 1620–1800* (London, 2009).

Spufford, Peter, *Power and Profit: The Merchant in Medieval Europe* (London, 2002).

Thomas, Keith, *The Ends of Life: Roads to Fulfilment in Early Modern England* (Oxford, 2009).

Vickery, Amanda, *The Gentleman's Daughter: Women's Lives in Georgian England* (New Haven and London, 1998).

— *Behind Closed Doors: At Home in Georgian England* (New Haven and London, 2009).

Wickham, C. J., *The Mountains and the City: The Tuscan Appenines in the Early Middle Ages* (Oxford, 1988).

Wrightson, Keith, *English Society, 1580–1680* (London, 1982; reprinted 1990).

— 'Mutualities and obligations: changing social relationships in early modern England', *Proceedings of the British Academy*, 139 (Oxford, 2006).

MARRIAGE, SEXUALITY, AND THE FAMILY

Barker-Benfield, G. J., *The Culture of Sensibility: Sex and Society in Eighteenth-Century Britain* (Chicago and London, 1992).

Behrend-Martínez, Edward, *Unfit for Marriage: Impotent Spouses on Trial in the Basque Region of Spain, 1650–1750* (Reno and Las Vegas, 2007).

Berry, Helen, and Foyster, Elizabeth (eds.), *The Family in Early Modern England* (Cambridge, 2007).

Brundage, James A., *Law, Sex and Christian Society in Medieval Europe* (Chicago and London, 1987).

Butler, Judith, *Bodies that Matter: On the Discursive Limits of Sex* (New York and London, 1993).

Carter, Philip, *Men and the Emergence of Polite Society, 1660–1800* (Harlow, 2001).

Coster, Will, *Baptism and Spiritual Kinship in Early Modern England* (Aldershot, 2002).

Crawford, Patricia, and Mendelson, Sara, 'Sexual identities in early modern England: the marriage of two women in 1680', *Gender and History*, 7.3 (1995), 362–77.

Cunningham, Hugh, *Children and Childhood in Western Society Since 1500* (London, 1995).

Darmon, Pierre, *Damning the Innocent: A History of the Persecution of the Impotent in Pre-Revolutionary France* (New York, 1986).

Fletcher, Anthony, *Gender, Sex and Subordination, 1500–1800* (New Haven and London, 1995).

Foyster, Elizabeth, *Manhood in Early Modern England: Honour, Sex and Marriage* (London, 1999).

—*Marital Violence: An English Family History, 1660–1857* (Cambridge, 2005).

Gatrell, Vic, *City of Laughter: Sex and Satire in Eighteenth-Century London* (London, 2006).

Gottlieb, Beatrice, *The Family in the Western World* (Oxford, 1993).

Harvey, Karen, 'The history of masculinity, *circa* 1650–1800', *Journal of British Studies*, 44.2 (2005), 296–311.

— *Reading Sex in the Eighteenth Century: Bodies and Gender in English Erotic Culture* (Cambridge, 2005).

— and Shepard, Alexandra, 'What have historians done with masculinity? Reflections on five centuries of British history, c. 1500–1950', *Journal of British Studies*, 44.2 (2005), 274–80.

Helmholz, R. H., *Roman Canon Law in Reformation England* (Cambridge, 1990).

Hitchcock, Tim, and Cohen, Michèle (eds.), *English Masculinities, 1660–1800* (London and New York, 1999).

Ingram, Martin, *Church Courts, Sex and Marriage in England, 1570–1640* (Cambridge, 1987).

Kelly, Jason M., 'Riots, revelries, and rumor: libertinism and masculine association in Enlightenment London', *Journal of British Studies*, 45.4 (2006), 759–95.

— *The Society of Dilettauti: Archaeology and Identity in the British Enlightenment* (New Haven and London, 2009).

Kertzer, David I., and Barbagli, Marzio (eds.), *The History of the European Family. Vol. I: Family Life in Early Modern Times, 1500–1789* (New Haven and London, 2001).

Kuefler, Mathew (ed.), *The Boswell Thesis: Essays on Christianity, Social Tolerance and Homosexuality* (Chicago and London, 2006).

Laqueur, Thomas, *Making Sex: Body and Gender from the Greeks to Freud* (Cambridge, Mass. and London, 1990).

Marcus, Sharon, *Between Women: Friendship, Desire and Marriage in Victorian England* (Princeton, 2007).

Outhwaite, R. B., *Clandestine Marriage in England, 1500–1850* (London, 1995).

—*The Rise and Fall of the English Ecclesiastical Courts, 1500–1860* (Cambridge, 2006).

Porter, Roy, and Teich, Mikulas, *Sexual Knowledge, Sexual Science: The History of Attitudes to Sexuality* (Cambridge, 1994).

Probert, Rebecca, *Marriage Law and Practice in the Long Eighteenth Century: A Reassessment* (Cambridge, 2009).

Shepard, Alexandra, *Meanings of Manhood in Early Modern England* (Oxford, 2003).

Smith, Heather, 'Women and marriage in the eighteenth century: evidence from the London church courts, 1730–1780', unpublished Ph.D. thesis (University of Bristol, 2000).

Stone, Lawrence, *The Family, Sex and Marriage in England, 1500–1800* (Harmondsworth, 1977).

— *The Road to Divorce: England 1530–1987* (Oxford, 1990).

Trumbach, Randolph, *Sex and the Gender Revolution. Vol. I: Heterosexuality and the Third Gender in Enlightenment London* (Chicago, 1998).

Turner, David M., 'Popular marriage and the law: tales of bigamy at the eighteenth-century Old Bailey', *London Journal*, 30.1 (2005), 6–21.

Weir, D., 'Rather never than late: celibacy and age at marriage in England. Cohort fertility, 1541–1871', *Journal of Family History*, 9 (1984), 340–54.

TOWNS AND THEATRES IN BRITAIN AND IRELAND

Barnard, T. C., *Making the Grand Figure: Lives and Possessions in Ireland, 1641–1770* (New Haven and London, 1994).

Beier, A. L., and Finlay, Roger, *London: The Making of the Metropolis, 1500–1700* (London, 1986).

Casey, Christine, *The Buildings of Ireland: Dublin* (New Haven and London, 2005).

Clark, Peter, and Gillespie, Raymond (eds.), *Two Capitals: London and Dublin, 1500–1840, Proceedings of the British Academy*, 107 (Oxford, 2001).

Hume, Robert D. (ed.), *The London Theatre World, 1660–1800* (Carbondale, Ill., 1980).

Kelly, Linda, *Susanna, the Captain and the Castrato: Scenes from the Burney Salon, 1779–80* (London, 2004).

Levy, Morris S., and Ward, John Milton (eds.), *The King's Theatre Collection: Ballet and Italian Opera in London, 1706–1883* (Cambridge, Mass., 2003).

Macleod, Jennifer, 'The Edinburgh Musical Society: its membership and repertoire, 1728–1797', unpublished Ph.D. thesis (University of Edinburgh, 2001).

Nelson, Claire, 'Tea-table miscellanies: the development of Scotland's song culture, 1720–1800', *Early Music*, 28.4 (2000), 596–620.

Price, Curtis, Milhous, Judith, and Hume, Robert D., *The Impresario's Ten Commandments: Continental Recruitment for Italian Opera in London, 1763–64*. Royal Musical Association Monographs, No. 6 (London: Royal Musical Association, 1992).

Shoemaker, Robert B., 'The decline of public insult in London: 1660–1800', *Past & Present*, 169 (2000), 97–131.

Stone, G. W. (ed.), *The London Stage, 1660–1800: A Calendar of Plays, Entertainments and Afterpieces. Part IV: 1747–1776* (Carbondale, Ill., 1962).

Styles, John, *The Dress of the People: Everyday Fashion in Eighteenth-Century England* (New Haven and London, 2007).

Walsh, T. J., *Opera in Dublin, 1705–1797: The Social Scene* (Dublin, 1973).

Wollenberg, Susan, and McVeigh, Simon (eds.), *Concert Life in Eighteenth-Century Britain* (Aldershot, 2004).

Wroth, N., *London Pleasure Gardens of the Eighteenth Century* (London, 1896).

OPERA AND CASTRATI

Barbier, Patrick, *The World of the Castrati: The History of an Operatic Phenomenon* (1989), trans. Margaret Crosland (London, 1996).

Clapton, Nicholas, *Moreschi: The Last Castrato* (London, 2004).

—— 'Carlo Broschi Farinelli: aspects of his technique and performance', *British Journal for Eighteenth-Century Studies*, 28.3 (2005), 323–8.

DelDonna, Anthony R., and Polzonetti, Pierpaolo (eds.), *The Cambridge Companion to Eighteenth-Century Opera* (Cambridge, 2009).

Dellaora, Richard, and Fischlin, Daniel (eds.), *The Work of Opera: Genre, Nationhood and Sexual Difference* (New York, 1997).

Feldman, Martha, *Opera and Sovereignty: Transforming Myths in Eighteenth-Century Italy* (Chicago and London, 2007).

—— 'Denaturing the castrato', *Opera Quarterly*, 24.3–4 (2008), 178–99.

—— 'Strange births and surprising kin: the castrato's tale', in Paula Findlen, Wendy Wassyng Roworth, and Catherine M. Sama (eds.), *Italy's Eighteenth Century: Gender and Culture in the Age of the Grand Tour* (Stanford, 2009).

Fraudsen, Mary E., '*Eunuchi conjugium:* the marriage of a castrato in early modern Germany', *Early Music History 24: Studies in Medieval and Early Modern Music*, ed. Iain Fenlon (Cambridge, 2005).

Freitas, Roger, *Portrait of a Castrato: Politics, Patronage and Music in the Life of Atto Melani* (Cambridge, 2009).

—— 'The eroticism of emasculation: confronting the Baroque body of the castrato', *Journal of Musicology*, 202 (2003), 196–249.

Gärtner, Heinz, *Johann Christian Bach: Mozart's Friend and Mentor*, trans. Reinhard G. Pauly (Portland, 1994).

Gilman, Todd, 'Arne, Handel, the beautiful and the sublime', *Eighteenth-Century Studies*, 42.4 (2009), 529–55.

Heriot, Angus, *The Castrati in Opera* (London, 1956).

Krimmer, Elizabeth, '"Eviva il Coltello?" The castrato singer in eighteenth-century German literature and culture', *PMLA*, 120.5 (2005), 1543–59.

Mazzeo, Antonio, *I Tre 'Senesini': Musici ed Altri Cantanti Evirati Senesi* (Siena, 1979).

Oldman, C. B., 'Mozart's *scena* for Tenducci', *Music and Letters*, 42.1 (1961), 44–52.

Rosselli, John, 'The castrati as a professional group and a social phenomenon, 1550–1850', *Acta Musicologica*, 60 (1988), 143–79.

# Index

Bernardi, Francesco, 'Senesino' 3, 28,
38, 45, 48, 83, 85, 183
Bernini, Gian 26
Bertoni, Ferdinando 37
Bettesworth, John, Dr 173, 190–1, 193
bigamy 171–2
Billington, Elizabeth 203
bisexuality 68–9
Blainville, Charles de 183
bluestockings 79, 81
Bologna, see Italy: Bologna
Bordoni, Faustina 78
Boswell, James 49, 70
Brent, Charlotte 64, 77
Bristol, see England: Bristol
Britain 43, 62, 70, 72, 86, 110, 144
British Muse 62
Brochi, Gio Batto 177
Brooke, Frances 83
Broschi, Carlo, 'Farinelli' 1–3, 28, 30,
33, 34, 48, 80, 83, 200, 201
Broschi, Ricardo 33
Brown, Lady 72
Bruncker, Lord 44–5
Brunelleschi, Filippo 177
Buonarroti, Michelangelo 7
Burgoyne, John, General 198
Burlington, Countess of 78
Burney, Charles 19, 51–2, 60, 87, 144,
164, 201
Burney, Fanny 79, 83, 99
Burney, Susanna (later Phillips) 79, 82
Burns, Robert 68, 150

Caffarelli, see Majorano, Gaetano
Calori, Angiola 40
Calvert, Peter 171
Campbell, John 151
Caravaggio, Michelangelo 17
Carestini, Giovanni 31, 48
Carlucci, Count 49
Carri, Guiseppe 209
Carter, Elizabeth 81
Casanova, Giacomo 159–60, 162
Castiglione, Baldassare 11
castrati 15, 16, 17, 18, 27, 28, 32–3,
35–6, 37, 38, 39, 42, 43, 45–6,
47, 48, 53, 69, 70, 82, 85, 108,

111, 128, 130, 138, 159, 174,
182, 183, 187, 204
and their Catholic faith 2, 111
and celebrity 26, 37, 47, 54, 60, 65,
66, 71, 94, 161,
as a curiosity 44–6, 47, 84
and emasculation 64, 76, 184
desired by men 16, 68–9, 73–4,
86, 88
desired by women 2, 67–8, 71–2,
73–4, 75, 79–86, 106, 137
and effeminacy 68–9, 75, 76, 199
failed careers of 37, 183
'family of choice' 33–4
fees paid to 1, 34, 35, 38, 48, 83
gifts given to 1, 48, 81, 82, 208
history of 15–17, 19, 44–5, 153
and impotence 79, 81, 103, 129
indeterminate sex and gender 73–4,
83–6
and infertility 33–4, 84, 85, 88, 141
and love affairs 56, 81–2
and marriage 136–45, 165
opposition to 3, 47, 62–3, 67–8,
85–6, 183, 199–200, 204
physiology 36, 44–5, 65–6, 71, 74,
75, 84–5, 141, 160
playing female roles 76–8
and their Protestant faith 45–6
recruitment by theatres 38–40, 47,
51, 77, 93
satires of 70, 71, 73–4, 75–6, 83,
84–5, 86, 88, 131, 206
and 'sexual double standard' 56,
78–9, 80–1, 82
and sexuality 17, 69, 75, 86, 94
singing technique and voice 3, 15,
16, 30, 45, 47, 74, 76, 77,
80, 82
temperament 2, 144
training 19, 23
see also eunuchs
castration 13–15, 18–19, 21, 31, 33,
69, 70, 74–5, 76, 78, 138–9,
178, 199
for aesthetic purposes 15, 219
and barber-surgeons 19, 20
hernias as pretext for 16

and the human voice 15, 18, 183
illegality and excommunication 13,
    15, 17, 19, 20
and manhood 3, 14, 76
and parental complicity 182–5
and political motives 14–15
and religious motives 18
self-castration 18
see also eunuchs
Catholic Church 68, 85, 110,
    187, 209
Catholic priests 12, 17, 109–10
Catholicism 9, 43, 45–6, 111,
    137, 142
  rituals 9, 187
Cecchi, Domenico, 'Cecchino' 17
Chamberlain, Lord 44, 47, 50
Charles I, king 42, 43
Charles II, king 75, 95
Charles III, king 28
Charlotte, queen 72, 154, 155
Chelsea, see England: London, Chelsea
Chichester Music Festival 158
choirs:
  church 26, 37
  Sistine Chapel, 16, 17
church courts 133, 137, 141, 145, 172,
    189, 197, 172, 173, 174, 176,
    179, 180, 186, 187, 189, 193–4,
    197
Church of Ireland 96, 97, 111
Cibber, Colley 32
Ciotta, Gio Senti 177
Cipriani, Giovanni Battista 203
Clarges, Louisa, Lady 79, 81
Clark, Sandys, Revd 170
Cocchi, Gioacchino 37, 39–40, 51, 53
coffee houses 49, 92, 118, 148
  Don Saltero's 42
  Prince of Orange 52
Collins, Mary 189
Collins, Samuel 189
composers 4, 15, 26, 29, 41, 48, 93
concert rooms 49, 63, 93
  Great Room, Dean Street, Soho,
    London 52, 59, 63
  Hanover Square Concert Rooms,
    London 63

Hickford's Great Room, Brewer
    Street, London 63
Pasquali's Rooms, Tottenham Court
    Road, London 63
concerts 61, 79, 98, 161, 168
  benefit 39, 52, 58, 59–60, 63, 66,
    91, 198
  private 1–2, 43, 44, 45, 49, 60, 61,
    69, 72, 204, 206
consumerism 42–3, 85, 98
consummation of marriage 13–14, 17,
    74, 129, 132–5, 140–4, 172,
    196–7
Conti, Gizziello, 'Gioacchino' 34
Conway, Henry Seymour 55–6
Cosway, Maria, Baroness 203
Cosway, Richard 203
courtship 108, 120, 193–4
Crawford, Peter 188
Cremonini, Clementina 146
'criminal conversation' 54–5
Cromwell, Oliver 95, 121
Curll, Edmund 137–8
Cuzzoni, Francesca 78

dancers 40, 41, 50, 51, 53, 200
Davys, Mary 99
Dawson, Joshua, Sir 102
Defoe, Daniel 59, 138
Devonshire, Georgiana, Duchess
    of 203
divorce, see marriage: divorce
Donaldson, Alexander 148
Donatello, see Bardi, Donato
Douglas, William 149
Dryden, John 80, 93
Dublin Courant 118, 119
Dublin Mercury 117–18, 131
Duncan, Mary, Lady 79
Dundas, Laurence, Sir 148

Eberardi, Teresa 60
Edinburgh Advertiser 148
Edinburgh Musical Society 147–9,
    150, 151–2, 159, 162
Egan, Patrick 110, 186
England 4, 9, 39, 40, 41, 42, 46, 47,
    51, 57, 60, 68, 69, 72, 78, 83,

Rauzzini, Venanzio 69, 81, 83, 204
Reginelli, Nicola 34, 35
religion 2, 27, 63, 68, 86, 121,
130, 139
evangelical revival 11
Renaissance anatomists 74
Renaissance period 15, 16, 18
Renaissance style 5, 11
architecture 7
art 175
poetry 7
reputation 75, 119, 151, 159, 164,
172, 188, 189
men, importance of 70, 115, 144
women, importance of 12, 79, 80,
81, 108, 122, 145, 146, 153
Reynolds, Joshua, Sir 203
Richardson, Samuel 98, 99, 100
Rich, John 47
Roman Empire 29, 44
Romanesque style:
architecture 5
romantic friendships 81, 82
Rome, see Italy: Rome
Rosa, Laura 40
Rossi, Ansano 176–8, 180, 186,
188, 192
Rossi, Giovanno 177
Rossi, Lorenzo 179
Rossi, Luigi Bernando 177
Rossini, Girolamo 16
Rothschild family 7
Rousseau, Jean-Jacques 183, 200
Rovere, Vittoria della, 7
Royal Opera House, see opera houses
and theatres: Theatre Royal,
Covent Garden, London
Royal Society of Science 44, 155
Rush, George 152

St Agata, church of 8
St Cecilia 46, 155–6
St James's Chronicle 119, 131, 152
St Paul 18
Salisbury, see England: Salisbury
Salisbury Musical Festival 91, 155,
157, 203
Salvi, Antonio 37

Samber, Robert 138
Sansovino, Andrea 7
Sardinia, see Italy: Sardinia
Savoy, Victor Amadeus, Duke of 35
Saxony, Electors of 43
Scarlatti, Alessandro 24
Scarlatti, Domenico 28, 93
Scotland 4, 164
architecture 147, 148
Edinburgh 68, 147–8, 149, 150,
151, 152, 162, 169
university 147
see also opera houses and theatres
Scottish ballads 149–50, 166, 202
Senesino, see Bernardi, Francesco
sensibility, culture of 70, 71, 72, 135
Setti, Guiseppe 179
Seven Years War (1756–63) 49, 62,
199
Shaftesbury, Anthony Ashley Cooper,
third earl of 11
Shakespeare, William 26, 135
Sheridan, Thomas 93, 198
Siena, see Italy: Siena
Siface, see Grossi, Giovanni
singers 63, 77, 176
female 78–9
singing technique:
alto 15, 30
bass 38
bel canto 29
falsetto 15
polyphony 15, 29
soprano 15, 30, 31, 38, 51, 201
tenor 16, 31, 38, 201, 209
see also female sopranos
Sixtus V, Pope 13, 15–16, 137
Smolensk, Russia 15
Smollett, Tobias 62, 73, 136–7
social mobility 4, 5, 12, 62, 92, 138, 159
Sorlisi, Bartolomeo 88
Spain 15, 16, 18, 19, 24, 27, 28, 95,
144, 155
Sterne, Lawrence 76
Sweden 46
Sweden, Christina, Queen of 43
Syler, Edmund 189
Syler, Elizabeth 189

310

Vienna, *see* Austria: Vienna
Vinci, Leonardo 24
Voltaire 148, 183

Walpole, Horace 55–6, 61, 164,
    176, 206
Walpole, Sir Robert 85
Weld, Catherine 143, 189
Weld, Edward 143, 189
Westmoreland, John Fane, Earl of 53

Whigs 45, 54, 78, 203
Wilbraham, Roger 174–5, 176–7, 181,
    186
Wilkes, John 148
Willett, Waring, Revd 170
William III, king 46
Winchester Music Festival 155
Wollstonecraft, Mary 135
Worcester, *see* England: Worcester
Wren, Christopher, Sir 46, 47